OMNIVM LVX CIVIVM

BOSTON
PUBLIC
LIBRARY

Namkwa

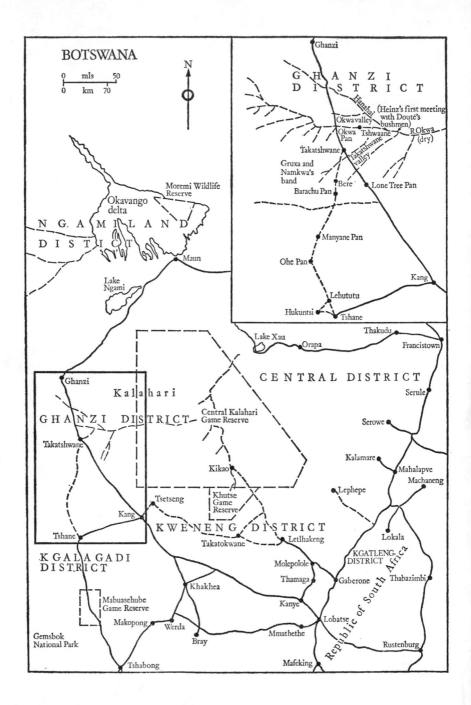

Hans-Joachim Heinz
and Marshall Lee

Namkwa

LIFE AMONG THE
BUSHMEN

WITH A FOREWORD BY
MARGARET MEAD

ILLUSTRATED

Boston
HOUGHTON MIFFLIN COMPANY
1979

First American Edition 1979

Copyright © 1978 by Hans-Joachim Heinz and Marshall Lee
Foreword copyright © 1978 by Margaret Mead

All rights reserved. No part of this work may be reproduced or transmitted in any form by any means, electronic
or mechanical, including photocopying and recording, or by
any information storage or retrieval system, without permission in writing from the publisher.

Library of Congress Cataloging in Publication Data

Heinz, Hans Joachim.
  Namkwa: life among the Bushmen.
  Includes index.
  1. San (African people) 2. Heinz, Hans
Joachim. 3. Anthropologists—Biography.
4. Namkwa. 5. San (African people)—Biography.
I. Lee, Marshall, joint author. II. Title.
DT797.H44 1979 301.29'68'1 [B] 79–346
ISBN 0–395–27611–X

Printed in the United States of America

V 10 9 8 7 6 5 4 3 2 1

To Raymond Dart, for his continuous encouragement and inspiration, and to my Bushman friends.

H.J.H.

Contents

Illustrations

Foreword

This book is a unique story of one of the more romantic episodes in the history of the encounters between a European scientist and a primitive people. The encounter began as a scientific expedition by a middle-aged parasitologist into the Kalahari desert, where he fell in love with a Bushman girl, became enamoured of Bushman culture, and returned again and again, to investigate new aspects of Bushman life, and finally to attempt to introduce the Bushmen to a settled way of life which would mediate their relationship to the impinging modern world.

The reason I have been asked to write this foreword is that I was there, there at the very moment when the structure of many years was falling apart, when the structure which he had built so hopefully was crumbling under the onslaughts of new forms of exploitation. I stayed at the little settlement where he had tried to introduce cattle raising, only for the Bushmen to kill an animal whenever they needed one for a feast. He started a school, but the teacher he had imported and who was later appointed a development officer for the Bushmen became an active opponent of what seemed to her a highly paternalistic rule.

I was on a brief lecture tour in South Africa in 1974 as the guest of the Johannesburg Marriage Guidance Society, which gave me access to chapters among South Africa's five castes. There is a fixed belief in South Africa that every visiting anthropologist will, of course, have to see Bushmen, and I did not wish to discourage this belief, although I had spent so many hours looking at uncut films on the Bushmen that I thought I knew a lot about them. But there is no substitute in film or book for the experience of standing, feeling like a giant even at my five-feet-two, towering over a tiny Bushman household.

Dr Heinz was my host, his Bushman wife Namkwa my hostess. During the three-day visit he introduced me to the whole range of his interests: his explorations of Bushman ecological knowledge; a paper he was just completing on his sociological findings that established wider ties among Bushman bands than had been suspected; the story of his participation in film making; and, finally, the ill-fated attempt to establish a sedentary base for nomadic people who had been so beautifully adjusted to a nomadic hunting-and-gathering life. Namkwa alone had bridged the gap. She, alone among her people, understood the advantages of building up a herd; she stood out in all her intrepid, uncorrupted integrity, as determined and resourceful as her German scientist lover. They faced each other over thousands of years of technological change, and she was equal to him, just as their union demonstrated the extraordinary cross-fertility of all human groups, for she had borne him a child.

The plot is not an unusual one: an educated German falling in love with some primitive, isolated people, going to live among them, studying them, and ultimately attempting to take charge of their lives. It is a temptation that is repeated again and again, to which all of those who come to cherish a people with a very different and vanishing way of life are subject. In a moment of transition, the foreign visitor, dazzling in his trappings of civilization, endearing in his interest and concern for the people's vanishing culture, takes charge. Inevitably today, his sovereignty will be short, as others take advantage of new styles of 'protection' for aboriginal peoples.

But the extraordinary contrast in size and the extreme simplicity of Bushman life in the Kalahari, the fact that Dr Heinz was using the most sophisticated instrumentation available, the drama of the newly won independence of Botswana, and the fact that he had to return periodically to his post and scientific support in South Africa where the new caste laws forbade any sexual relationships between Africans and Caucasians – all these make this an unusually poignant story.

Dr Heinz has strung his ethnological knowledge, of which he acquired a great deal during the years he went back and forth between his two lives, on his personal relationship to Namkwa and her kin and band. The ethnological side-comments on Bushman behaviour are all the more valuable. There is a delicious passage when he asks why he alone, and no other adult male, is allowed to witness a female initiation ceremony, and is told that he, a scientist, a father, a wounded veteran of European wars, is only a 'boy-child', not really a man, so his presence doesn't matter. He then spends a long time, interspersed with reading about the tortures administered to male initiates in other African societies, persuading the Bushmen to initiate him, finally succeeds, and keeps the secrets as he has sworn to do. One can only hope that he has written the details down somewhere safe, for in twenty years, by his own account, the old ways will have vanished under the pressures of modernization, economic exploitation, and even tourism.

The book is extremely honest, often angry, self-revealing; and through it all, Namkwa, his little Bush wife, shines brightly, glowing, as he used to describe her. Not unless we some day encounter men on some distant planet are we likely to be afforded such a drama.

Today, when many young people find the discipline and behaviour of anthropologists, as privileged strangers, too cold and distant for their liking, they may well revel in a kind of research which depends upon keeping the mother-in-law taboos oneself.

MARGARET MEAD

The American Museum of Natural History
New York 1977

FAMILY RELATIONSHIPS OF THE PRINCIPAL BUSHMEN

Abé. Wife to Douté.

Bolo Bolo. Son to Duce; sister to Kamka.

Douté. Husband to Abé; elder brother to Thauxum.

Duce. Father to Kamka and Bolo Bolo.

Geitchei. Wife to Tasa; aunt to Nkanaki; sister to Theugei and Nxabase.

Gruxa. Husband to Simmertchei; father to Namkwa and Nkasi.

Guanaci. Wife to Xauko.

Kamka. Daughter to Duce; sister to Bolo Bolo.

Kesi. Wife to Nxabase; mother to Tkose; sister to Tasa.

Kwé Kwé. Niece to Douté and Abé.

Kxei Kxei. Father to Thxale; father-in-law to Nkasi.

Namkwa. Daughter to Gruxa and Simmertchei; elder sister to Nkasi; wife to Dr Heinz.

Nkanaki. Daughter to Theugei; wife to Thomate; niece to Tasa.

Nkasi. Daughter to Gruxa and Simmertchei; younger sister to Namkwa; wife to Thxale.

Nkisa. Daughter to Xamxua.

Nkobe. Wife to Thauxum.

Ntchumka. Father to Shucre; brother to Xauko.

Ntonno. Husband to Shucre.

Ntumka. Husband to Thakum; Dr Heinz's young 'teacher'.

Nxabase. Brother to Geitchei and Theugei; husband to Kesi; father to Tkose; brother-in-law to Tasa.

Shucre. Daughter to Ntchumka; wife to Ntonno.

Simmertchei. Wife to Gruxa; mother to Namkwa and Nkasi.

Tasa. Nephew to Gruxa (but in the same age group, therefore 'uncle' to Namkwa); husband to Geitchei; uncle to Nkanaki; brother to Kesi.

Tchallo. Younger brother to Tasa and Kesi.

Thakum. Wife to Ntumka.

Thamae. Dr Heinz's interpreter from Ghanzi.

Thauxum. Younger brother to Douté; husband to Nkobe.

Theugei. Sister to Geitchei and Nxabase.

Thomate. Husband to Nkanaki.

Thxale. Husband to Nkasi; son to Kxei Kxei

Tkose. Daughter to Nxabase and Kesi; husband to Txaunxua.

Xamxua. Father to Nkisa; Dr Heinz's old 'teacher'.

Xauko. Husband to Guanaci; brother to Ntchumka.

Prologue

A small, almost lifeless flame, barely giving warmth, flickered in front of us. Around me, the band of Bushmen hunched in the shadows, their squat outlines against the sky, clicked their percussive tongues in strange conversation. Straining to catch a meaning in the rhythm, I hardly noticed the incessant high-pitched cry of giant corn-crickets, or the two jackals, howling across the bush. What I felt was the thump-thump of my own excitement; for my hopes, and I think I sensed it, my future, were being decided in the exchange of clicks around the fire.

Next to me sat Thamae of Ghanzi, my interpreter. The twelve hours I had so far spent in his company had given me confidence in him, and I edged closer. But I was no nearer to understanding what was happening.

The fire subsided into a red glow. A hand came out, pushed one of its three firebrands closer to the centre of the heat, and a bright flame leaped to throw out some light. Now, suddenly, the soft line of faces in profile changed into grotesque masks lit from below, with long black shadows above nose, cheekbones and eyebrows. I could see their wrinkly bellies, dust-dulled and ash-coated; their shins scarred by years of burns caused by cowering too close to the coals on cold Kalahari nights.

In this weird setting, among these earthiest of folk, I felt my intrusion and sat apart, a stranger. But it was I who had chosen to enter this world of the Bushmen of Botswana, or Bechuanaland as it was then. And there was no turning back.

Leaning against the inner circle round the fire, the women of the group sat in a second circle. Most were old and wrinkled, riddled with shadows. But one looked a child, with long head and fine features. Could this be Gruxa's elder daughter, who had been described to me earlier? Then I saw her better, as another woman's shadow moved from her face. I couldn't take my eyes off her. She glowed in the firelight, beautiful but completely impassive. She wore a dirty old handkerchief tied in a *doek* behind her head, and drawn down over her eyebrows. A tasselled skin hung over her shoulder, leaving one breast bare.

Though I tried to follow the direction and mood of the men's talk, the girl became my main interest. It was the face that held me. It was quite different from the features of those Bushwomen I had seen up to now, or would meet in the future. She sat unmoving and unmoved, inscrutable, but she stirred designs in my mind.

Her name was Namkwa.

That was how it all started. The matter under discussion was my admission to the Bushman band. I could have, like some other anthropologists and scientists, assumed my scientific prerogative and plonked myself down on their privacy. But I am grateful that I stifled such inclinations.

I know that I can be accused of being Machiavellian in my research, that I was simply using these people for my own advantage, that I was prompted and remain prompted by some sexual perversion – how else could I lust after a Bushwoman? I also realize that some might point at this book and say that if ever anything amounted to an invasion of privacy, this does.

In truth it is not like that. I know, or I hope, that this book has some scientific validity. I know that this is a very intimate story about a people, and a woman, who can hardly know how deep I try to go. I also know how much of a personal confession it is. Above all, I know that if I thought there was any prospect of hurting the people involved, it would never be published.

If I were to vindicate its publication beyond whatever merit it might have for its social-anthropological detail, I would say that it was an attempt to say something worthwhile, to contribute to the understanding of people long misunderstood and too often regarded as zoo exhibits. If I have got anywhere along the way to establishing them as real people, and not simply as 'living fossils', or creatures to gawp at under an anthropologist's microscope, it has been worthwhile.

I write this knowing that my part in the story is not always praiseworthy. I have made lots of mistakes, acted irrationally, immaturely and often out of pure self-interest. I also started out with little consideration for the effect I would have on lives free from the stresses I introduced — as though life weren't hard enough for them already.

In my defence, I could not foresee the turbulence and tensions I would let loose, and once involved there was no turning back. I became a prisoner of not only my ambitions and my stubborn fight against the odds, but a prisoner of these Bushmen, and one of their women as well.

I was bound to them as surely as if they had cast a spell.

ONE

My Early Life

I had come a long way to my meeting with this Namkwa and her people, who were to have such a profound influence on my life. When I first saw her in the firelight, she was no more than eighteen. I was forty-four, born in 1917 in Leipzig, Germany.

My father was a man of considerable intellectual capacity, interested in philosophy, history, geography and art. The eldest of four brothers, he could not devote himself to these interests, but had to enter the ceramic business established by his father. It was a flourishing concern, for my grandfather had been an enterprising potter.

World War I, however, proved disastrous for the family fortunes, and the fact that my father had married the wealthy daughter of my grandfather's largest client, Robert Froehlich, did not save the pottery business from collapse. Fortunately Herr Froehlich's enormous stamp collection enabled my father to open a philatelic shop, and for a while he eked a living selling stamps until he was able to emigrate and take his technical knowledge to the United States.

When I was seven years old my mother and I followed. We lived in Trenton, New Jersey, where I grew up more American than German. My parents did foster my tribal attachment to Germany, however. I continued to speak German, and absorbed some of the traits that were inherent in a European upbringing.

My father was kind, good-natured, methodical and dogged. He taught me the value of restraint, and an abiding respect for punctuality. But he was uninspired. My mother, without my father's sense of humour, was the disciplinarian. She was also the artist of the family. She had a beautiful voice, and might have gone into opera had her father not frowned upon so lowly a career. From her I inherited my love, and whatever little talent I have, for music. While my father's inclination was to play Bach's *Well-Tempered Clavier* ad nauseam, my mother and I spent many evenings (particularly party nights) running with much feeling through the likes of Lehar, Strauss and Stolz. She played and sang, and I accompanied her on the violin, an instrument which I played for many years with enthusiasm and devotion.

Away from parental influence, it was my American experience that was the major factor in my early development. We lived alongside the great Delaware River, source of the Fenimore Cooper *Leatherstocking* tales, and the mainstream of a Trenton child's life. If anything, my early days in Trenton were a test for survival. The memories of the war had not yet been erased, and neighbourhood children, echoing the prejudices of their parents, jeered and teased me to the point of misery.

Ironically, my only ally was a Jewish boy, Sidney Rosenthal, who stuck by this German underdog. But even with Sidney I could hardly assert myself against all the kids collectively, and since my father ignored my complaints and simply kept shoving me back into the street, I took to catching the boys and beating respect into them individually. This way I became accepted as one of their gang, and there was no more trouble.

Together we hunted and fished and rode the Delaware in canoes. Our lives were very much circumscribed by that river, and summer and winter we were seldom away from it. We built a hut on one of its islands, tasted camp-fire cooking and the escape from civilization. It flowed for us with a great deal of romance, but we also took much of it for granted.

On Saturday evenings we either gathered in our den to clean our guns and tie our flies – or we went to the back of Jake's gun and fishing-tackle shop to 'chew the rag' with the local cronies.

Here, on worn benches, around an enormous stove, we sat fascinated among the folklore. What a marvellous anachronism was Jake's shop: a place more suited to the stories of Mark Twain than to downtown Trenton in the 1920s.

Jim, a black man, was my hero, and my friend. It was a privilege to go out with him, for my pleasure was to be at his side. But the greatest moments were those when he came over to tell me that he was going racoon hunting. He had an excellent pack of dogs, and they seldom missed the scent. One night, however, he made the mistake of taking along a bitch on heat, and the best male couldn't concentrate on searching for 'coon' spoor. Jim just caught the dog, masturbated him, and the hunt went on. This bit of practical know-how apart, Jim had a remarkable way with his dogs, and I learnt much from him.

I was a frequent visitor to his home, and was also made welcome in the neighbours' homes. They fed me innumerable cups of coffee, and hot pancakes, and although I was only a youngster, I was accepted as an equal. These were honest, religious, warm and upright people. It never occurred to me that they were different because they were black.

Other interests also flicked at my character development. I was fascinated by the ways and customs of pre-literate man, particularly the American Indians, and I can now recognize the first stirrings of the ethnologist in me. One special interest was Indian beadwork, and I would fiddle for hours with designs copied from the painstaking descriptions of Ernest Thompson Seton.

Although I enjoyed my friends, I often took time off from the gang to be a loner, going off without any strict schedule to restrict me. Some nights I would climb down the rain spout, slip down into the river and explore the night in my canoe; lie listening to frogs and crickets, the splash of fish rising to moonbait, the flap of muskrat tails and the hunting hoot of owls.

Most times I took along as companion Treff, my English setter. But, once, after the high school graduation ball, I went down with pretty Elsie Layton. There among the night we felt the sounds and touched hands, sensual ripples lapping round our innocence. When I crept back home my mother was waiting with a rolling pin of rebuke. She beat her morality about my ears, and threatened to lay into Elsie as well. I was mortified. She just did not understand.

My parents could not afford to send me to college after my graduation from high school. My father had chosen the wrong time (and the wrong associates) to go into business on his own. Instead I decided to return to Germany, which despite my father's application for American citizenship (it was refused) was still something of the Fatherland in our minds.

Hitler had arrived by then, but the calumny heaped upon his

Nazism merely stimulated my latent patriotism. In my immaturity I saw Nazism as synonymous with the beloved Germany of my imagination — a figment in which the concept of 'my country right or wrong' had a noble ring. At least I was curious to visit the land of my birth.

Somewhat impulsively I went to New York to look for a job on a ship going to Europe. I found a job easily enough, as coal passer on a German tramp steamer.

But it wasn't exactly what I'd hoped for. I had to shovel 15 tons of coal a day, and only my word of honour that I would be a diligent coal passer and wouldn't skip ship convinced the engineer to take me on. He was wise, for my initial dismay when confronted by the work tempted me to desert at the next port. There were to be many ports between New York and Germany, because we steamed in the other direction. For a year we plied the trade routes of the Pacific and the Far East, and I crossed the line into manhood.

I gave myself in high fever and in health to shovelling coal in that bunker down below. But I also scraped on my fiddle in the boiler-room one Christmas Eve, played *Stille Nacht, Heilige Nacht* on an upturned shovel, and went AWOL in Bangkok. I met strange customs, and odd people, opium addicts, layabouts and lepers, and once I had to leap for my ship as it left dock in Venezuela. In Galveston a whore sat on my lap, and talked about the world. When her mother called her away for a customer she begged me not to leave. She would 'do it quick'. She came back then, that girl, and has kept on coming back all these years, a wispy thing in my memory.

My stay in Germany, when we eventually arrived there, was brief, for I had decided to return to college in America. I had little contact with the politics of Germany, although I did catch a glimpse of Hitler at Berchtesgaden, and experienced the jubilant hysteria that surrounded him. But it was the beauty of the Bavarian Alps that captivated me, and they were to lure me back to Germany.

On my return to the United States I entered Dartmouth College. I roomed with Bill Hutchison, a Catholic conservative sportsman, and Tom Braden, an atheistic, intellectual parlour-communist. In our rather unholy triumvirate I played the fascist, but more out of defiance than as a genuine and knowledgeable defender of the Nazi faith.

In keeping with my schoolboy activities, I was an active member of the Dartmouth Outing Club, and of 'Cabin and Trail', its governing body. For us it was hard to come down off our mountains, real or imaginary, and our standing complaint was: 'It's hell the way college interferes with our mountaineering.' I kept on looking beyond the ski slopes of New Hampshire, clear to the Alps.

To get to them I joined the 'Junior Year in Munich' programme and at a time when peace was falling apart and Chamberlain waving his famous piece of paper from Munich, I and other care-free students waved goodbye to the States.

Our Atlantic crossing was riotous. We were seldom in bed before 6 a.m. or up before noon. And I fell in love. The girl was Margaret Reichart, called Gretel, a refined young Smith student of German stock. In return she loved me, and together we experienced the shock of profound disillusionment with Hitler's Germany. Still it was not enough to force me to turn my back on the Fatherland, or avoid *Arbeitsdienst*, and military service. I didn't want to be branded a fugitive from my duty. Besides, Gretel and I rationalized that it would be better to interrupt my studies then rather than later on. It was hardly a wise decision. War was imminent. Gretel had to return home, and when her father tried to get her to Germany again so that we could marry, the holocaust had already begun. The war reinforced all my misgivings about Nazism, and in time my feelings found expression among like-thinking comrades, particularly those I encountered in the Interpreters' Unit in Munich. Its record as an anti-Hitler resistance unit in that city is well known.

Nevertheless I did bleed for Hitler. In the latter part of the war I was sent to Sardinia as a member of a task-force. There we were surprised by the Badoglio Uprising, and in one of the skirmishes that ensued I was wounded. The three comrades alongside me were killed.

Sent back to Munich for convalescence I nearly died, not from my wound but typhoid fever and malaria. My doctor failed to recognize the malaria, but fortunately a nurse sent a bloodsmear to the laboratory, and once it was diagnosed and treated I began my recovery. The nurse who helped save me was Marianne. Before the war had ended, we were married.

After the war I carried on the work I'd started in animal behaviour, and, while I completed my thesis, Marianne was our breadwinner. In a small room in Munich she also became pregnant. Ralph was born and brought another dimension to our life. Now as mother, breadwinner, wife, Marianne's capacity and opportunities for sacrifice increased. Not that I noticed. The shameful thing about our lives was that I simply took her selflessness for granted.

I obtained my Ph.D. degree on the back of an insect, the meat fly. I had studied his instinctive behaviour, his manners and his methods, his physical characteristics, his intellect and drives. But in a war-shattered time no one seemed particularly interested in this sort of research. The father of modern behaviourism, Conrad Lorenz, had disappeared into a Russian P.O.W. camp, and I had become a war orphan in science.

Armed with my peculiar knowledge I decided to try and turn my training into profit, and one opportunity that presented itself was to enter the realm of insect control. For some time I had been interested in the tropics so I went to Hamburg and joined the Institute for Tropical Medicine, where Dr Fritz Zumpt took me under his wing. An eminent systematic entomologist, he wasn't concerned with any Lorenzian notions about the psychological behaviour of flies, and he gradually devitalized my zoological enthusiasm. I became, so to speak, his gun-bearer.

My move to Hamburg and association with Dr Zumpt proved fateful. Post-war 'influx control' regulations prevented Marianne and Ralph from coming with me, and they went to live with my parents, who had returned to Germany after their repatriation from American internment. Separated from my family I embarked upon an affair with Gerda, a refugee from East Germany. It started as a 'fried potato' affair – in those days a man needed a girl to help supplement his meagre rations. Although our relationship was hardly destined to last, her hold on me, assisted by my susceptibility for the other sex, was enough to destroy my marriage.

I convinced myself that Marianne was not worth it. Her formal education was sadly lacking and I told myself she was my intellectual inferior. Perhaps I was looking for excuses for my behaviour, but in any event this was a stupid rationalization, and I have lived to recognize the hollowness in such conceit. My son, justifiably, grew to resent his father for this, and the price I have had to pay for sacrificing Marianne has been to lose some of the love and respect of my son.

Faced with the mess of the lives around me, I snatched at the escape that came my way. It came in a call from Dr Zumpt, who had gone to South Africa, and who now offered me a post as parasitologist at the South African Institute for Medical Research. I doubt that Fritz's motives were based on pure professional considerations, for I was ill-equipped for such a job. Nevertheless, bolstered by a crash course in parasitology, I fled from post-war Germany to become head of the Research Institute's department of parasitology.

My job at first was a synthesis of bluff and application. In time I dropped the bluff and replaced it with proficiency, but the job excited neither enthusiasm nor dedication. I was a field worker by inclination: something my colleagues and superiors at the University of the Witwatersrand Medical School (which I joined, honourably, later on) failed to appreciate.

Had they done so, I might possibly have made a significant contribution in the field. As it is, I think I gave value as teacher and lecturer. Certainly I tried to impart to my students an understanding and enthusiasm for their subject which reached beyond their textbooks, into first-hand field experience. Nor do I think I failed, for there have been rewards.

One of my early problems, my job apart, and rather predictably, was a woman, a theatre sister from the Johannesburg General Hospital. The affair was dramatic and humiliating. I didn't fancy being burned again, and crept away from womankind. I secluded myself in a small room in Braamfontein, and drove my despair and spare time into study, reading and music. I played the violin with extreme passion and remarkable endurance. For five hours a day I fiddled my way to peace of mind. Just me and my cocker-spaniel, Asta.

Like my other relationships, this affair with myself, the recluse, wasn't to last. The diversion came again in a nurse's uniform – as if I hadn't been warned. A cousin, Paul Vollrath, who was living in South Africa, and whose motives I accept were most noble, brought round two German nurses recently recruited from abroad. One was homely, and the other was Ingrid.

In view of my weakness it was probably inevitable, but Ingrid inveigled herself into my seclusion and became an integral part of it. She ministered to my needs, and provided intelligent company for my mind. Ingrid was a girl who knew what she wanted, and it was soon also clear to me what she wanted. She led me unprotesting through a divorce from Marianne into a marriage which was supposed to dissolve the differences which had reared in our informal relationship. Instead they were formalized into marital squabbles and an abrasive association which I endured for eight years, largely because I feared the disgrace of a second divorce. Our incompatibility embraced our friends, and I found myself becoming steadily isolated, more and more depressed.

I turned to a psychiatrist for help. But instead he tore apart what remained of my self-confidence. He led me to believe I was abnormal and the effect was traumatic. With my equilibrium destroyed I staggered around groping for a straw ...

It was then that I turned to the vastness of the Kalahari for escape, for distraction, and as it happened, for enrichment.

TWO

From Boskopman to Bushman

Shortly after joining the University of the Witwatersrand Medical School in 1961 I accompanied an expedition of scientists and students to Botswana. The purpose of the expedition, led by Professor Philip Tobias, one of the world's leading experts on the evolution of man, was to study numerous facets of the biology as well as the anthropology of the Kalahari Bushmen. Officially my brief was to survey the parasitic fauna of the Bushpeople. Off the record I was simply hunting a change, for I had knowledge neither of the land nor of its people, let alone the potential benefits of such a study. I certainly had no inkling of the fascination that waited for me.

That caught alight around our evening camp-fires, while our bread baked. Professor Tobias, who has the knack of making fossils come to life, reared pre-history before us, took us through the broad history of man in Africa, and the special role played by the Bushmen. Later, back in Johannesburg, my curiosity was compounded listening to that grand old man Raymond Dart, and others such as Piet Beaumont. And as I learnt and delved into the background of these little people my simple fascination deepened with understanding, and knowledge.

Not only did I have the benefit of minds pre-eminent in this field of man's history, but I was also stimulated by the proximity of the sites where some of the world's most exciting discoveries have been made.

Only a few miles west of Johannesburg were the Sterkfontein caves, and three hours to the north those of Makapansgat. Here the very earliest hominoids, the Australopithecines, were found, along with a profusion of their bone tools. Here among the pickings of pre-history I found a new direction for my life.

Australopithecus was a creature upright in posture, with a small brain of some 450 to 600 cubic centimetres, or about one-third of ours. He was a cave-dweller about three million years ago, and although his skull has appeared in various parts of Africa he was first unearthed by a labourer in Taungs in South Africa, and described by Raymond Dart. Some people say Australopithecus was an ape-man, and distinguishable from his successor, the man-ape, Homo habilis, who existed around two million years ago.

The discovery of Homo habilis was the result of chance and considerable toil. In 1911 a German entomologist named Kattwinkel stumbled upon Olduvai Gorge, in Tanganyika (he nearly fell into the gorge in pursuit of a butterfly), which turned out to be a sort of paleontologist's paradise; a treasure-trove of animal skulls and bones and bits and pieces. After World War I a German paleontologist, Reck, handed this discovery over to Dr Leakey, who made it his life's work to search for traces of human activity. Years of frustration were finally rewarded in 1959 when Mrs Leakey suddenly uncovered part of a skull. 'Oh, you dear boy!' she exclaimed. And since then, despite the high-sounding and scientific label, Australopithecus boisei zinjanthropus, they attached to the skull, the affectionate nickname 'Dear Boy' has stuck.

He was identified and described by Philip Tobias, the brilliant young scientist who succeeded Dart at the University of the Witwatersrand at Johannesburg. Dear Boy's brain, though still small, had a 650-cubic-centimetre capacity. While the older Australopithecus had used the long bones of animals as weapons, splintered bones as gouges and knives, and his upper jaw and teeth as scrapers, it was apparent that Homo habilis was more advanced and had begun to prepare and use stone tools, and in a way to think and act like a man.

The successor of Homo habilis was Homo erectus, who lived about 750,000 years ago. Because Homo erectus was discovered earlier than both Homo habilis and Australopithecus, and furthermore inhabited the Far East, men of science believed the cradle of man to lie in the Orient. They relied on the Peking man, and the Java man, whose brains had increased to 1,000 cubic centimetres, and who were clearly at home with stone tools.

German Neanderthal man, a successor of Homo erectus who lived 250,000 years ago, was actually the first hominoid to be discovered, at about the time of Darwin. Nobody took this prehistoric man seriously, and all sorts of unlikely explanations for his existence were advanced, but subsequent finds showed that he had brothers in southern Africa, where Rhodesian man was found at Broken Hill.

Neanderthal man's anatomical proportions were relatively sophisticated; he had a brain capacity of 1,500 cubic centimetres, and showed very pronounced brow ridges. It was he who prepared the anatomical skeleton for his successor, Boskopman.

Boskop lived about 100,000 years ago. He was probably the first creature to become aware of his ego, and the difference between the states of life and death. Evidence of this has been gleaned from, among other things, the discovery in the Border caves of northern Zululand and eastern Swaziland of a child buried some 50,000 years ago with a pendant around its neck. The fact of the burial is significant enough, but the deductions to be drawn from the pendant are irresistible. Not only did the parents or friends of the child respect its ego, but it is also clear that at this time a desire for eternal life had emerged. Cave drawings of perhaps the same period are additional proof of this.

Later examples of rock and cave art, estimated to be 30,000 years old, show clearly that man could then symbolize freely. The haematite and specularite pigments found by Beaumont in the Lion Cavern site at Ngwenya iron mine and radio-carbon dated by Vogel indicate that these prehistoric men had also become traders and miners, because the pigments have been found in Border Cave, 100 miles away from the nearest known red ochre mines.

It is therefore probable that language as a form of communication also evolved in Africa among Boskop types, and that their social system laid the basics for human society as we know it. They give the lie to the theory that the Black African continent was an evolutionary backwater, and that our version of modern civilized man emerged out of Europe or Asia.

Indeed many scientists now accept that the early communities founded in Africa could have provided the patterns of culture elaborated in Europe and elsewhere. It is a theory, incidentally, that came intuitively to Darwin, and with evidence to twentieth-century scientists.

Down from the Boskop-type, the genealogical table of man shows the evolution of the different races, the Caucasoids, Mongoloids, Negroids, and Capoids. But of these only Capoid man – the Bushmen and Hottentot peoples (who split about 10,000 years ago) – have a direct link with their Boskop ancestor.

In the light of this, it is not surprising that Bushmen are sometimes referred to as 'living fossils', but such a label is, at best, misleading, for it tends to belittle their high intellectual ability. Nevertheless, the fact is that the Bushmen are a living link with fossilized man, and in a schematic representation of evolution the Bushman is certainly in a position of unique scientific interest.

At one time he was spread far and wide over southern Africa. Thanks to their evolutionary side-shoots, Negroids and Caucasoids, who set about decimating their Capoid brethren in historically recent times, they are now virtually confined to South West Africa, Angola and Botswana, most of them in the Kalahari Desert.

No one can be really sure whether the Bushmen living in the Kalahari today are remnants of people who fled into this inhospitable region to escape extinction, or whether they were there all along, safe in a cruel environment where nature was their sole enemy in the never-ending hunt for survival.

This was one of the questions raised on my first venture into the land of the Bushmen. Then the parasitologist in me led me to believe that these desert-dwellers were refugees from elsewhere, because of the parasites they harboured. My early assumption was not to last, and today I am inclined to agree with those, like George Silberbauer, former Bushman Survey Officer for the Bechuanaland Government, who believe that the Bushmen's adaptation to their special environment, notably their extensive knowledge of plant life, is attributable to having lived under worsening climatic conditions for thousands of years.

In other words, the Bushmen were living their desert life long before the first Negroid intrusions into southern Africa about 1,600 years ago. No wonder then that the Kalahari is their special preserve, and small wonder that this dilettante ethnologist should have felt the fascination in his meeting with these survivals from the past.

THREE

Into the Bush

For all the novelty and wide-eyed wonderment of my first expedition, I found myself critical of several aspects of the organization. I was also somewhat appalled by the indifference shown to the daily needs of the dozens of farm Bushmen who were the objects of our numerous tests and measurements. For the sake of science they were expected to put up with our curiosity all day, for hours on end. And I'm afraid our intellectual concern did not embrace much thought of providing for their daily wants. In the event I resolved never again to join a team trip into the interior, and I told myself that I should pick very carefully anyone to accompany me on any future ventures.

Other lasting impressions of that first trip include my meetings with two men: George Silberbauer, whom I'd heard so much about, and Freddie Morris, who, with respect, I call a 'white' Bushman.

As Bushman Survey Officer in Her Majesty's Bechuanaland Protectorate, Silberbauer was a man of some authority in the Kalahari. The aura created around his personality by Philip Tobias was so vivid that we all considered him to be an inexhaustible fund of Bushman ethnological information.

He was continuously being referred to or quoted. Consequently there developed in me a respect for the man that was on the way to reverence. It never got that far. Regrettably, he lost my respect, not only because he regarded me as an interloper, but also because I felt he thought me his enemy.

It was different with Freddie Morris. I was fascinated by him, and his way of life; his example influenced me in my subsequent years of work in the Kalahari. Here was a man of understanding and compassion, who had grown up among the Bushmen of the

Ghanzi farms, and who knew the XKo. He could walk, hunt and talk like a Bushman. But he could also talk for the inquisitive academic, drawing bushlore from an inexhaustible storehouse of experience. His experience was widened by his association with Bushwomen, and he had been married several times. Some of his wives he 'threw away' because they were unfaithful, others died. All gave him fine children. Their features are among the most interesting I have seen in Botswana.

Our first meeting stimulated my interest in the Bushmen, and by the time our expedition reached the Okwa valley, just 18 miles north of Takatshwane, home of the XKo, I wanted to immerse myself in the life and lore of these little people.

I asked Professor Tobias if I could leave the expedition for a few days and remain behind. To my delight he agreed quite readily, and it was decided that I would be picked up again three days later.

I had already told Thamae, the interpreter we were using, that I wanted to join the local group, and he passed this on to them. My acceptance was aided by an incident which had occurred a few days previously. One of the Bushmen required urgent hospitalization, and after I had treated his illness as best I could, I stopped a transport lorry en route to Ghanzi. The driver at first refused to take the sick fellow, but my harangue induced him to change his mind. This established me in their estimation as something of a Samaritan, and long before the patient reached Ghanzi the news of my good deed had reached the XKo Bushmen, whose hospitality I was seeking.

I was far from home those first three nights I lived solo among the Bushmen. It was a strange experience, and I was the oddity. All six foot two of me, I was an object of curiosity, standing tall like some baobab among the Bushmen, and feeling more like a Balboa catching his first glimpse of another ocean of life. It didn't matter that others had come before me. This was my discovery.

I can't remember all my new companions, but Baynette, a farm Bushman with a smattering of Afrikaans, was one of them. And so was Douté, the same conniving Douté who was to play such a significant role in my Kalahari life.

Among those with Douté were his wife Abé, Nkisa, a striking girl and the subject of a haunting story, Kwé Kwé, a charming

enfant terrible, and Nkobe, the wife of Douté's younger brother,
Thauxum, who was away on a cattle drive.

It was Nkobe whom Douté delegated to care for me. Whether
it was Thamae's idea, or Douté's own, I don't know, but there
was no mistaking Douté's only slightly disguised suggestion that
I should sleep with Nkobe. I might have been contemptuous had
I then known his motive, or that he was offering me his sister-
in-law.

As it was, I thought Nkobe to be particularly uninspiring.
Neither her face nor her form was attractive. She was heavy and
too stocky, with a bulldog jaw and none of the gracefulness of
movement I have come to associate with most Bushwomen.

But she was willing, and looked after me well enough. More
than that, her presence gave me an indication of the advantages to
be gained from having a female helpmate in the bush.

That first evening she collected the wood, and as night fell
other villagers squatted around, sharing the food, tea and tobacco
I had brought. Bushmen laugh easily in the presence of such
plenty, but gradually the chat and laughter died down as one by
one the villagers rose and went off into the night. When they had
all gone Nkobe rolled herself into her blanket on one side of the
fire, and I crept into my sleeping-bag on the other. Cushioned on
eiderdown and wellbeing I fell asleep, but was suddenly jerked
wide awake by a repetition of loud grunts passing just beyond the
firelight.

'*Xui!*' said Nkobe, who waited for the grunts to travel on
before putting her head down again. I didn't know then that *xui*
meant leopard, but I was terrified. I hadn't got used to bush
noises, and I lay there haunted by the monsters of my imagination.

When I awoke Nkobe had already started her day. I got up and
was preparing my own coffee when I saw a column of Bushmen
trailing down into the valley towards my camp. I watched them
as they crossed my hearth, and began carefully rolling my
sleeping-bag, packing my things and placing them in a neat pile.

Then Baynette beckoned me to sit near the circle they had now
formed. Douté lay on one side facing Baynette. With their faces
down they began a lengthy discourse, clicking away at the earth
while the others, women and children, sat quiet and serious. After
some time Baynette raised his head and said in Afrikaans, 'It's all

right, Baas.' I interpreted this ceremony as a prayer to their God who, it appeared, now approved my presence among them.

Immediately this was done, everyone rose. Each took a piece of my baggage, while Douté encouraged me to follow them. We eventually reached their village, and Nkobe set about hollowing out a sleeping nest under a bush just behind that of Douté. For privacy and protection against the wind she placed, upright, tussocks of grass at the head of the nest.

On that night as on the previous night, Nkobe looked after the fire, cooked the food I produced and slept nearby. Once again, but not so fearfully, I listened to the night noises. I also heard the growing clamour in my mind of a dream long dormant. Three days weren't long enough to build the dream, and they passed all too quickly. The Land-Rover came and fetched me, and as I waved I said, 'Auf wiedersehen.' I was determined to come back.

FOUR

The Road to Ghanzi

Long before we reached Johannesburg I was planning to return to the Bushmen. I decided I would use my profession as the means. I knew nothing about the disciplines of anthropology or ethnology, but I was a parasitologist. As such I had been programmed for the study of human parasitic diseases, and the Bushmen of the Kalahari presented themselves as a legitimate and worthwhile area for research. My first excursion had proved this. The problem was to convince others, and raise the necessary funds.

Meanwhile life with Ingrid was increasingly unpleasant; our marriage was buckling under the stress. Ingrid blamed our cramped living conditions, and I set about designing and then building a house for tranquillity. I worked on the house in the early morning, in the afternoon after work and at weekends. Ingrid often assisted me, but the work was taxing in the extreme. It meant rising at four in the morning, driving through Johannesburg on a scooter (to cut down expenses), working on the house till eight forty-five, then chasing off to the laboratory, back again after four and getting home after dark for a sleep before the next day's repeat performance.

On one of my morning runs I had a collision with a car and found myself in hospital for several weeks. Lying in hospital I had ample time to think about my return to the Kalahari – a therapeutic prospect.

For my troubles, more particularly my pain and suffering, I was paid a tolerable sum in damages, which I quickly pigeon-holed for my first solo expedition. It was the sort of money that could help me to buy a vehicle equipped with the necessary four-wheel drive. I found the vehicle, an old war veteran in a panel-beater's shop. It was a Willys jeep, still full of spunk, but in need of an overhaul. It cost more than my compensation money, but at this point the first of my many fairy-godmothers appeared, in the shape of an Italian businessman, Dr Folli, who was prepared to help me financially. I also scrounged material assistance from the spares department of Willys, and practical aid from Stanley Motors, a big automobile firm. Soon my jeep was rehabilitated, and roadworthy.

Ingrid and I moved into the partially completed house, but our relationship remained unchanged. The more despondent I became, the clearer the desert loomed as an oasis of escape. The prospect of getting away from it all lent vigour to my preparations. I worked methodically: procuring water tanks, assembling camping equipment, selecting non-perishable emergency rations, increasing my petrol capacity, packing first-aid equipment and the scientific implements and apparatus I would need.

Dr Folli and his stepson Vincent took considerable interest in my planning. I explained to them that it was the purpose of this expedition to follow up some of the parasitologically interesting findings of my Tobias trip. Two puzzles had emerged from my research. Firstly I had found that a considerable number of Bushmen were infected with hookworm. This was surprising, because the hookworm, an intestinal parasite, is notorious in humid tropical and sub-tropical countries. It was against the cards that it should survive or prosper in the hot, very dry climate of the Kalahari. What then was the life-history here in the Kalahari of this organism? What was its significance as a pathogen?

Secondly, why was it that I had found in the most unsuitable specimen for examination, the urine of Bushmen females, such a high proportion infected with a one-celled organism of the genital organs, Trichomonas vaginalis? In our world this parasite has been responsible for much stress, frustration, and despair among women because of its refractory response to chemotherapy. What was the actual incidence among Bushwomen? Was it pathogenic amongst them, and if so, how did they cope with it?

A third investigation was to be added to these. It was well known that the cholesterol content in the blood of 'native' peoples living off the land was low, and that these did not suffer from heart disease, which is such a killer in white society.

Dr Bersohn, a biochemist of the South African Institute for Medical Research, discussed this with me. I volunteered to live completely in accordance with the Bushmen's diet, and see what effect it had on me. The idea intrigued me immensely, although I had no definite plan on how to carry out the conditions of the experiment. I would need to fly a bi-weekly blood-sample to Johannesburg, a big enough problem. But first I'd need someone who would actually provide and advise on the Kalahari cuisine.

All in all I was satisfied I had a hefty scientific programme. The thing was to get there and carry it out.

Vincent Folli, in the meantime, had become imbued with the idea of lion hunting in Botswana, and we planned to travel together, he in his Willys van, and me in my jeep. We set off on a cold and frosty Highveld morning, the Follis' van leading the way. My open vehicle was bitterly cold, and I had forgotten my gloves, but I was too excited to care.

At Swartruggens, halfway to the border, we stopped for a hot drink, then went on. In those days of the Bechuanaland Protectorate there were no border patrols or wire fences, and we drove straight on to Lobatse, and further into the interior, past the deceptive Sukuma Pan flimmering with water which was not there.

Twenty miles on we came to a genuine watering-hole, and stopped for lunch. Here a stately acacia extended itself in welcome, and we sank into its lush green shade. That was then. Today, for miles around, not a blade of grass is visible. The overgrazing of local cattle has taken its toll, and only a few straggly bushes survive the nibbling of ever-hungry goats. Now only the best of drivers manage to pass this dreary place without getting stuck in its loose heavy sand.

A bare 40 miles further on, not far from Muramush Pan, we decided to call it a day, and Vincent went off to shoot his first springbok at the edge of the depression. That evening we ate springbok steaks, and round our crackling fire shared anecdotes to the glug of beer. I relaxed and counted my good fortune in stars. I didn't know that my Willys would play up the next day.

Fortunately my engine trouble wasn't anything of major significance, but I had to slow down to an average speed of 15 mph. Rather than hold up the Follis' van I insisted they push on, and not worry about me. I watched their van disappear. I was alone.

For a while driving demanded all my concentration. The road was nothing more than a sandy track, with two endless parallel spoors divided by a high, equally endless, hump. In parts the sand was soft and deep, and I frequently had to engage my four-wheel drive.

Gradually I became more expert, and could anticipate the more troublesome sections. I shifted gears around with confidence almost automatically, and at my strolling speed I took in more and more of the country about me.

It was not as bare and featureless as I'd expected. Open patches tussocked in grass, bush, clumps and bunches of trees in no order of succession came up to me, watched me go by and ambled off in my rear-view mirror. Here a pair of big brown ears betrayed their owner peering warily from behind a bush. There a spurt of tiny antelope spun out of sight. Another glimpse caught the minute steenbok in beautiful surprise. The smallest buck in the Kalahari, he teems with grace. Several times he stopped and with a bravado born of the inquisitive watched me plough on. His slightly bigger brother, the duiker, wasn't so accommodating. I only learnt to recognize him from his darker colouring, and the white flag below his tail which he flies in retreat.

For miles, it seemed, the same set of hornbills followed me like seagulls above a boat. In fact they were different flights, each disturbed in turn as I went past, rising from their perches on a few strokes of their wings, and gliding and dipping to pull up on the next clump of trees.

A bluish-silver flash that turned into a lilac-breasted roller raced across my path, and not far ahead I saw a sooty-coloured balloon-like thing that floated up and dropped again.

This was the bush korhaan, which during its mating display throws its head back and allows itself to fall almost to the ground before expanding its wings and sailing to a safe landing. Then an ostrich, just like a chicken and hell-bent for somewhere, raced to cross the road in front of me.

Wherever I looked I saw something different. The clouds rolled and puffed themselves into portraits on blue. Even the trees twisted themselves into forms filled with abstract fantasies, and thorny, outstretched arms scratched the sides of my jeep. In daylight there is no hostility in this sort of company, at least not while your wheels keep turning. But when your engine fails the bush takes on a frightening aspect. Trees pull in their shade, the drought spreads itself before you, and fear shrivels your blood. When you are lost it is a nightmare, a hideous game of blind man's buff. There are no landmarks, only whispering bushes and a tittering silence all round. Whichever way you turn you are facing thirst.

Such experience was beyond me my first time out, and I drove on blissfully, almost satiated by too many surprises. Then suddenly I came upon a sight I'd heard of, so rare I shall perhaps never see it again. Far off on a grassy plain I saw a vast brown column flecked with white. As I drew nearer a wave of agitation passed through the mass, and as it reared I realized I was gazing at thousands of springbok. Without slowing down I came closer, and was almost alongside when they rose in a living bridge in front of me.

They leapt in a continuous line across the road, so close together their arc was unbroken. It was unreal. As I moved along so the bridge moved with me, until the last of the antelope had tucked in its legs and sprung in suspended panic to the safety of the other side.

I was entranced. My tiredness vanished, and all I could see was this mirage, leaping and leaping and leaving me stunned.

Reality was pressing me on to Ghanzi. There I had to find Thamae, the interpreter, and start my work. It was essential that I worked quickly, completing my experiments and examinations and renewing contact with Douté and the other Bushmen I'd met in the Okwa Valley. I didn't have much time available, and it was only by taking back results that I could assure myself of future trips.

The further I drove the heavier became the sand, and the slower my progress. The sun went, and darkness set in. Springhares, eyes as bright as light-reflectors, bounded out of my way. A black-backed jackal ran with my headlights down the spoor ahead of me. Owls, nightjars and plovers resting on the sand of the road jumped clear as I drove them down. But I slowed down respectfully for a porcupine treading through the spoor.

The night wore on and on and I had ample time to think about my third task, the food experiment. I knew from what I'd read and learnt during my brief encounter with the Bushmen in the Okwa valley that food-gathering is primarily the task of women.

If I, therefore, could induce the Bushmen to place at my disposal a Bushgirl who had no other responsibilities to occupy her time, I would have someone who could not only collect the veld-foods for me but cook them as well. In addition, as Nkobe had done for me before, she could look after all the other household chores.

The more I thought of this plan, the more it appealed to me. I put it together with my childhood fascination for the Indians. Perhaps here was an entrée into a Bushman family, and with it an insight into their life and customs. From behind my steering wheel and my ignorance it all looked very easy. Maybe it would require a contract with the girl or her parents. Hah! A simple proposition.

That decided, my self-satisfaction sank steadily into fatigue. In the featureless dark I seemed to be getting nowhere. Ghanzi was a myth, and I was a wound-up robot winding down.

Somehow I kept my eyes open, and eventually picked out the first fence-post marking the start of the Ghanzi farms. Twelve miles to go. In a stupor I rolled into Ghanzi at first light.

I drove directly to the home of Dr Asbjorn Jensen, where I knew I'd find welcome and rest.

Asbjorn, a Danish veterinary officer, wasn't at home, but his faithful Nabuki rose, let me in and made up a bed. I declined her offer of food and a beer from the fridge. My only thought was sleep. That came without my remembering getting into bed. The next thing Nabuki was violently shaking my shoulder.

'There's a policeman outside, wants to see you,' she said.

'Tell him to go away. I'm sleeping.'

Nabuki came back and shook my shoulder again: 'He says he wants to see your passport.'

'Tell him to come here, I'll show it to him,' I said.

Nabuki returned a second time: 'He says he can't come in, you must come out.'

'Then tell him I'll see him at his office when I get up.'

Nabuki's patience was infinite. She returned a third time: 'He says you must come out now.'

I swore, got up, dressed and stamped swearing into the sun. Twirling his cane, leaning against a post, was the officer, reeking of petty officiousness. I showed him my papers, which he studied with painstaking efficiency. I kept my temper, and he eventually said 'thank you' and left. I had no wish to antagonize anyone on this expedition, and Heaven knew that I would have much more cause in the future to keep circumspect and on the safe side of this sort of officialdom.

My first task in Ghanzi was collecting and examining the stools of the farm children attending the Ghanzi boarding school. All those found to be infected with hookworm were later treated and dewormed. This mission only took two days, but it gave me the opportunity to become acquainted with the names of a number of Ghanzi families.

Ghanzi is a peculiar settlement. It is primarily the administrative centre for farms which extend some 70 miles to the north, and a further 12 miles to the south. It is the only chiefly Afrikaans-speaking community known to me that lacks a church. Its isolation has led to its being described sometimes as the loneliest white settlement in Africa. These days its pace has quickened slightly, and it is a mélange of government officials, traders and farmers, of Kgalagadi, Herero, other Bantu tribes, a variety of Bushmen, mostly Nharo, and a representative collection of many types of miscegenation.

The first European came to Ghanzi about 120 years ago. But there is evidence – scrapers, points and blades, flakes and cores – of man's presence in the area since the earliest Stone Age. In the late eighteenth century a breakaway group of Ngwato Bantu tribesmen arrived under the leadership of Tawana, whose name the tribe bears to this day. Although Maun, much further north, became the centre of Tawana land, cattle posts were maintained as far south as Ghanzi. When the Kololo, a Sotho tribe, invaded the area, a breakaway group of the harassed Tawana gathered up their cattle at Ghanzi, and fled to the Chobe River far to the north.

Around 1830 Mzilikazi's Matabele warriors arrived in eastern Bechuanaland from Zululand, and pushed the Ngwaketse people further into the Kalahari, as far as Ghanzi, before the Ngwaketse continued southward.

Later Ghanzi became a well-known watering place for half-caste Hottentots, hunters from Griqualand who wandered far into the desert in search of game. It was their language which some say gave Ghanzi its name: a term meaning 'very large, yet very small'. It sums up Ghanzi rather well. It's a place that looms large in the lives of the people around it, but really it is not much more than a few houses, a hotel and a couple of stores. The Griqua description, however, came from the discovery that despite the surface indications of a plentiful supply of water there was, in fact, very little.

The first European traveller who wrote about Ghanzi was Charles John Andersson, who in 1855 pioneered a route from Walvis Bay to the newly discovered Lake Ngami. He found Ghanzi, and reported ample evidence of elephant and rhinoceros. No one today would associate Ghanzi and its environs with the presence of these huge pachyderms.

Andersson mentions a trader and hunter, Moyle, who had arrived in Ghanzi as early as 1852. Another trader who probably preceded Moyle in the same year was Joseph McCabe. Neither of these, or other travellers, stopped to settle.

The first settler was a Transvaal Boer, Hendrik van Zyl, who obtained authority to set up his headquarters at Ghanzi from the Tawana chief, Moremi. He asserted his right to a monopoly of the whole of the hunting grounds in the district, and turned away many whites, including other Boers, on their way to these grounds. Stories about van Zyl slaughtering hundreds of elephant and trekking out the ivory are legion, and this activity may have contributed to his violent death at the hands of one of his native servants, probably at the instigation of Moremi.

Among other names associated with Ghanzi is that of Cecil John Rhodes (Cecil 'Dusty' Rhodes, of the same family, still farms in Ghanzi today). In order to establish a buffer zone against German eastward expansion from South West Africa, Rhodes settled a number of chosen Boers from the Transvaal in the Ghanzi area. These settlers and their descendants account for most of the present-day owners of Ghanzi farms.

It was at the bar, the general store, the District Commissioner's office and at the landing strip for the mail-plane that I became acquainted with some of the farmers. Maybe it is because people

are so few in the Kalahari that those who live there appear to have
personalities packed with character and eccentricity. Or it might
be that outlandish places only attract extraordinary people. Maybe
these were ordinary men after all, and only the impressionable me
turned them into the Kalahari equivalents of Somerset Maugham's
monsoon characters.

From the earliest days of the white settlers, the farmers have
employed as servants or cattleherds the Bushmen they found on
the land allotted to them. European children have grown up with
the Bush children, and have learned to speak their language. The
general attitude of the farmers has been paternalistic, and one now
finds a second or even third generation of 'tame' or farm Bushmen.

Besides these, other Bushmen have come on to the farms during
lean seasons in the veld. They profit from work on the farms, and
may even be permitted to tend the cattle and drink their milk.
These periodic visitors are the 'semi-tame' Bushmen. The 'wild'
Bushmen are those who have never visited a farm, and it was a
band of these, unadulterated by association with white farm life,
that I was hoping to join.

For someone like myself Ghanzi was the obvious place to
begin. It is the focal point of Bushmen in the western Kalahari,
not only the 'tame' but the 'wild'. By geographical coincidence
the three major language groups come together in Greater
Ghanzi: a fact appreciated by the numerous scientists of different
disciplines who have come to Ghanzi over the last seventeen
years.

The differences in language between the three groups are
significant, and have been large enough to prevent a wide diffu-
sion of cultures. In Ghanzi, however, considerable mixing has
taken place, and Nharo is spoken sufficiently widely for it to be
the Bushmen's lingua franca.

Nharo, the language of the Nharo Bushmen, is the central
language spoken also by the Gwi and others who live to the
north in a wedge that goes through Greater Ghanzi. It is a four-
click language with grammatical features more closely related to
the language of the Nama Hottentots than the four-click language
spoken by the XKung and Kaukau who populate the northern
farms and land to the west. I was interested in the XKo, who

were part of the southern group whose 'backyards' fringed the southern farms of Ghanzi. They speak a five-click language which has all the grammatical attributes of a typical Bush language, but which clearly differentiates them from the two other groups.

It was also a language of which I knew not one word. Consequently employing Thamae the interpreter was imperative.

I located him without difficulty at the segregated African school at Ghanzi. (There was no integration of races in the Ghanzi boarding school in those days, and when years later it was enforced by the independent government, the whites of Ghanzi preferred to see the school closed and their children sent to school in South or South West Africa.)

Thamae was the son of a Nharo Bushman prison warder, and spoke English fluently. He only had a smattering of XKo but his Nharo and his feel for Bush languages would, I knew, be invaluable. A moody, intelligent man, he had a strong personality. But he drank heavily and increasingly, and it was sad in the end to see him so undone by his addiction.

He also had an insatiable appetite for women, which was hardly dulled by taboos. He flirted compulsively and indiscreetly, and this led us into minor crises that I would have preferred to avoid.

Together Thamae and I scoured the southern Ghanzi farms, feeling our way from one cattle post to the other, and asking after Douté or any other Bushman from the Okwa valley group. According to our information at each post, we were just a few days behind them, and it was simply a matter of time before we caught up with Douté and his wife Abé.

When we did, Douté immediately recognized us, and appeared pleased to see me. He agreed at once to take me back to the XKo Bushmen, but said we would not find those whom I had met.

For various reasons they were dispersed just at that time. He suggested that he take me to Takatshwane, an old river-bed about 20 miles south of the Okwa valley. Not altogether encouraged, I took Douté back to Ghanzi. Abé came with us, and to my delight so did the elfin Kwé Kwé, Douté's small niece who had charmed me before.

In Ghanzi I arranged for a lorry to help us get to Takatshwane, for my jeep was too small for five passengers and all our baggage.

Meanwhile Thamae told Douté of my plans, and explained my
need for the services of a Bushgirl to collect veldfood and cook
for me. He also told him I was eager to be accepted by a Bushman
family in order to learn and understand their customs and ways.
I don't know how successful he was in articulating my ideas, but
Thamae assured me that Douté thoroughly understood them.

We headed south from Ghanzi, with Thamae and I riding high-
spirited in the jeep. Just before we reached the last farm we came
upon a large group of Bushmen drawing water at a cattle trough.
Thamae, who seemed to know a lot of them, particularly the
girls, soon had them animated and chatting and laughing with
him. He took a guitar from one of the group and began playing.
Not to be outdone, I fetched my violin, and joined him in an
incongruous duet.

We turned our act into an entertaining evening, and we made
a lively scene around the cattle trough. But I fear the Bushmen
thought our performance a little odd.

Eventually we put down our music to push on into the night.
At Okwa, as Douté had thought, we found no one, and decided
to drive on in hope to Takatshwane. As we reached Takatshwane,
the lorry accompanying us pulled up, and we transferred Douté,
Abé and Kwé Kwé to the jeep for the last mile or so to the village.

It was well after midnight when we descended upon the sleeping and unsuspecting band of Bushmen.

To the Bushmen the rumble of my jeep arrived like an alarm
clock going off. Even before we had climbed down figures were
converging on us from nowhere. They stood around us, some
holding flickering torches, and all with inquisitive faces. Douté,
taking command, sent a couple of the younger men scurrying to
the back of the jeep to unload and skin a steenbok I had shot along
the road. Then he introduced us, simply saying who we were and
that he had something important to discuss.

He spoke as a person of some importance. Immediately a
collection of glowing sticks from surrounding fires was arranged
among us, blown to a short burst of flame and left to warm in
ember. The inner circle around this fire were mainly men. I could
make out a few women sitting a little further away, just beyond
the circle of dim light.

Douté began his talk, and the Bushmen listened attentively.

Eventually one of the older men, with what looked like a saddle-nose, began replying. On the trip down Douté had mentioned with enthusiasm the possible availability of a Bushgirl, the daughter of a man called Gruxa. I decided that the man speaking must be Gruxa. But I couldn't make out what was going on, and Thamae, for all my trust in him, had lost the drift.

In the dark I felt helpless, and clutched for clues in the mood of the talk. It was then that I first saw Namkwa. Here was a woman who would be different, a deviation from my civilized norms. A woman untouched by hands that have plucked violins or fiddled with whores. This was the romantic speaking, for the scientist in me was quiet. I think that had he objected I would have stilled his doubts, for romantics can rationalize as well.

Later I was able to rationalize my involvement in more scientific terms, and in results. I had to, for there were others who found my methods objectionable. They favoured objective, impersonal, research. Even some scientists who were on the side of partici-patory field work screwed up their noses and thought my participation went beyond academic propriety. And some were simply racialist. Had I known all this around that camp-fire I might have balked, but I didn't think beyond my immediate hopes. I was caught in my own excitement.

Meanwhile Thamae was interpreting a mood of his own. He had caught the eye of another young girl, and while Douté and the village elders talked on, Thamae turned his attention to charm and conquest. Shucre, the girl, was not completely averse to his advances. She dropped her eyes in coy awareness, and lifted them timidly again for more.

Somehow I became aware of a slight commotion among the men, and one man in particular seemed to seethe as he watched Thamae's behaviour. I couldn't mistake the jealousy, and when the man got up and came back with his bow and arrow I sensed serious trouble. The feeling moved around the circle, missing Thamae, who was oblivious of the change of mood. For my safety as much as his, I warned him off, and the tension eased.

When I got to know these people better I learned that old Kxei Kxei, the agitated one, had indeed harboured sinister inten-tions. For some time he had been 'feeding' Shucre, that is hunting and collecting food for her with the intention of marrying her when she got a bit older, and he felt his rights were being in-fringed. In any event, his hard work at courtship was in vain, for Shucre never did agree to their marrying.

Kxei Kxei's potentially violent reaction was not altogether extraordinary. It is true that the Bushmen are a harmless people, and peaceful enough at heart and home, but, like most people, they have a violent streak and a fighting spirit.

The XKo, by reputation, were among the more hostile Bush-men, and old Ghanzi farmers maintain that only forty years ago a one-man trek through XKo country was a hazardous under-taking. I was told of one farmer who was nearly pulled from the cab of his truck by two Bushmen. I also heard there were cases of actual killing, and cattle stealing, and attacks on police sent out to arrest culprits.

Some of the old men I came to know and regard so highly were said to be wild in their youth, and the memory of Musomo, Douté's father, is very much alive. He was shot dead after he had half-killed a Hottentot policeman and left him tied to a tree as a meal for the hyenas. Nor was Musomo the only one killed before the XKo were finally tamed into submission and turned friendly.

Bushmen, I discovered, grow friendlier on full stomachs, and once Thamae had tamed his ardour and the men had started munching at the steenbok I'd brought, their talk became patently more congenial. Youngsters had skinned and disembowelled the buck, and with diplomatic largesse I'd indicated that it be pre-pared and shared around the fire. This might not have endeared me to them, but it was enough to make the Bushmen feel obliged and clinch things in my favour.

As they sliced pieces from the roasted carcass I caught the name Namkwa mentioned several times, but no one turned to her, or asked her opinion. She simply sat there seemingly uninterested in the discussion. I don't recall her moving at all. Nor did she react when Gruxa finally said he was willing to allow his daughter to live and stay with me during my visit, but this was only his decision, because his wife was somewhere in the bush collecting veldkos, or wild bush food. She would have to put her seal on the arrangement.

This didn't bother me; I was confident that my acceptance was definite. I made noises of gratitude which Thamae translated into clicks. Namkwa just sat there, and remained sitting there until all the Bushmen had slipped away to sleep what was left of the night.

When she stirred I was astounded by the gracefulness of her movements. She stood silently in front of me dressed only in a tasseled duiker-skin, her fawn colour contrasting with her white ostrich-eggshell beads. Only the dirty old handkerchief on her head demeaned her native dignity, and when I removed it and threw it on the fire she made no protest. She was too afraid.

With Thamae's help I prepared a sleeping place, spread out my groundsheet and unrolled my sleeping-bag. Namkwa sat beyond the groundsheet with her back towards me, and when I talked to her she sank into a curl on the sand, her hands tucked under her head. Softly I tried to coax her on to the groundsheet, but she was still too afraid. I pulled out a spare blanket from under me and put it over her. Once again I tried to persuade her closer to share the groundsheet. Slowly she gave way to my persistent and gentle persuasion until her body no longer lay on the cold ground. I felt nothing but tenderness for this small creature now sharing my bed, and knew that I could do no more. I stroked her head and went to sleep.

FIVE

Namkwa ...

I awoke that morning, the first in our lives together, with the lilt of an unusual melody in my ears. I lay with closed eyes, afraid that opening them would stop the sound. I opened them, and the tune was still there. Namkwa had gone. Then I saw her over at her father's fire playing a dongo, a small instrument probably best described as a hand-piano. She had her eyes closed, and her head and body swayed to the music. At first I thought she was repeating, again and again, the same short tune, until I discerned very slight modulations following each other as if she was groping for new variations. The subtlety in such simplicity was entrancing, and Namkwa had taught me her first lesson: an appreciation of dongo music.

I watched her for a long time, swaying there, a bush melody in herself. Her olive-fawn skin shone smooth in the early sunlight, and her rhythm seemed to run from slender fingers up through her body, her arms and shoulders into the expression on her face. She still wore her meagre duiker-skin, and her ostrich-eggshell genital apron was tucked between her legs. Strung round her neck was a necklace of brightly coloured beads. This was all she wore. I could see her breasts, firm and protruding and embellished by large areolas. Again I was held by the clean-cut features of her face, and the line of character it revealed.

Abé saw me rise from my bed, and called out to Namkwa. Only when she was ready did she stop her music, get up and start gathering some firewood. Thamae, who was also up, gave Abé some coffee and some instructions. Namkwa returned with a glowing piece of wood, and a few straws of dry grass, and in a matter of seconds had a fire going. Then she sat on one side as if all this was of no concern to her. She didn't say a word, and I felt too shy and too stupid to try any sort of conversation with her. It was Abé who took over the household, and Thamae saw to it that we were both watered and fed.

After breakfast I decided to return to Lone Tree Pan, 22 miles away, and collect some important baggage, including tobacco I had left there. I asked Namkwa to come with me, not expecting her to agree. But she got up immediately, called her little sister Nkasi, and both were ready to leave. Curiosity, it would seem, was stronger than fear.

The 22 miles from Takatshwane to Lone Tree Pan is one of the heaviest stretches along the entire Ghanzi–Lobatse road. The day was warm and the engine hot. The two girls chatted incessantly, but directed not one word at me. I didn't mind, for they were obviously enjoying themselves. A few times they indicated I should stop, and then they bounded out to collect tsamas that they had spotted. Tsamas are watermelon-like fruit, and the main source of water for Bushmen during the dry season.

We arrived at Lone Tree Pan and were surrounded by a swarm of clicking Bushwomen. They crowded round the two girls, clucking with admiration and envy while Namkwa and Nkasi preened themselves on this attention.

Our return trip was tedious and tiring. The temperature had risen sharply, the sand was heavier and the engine boiled. Twice we had to stop, but this mattered little to my passengers. They were as perky on their return as they were when they set out. After all, a journey in a jeep is a novel happening in a Bushman's life, and their experience held the promise of greater prestige in the eyes of their peers.

When we climbed down a little elderly woman whom I had not seen before came to greet us. It was Namkwa's mother. She looked at me closely, and I wondered what she was thinking. I learned later that she hadn't been enchanted by the idea that her daughter should be allocated to this stranger, and she had flatly refused to have anything to do with the windbreak and sleeping place that Douté had asked the women to build for us.

According to Thamae there had been a lengthy discussion while I was away between Douté, Gruxa and Namkwa's mother. Douté had overwhelmed their objections, and won the battle for their co-operation. It was up to me to win their sincere consent.

Here Namkwa and Nkasi helped. They returned so patently happy with their trip that their mother's fears were partly allayed. In fact, she dropped her passive resistance, and even helped to enlarge the windbreak, and the next day build it into a proper Bushman hut. Namkwa had no part in this, neither did any of the younger girls. This was a job only for the older women.

They brought strong 5-foot pieces of wood and planted them closely in the ground in a circle. They laid other pieces criss-cross to strengthen the structure, and then stuffed and covered the web, rather haphazardly, with tussocks of grass which the old women had collected and carried in their big skin capes.

The building of the hut was significant. It was the symbolic seal of approval placed on my union with Namkwa. This was the marital bed.

My role in all this was not altogether a passive one. I had come with my simple enough idea of getting a Bushgirl to find for me, and had now expanded it into a proposal of marriage. I had told Thamae of my feelings, and once again he had passed them on to Douté, who came back to say the Bushmen would 'marry' Namkwa to me. I was delighted, for the more I studied Namkwa, the more I was convinced that this was what I wanted.

The fact is that she was no ordinary Bushwoman. To me she lacked the typical smell of a Bushwoman; she stood out from the others in her cleanliness, her stature and bearing. As young and timid as she was, her natural self-assurance came through, and offered a challenge. I wanted to bring that spirit out.

All this going on in my head wouldn't have concerned Namkwa. Although she spent more time at her mother's skerm than ours she had apparently resigned herself to the circumstances, thinking that I was leaving the next day. When the tomorrow came, and I stayed, only then did it dawn on her that she had gained a 'husband'. She was not so easily rid of me. When we grew to communicate, she told me that the only feeling she had for me then was fear. She had heard of white men taking Bushwomen, but she never thought it possible that one would actually come to her. When it happened it was only her fear, and to some extent the command that she should sleep with me, that prevented her from objecting.

'We were never properly married,' she said. 'We never had a

period of *hu'u* [betrothal] when we should have stayed and slept apart. It was all so different with you. Your people should have visited my parents with meat, and eaten with them, and they should have exchanged gifts. You had Douté to speak for you, but I never asked any of my friends to speak for me.'

'Yes,' I said, 'but your mother and father agreed.'

'But you know that Tasa, my old relative, was never asked, and he still talks about this.

'Besides, you know I never took my *xobbi* [her bag in which she kept most of her earthly belongings] to our house. And besides, I was just told to sleep with you. No one ever took me to your house, no one ever brought you to our house.'

'Yes, I agree, but then you know that parents can determine who their girl should marry.'

She scoffed: 'Oh don't say that! They can do this, but only if the girl agrees, and I should never have agreed. It was just fear of you that made me agree.'

'Then you *did* agree!'

She hit me, and we left it at that.

In retrospect, she was right. It was different with me. I had barged into their lives, and tossed their customs into confusion with my impetuous proposal. Certainly there was no ceremony to speak of with us and in retrospect I suppose we never were properly married. I was simply told that our sleeping together with the parents' consent was all that was required. Otherwise there was an attempt to advise me on some of the niceties. Thamae suggested I should think of a present to give Gruxa, and perhaps one for the mother to 'tame' her.

I gave Gruxa a new solid chopper, an ideal gift, I thought, and to Namkwa's mother I gave an assortment of string beads. Both seemed satisfied, but Douté pouted with dissatisfaction, and hastily I told Thamae to thank him for what he had done, and promise him a gift when I left.

I thought the gifts were necessary consideration for the parents' consent and an expression of gratitude. On one of my later trips, Xamxua, my teacher, pointed out that even the conveyance of the gifts had been bungled. He made it clear that I had not properly compensated her parents for their loss or secured Namkwa with my present. The chopper should have been given to Namkwa, not Thamae, to pass on to her father. This way it would symbolize the fact that the groom had become a relative of the father-in-law's group.

For this reason there may also be a passing of presents, beads, pots, knives, or weapons, from the bride through the groom to his parents. On a subsequent visit, Namkwa made such a gesture. She insisted I give my mother a string of beads from her, and so expressed her willingness to belong to my family. A bride will also claim a present, and a hartebeest or gemsbok skin were usual. Today Namkwa, like other girls, would prefer a woollen blanket. Her wedding present was a bright red doek, or headscarf, to replace the dirty handkerchief I removed from her head.

I was amused to learn from Xamxua that Bushmen have a sort of leap-year marriage. He did not love his wife, yet when she stole his weapons and placed them in her hut, he knew that this was a form of proposal and he had to accept her as his wife.

It is not usual for younger couples to arrange their marriages alone. They employ the assistance of their parents, friends or a relative with whom they are on particularly friendly terms. It was perhaps because of the absence of these that Douté undertook this role on my behalf.

I learnt in time that motives or reasons for marriage in a XKo society (or any Bushman society) differ from ours. Love is generally a minor consideration. 'She will learn to love me,' a boy will say. Security is of far greater importance. The man must be able to provide for his wife, and she must be able to collect food abundantly. Looks are unimportant, but in a land of periodic drought both sexes fear getting thin and dislike skinniness in the other. The girl wants a man with an even temper, not given to outbursts of anger during which he might strike her.

This is a preference shared by the man as well in his appraisal of his partner. Each expects the other to be kind, especially to children, and restrained. A girl wants a diligent man who provides her with plenty of food, skins and tobacco. A man wants a girl who works well and builds a house and performs her duties, collecting food, water and firewood, to his satisfaction. Girls appreciate skills in a husband if they increase his status, and thereby theirs.

Thus a Bushman's motive for marriage is primarily economic.

Both sexes are so preoccupied with food in a difficult environment that the good provider is the best choice. The best collectors are often older women, who can easily find a younger suitor. A good hunter makes an ideal match.

There might also be sexual motives behind some unions, but generally the Bushmen do not see marriage as a necessary precondition for intercourse. Nor does the Bushman expect his wife to be a virgin, as might chauvinistic males in our 'civilized' societies. Virginity is neither essential nor general.

Although Namkwa has always emphatically maintained that I found her a virgin, most children start early, and go into the bush to indulge in sexual experimentation. When a girl reaches puberty she is not by convention required to show avoidance of sexual activities, but while having full licence in sex matters girls do come across practical obstacles to their indulgence: there are usually other people about, especially younger children, who play around in the same house without respect for privacy. Besides, the sand tells tales – Bushmen read its impressions like a book.

Sexual intercourse in the bush, even for married couples, is not approved, though it does occur. For a boy to get his girl they must connive to be at home while the others are out hunting or collecting food. Boys will set off on the hunt, then slip back. Girls will say they are ill and must stay behind. So sex has a way.

Because Bushgirls have long periods of sterility, pregnancies are rare, and therefore not inhibiting. The only other curbs on an unmarried girl are the taboos on sex before puberty and incest. There are also avoidance taboos during menstruation.

It was soon obvious to me that even in such a small community expected and actual behaviour do not always coincide. One evening Thamae was amusing the Bushmen sitting around our fire. Suddenly there was a howl, especially from the girls. At the time Thamae was not fully aware of the kinship ties of the surrounding group, and in his ignorance he teased Thxale, saying that Thxale had had intercourse with Nkanaki, who was in fact his niece. Despite the strict taboos between the two, the girls' reaction was not so much reproof of a shocking act as an exclamation of surprise that it should be spoken about in public.

It was in this somewhat laissez-faire atmosphere that Namkwa had grown up, but she came unpractised and reluctant to my hut.

Around the fire she affected the same lack of interest she had displayed on our first night. She hardly participated in the cooking, but left it all to Abé. And although I didn't know it then, she ought to have sat on my right, between the hut and the fire. Nor did I attribute any significance to the fact that Namkwa's mother sat outside the fire circle.

Abé prepared some meat which had been given to me, and roasted a long stringy tuber. The meat was tasty but the root was bitter. Only hunger prompted me to eat. Namkwa said little, but gave her mother portions of everything we ate, and everyone else at least had a lick of the pot. Tea ended our meal, and one by one, as before, the guests got up and went off until only the two of us were left.

Namkwa pulled out a conical piece of tin, filled it with tobacco and smoked it like a pipe. I said nothing, just watched her as the fire sank to embers. Then she rose and entered the hut. When I peered in she had curled herself up on the blankets at the far side of the hut. She was nowhere near sleep, and I could sense the thoughts racing through her head. Should she get up and run away? That would be useless; where would she hide? I would fetch her, and might then hit her. I was so big. When I entered the hut she realized there was no way out. I was alone with her, and she was there to let me do what a man would want to do. In the morning it would be over.

She was lying on her side, with her back towards me. Gently I covered her with the kaross, a blanket of jackal skins, and lifted her head on to the pillow. She did not resist. Under the cover I lay against her, and put my arm around her. I felt her coarse, cold duiker-skin against my chest. Slowly I lifted it, stripped it from under her, and slipped it over her head. Her shoulders were icy from the cold outside, but her body was warm. She lay on her side, and I could feel the round of her warm buttock against my thigh. But she lay unmoved.

Gently I tried to get her to turn round, but she wouldn't and each time turned back to her original position. With great care I nibbled at her ears, fondled them with my lips and ran kisses around the nape of her neck. But when I tried to turn her face and kiss her mouth she struggled violently.

Her lips were tightly pressed together, and when I let her she turned once again on her side. But this time she pushed her bottom out towards me.

I then began fondling and stroking her body. Around her breasts and down to her waist I met her eggshell beads, and felt her front genital apron – her *k'gu* – still tucked between her legs. As I stroked her thighs I could feel her leg muscles contracting. The little apron became lodged all the more securely. I tried again to turn her on to her back, but she wouldn't relax. Yet each time she rolled back she moved to push out her buttocks towards me. On top of her resistance such a basic gesture was highly erotic. I was aroused anyway, for even if my love-play hadn't been altogether successful on Namkwa, it at least had the effect of urging on my own passion.

Now I dropped gentle persuasion, and forced her over on to her back. She lay there, almost infant-like, with her head on one side, her hands up above it. She didn't move, nor utter a sound but turned her head violently when I tried to kiss her. In this position I lowered myself into her. My coming was a culmination, and a release from lust. I lay by her side, holding her, and drawing her closer to me until we nestled spoon-tight together.

I like to think I gave her comfort then, and afterwards we always fell asleep like that, turning in tune with the other through the night, and waking with the same closeness.

It could have been different that first time. We were both victims of our ignorance, and the traditional techniques of our own kind. With typical missionary ardour I thought only in terms of the man on top. And I was impatient. I didn't know that a Bush-girl indicates her willingness by proffering her buttocks, and that this is the most common position for intercourse. Couples sleep that way in their efforts to keep each other warm. Besides, Namkwa was a virgin, and knew no other position. As she confided later on, she was also frightened at what I should do to her. But when I had done it, it was good that it wasn't as traumatic as she might have feared.

The sun was rising when I felt Namkwa stirring. She rose, strung her cold duiker-skin over her bare shoulders and went out. From the roof of our hut she pulled some grass, dug out the glowing embers from the ashes of the previous night's fire, and expertly blew the grass into a flame. This done, she lit her pipe. Silently she puffed at it, savouring its smoke, and staring in front of her.

Soon Abé came round to make coffee, but there were no signs of a Bushman breakfast. (There was absolutely no schedule of meals, and sometimes I was left all day without a thing in my stomach.) Finally, when I'd given up the thought of food for the time being, Douté arrived with the tongue of a steenbok, probably the one I had brought. It was deliciously soft and juicy.

The Bushmen had prepared a bed of glowing coals the evening before and then raked these into a large hole over which they placed a few branches, then the buck's head, more branches, some more coals and a blanket of sand on top. All night the head stewed like this. When uncovered in the morning the skin was simply peeled off with the ashes, leaving the skull with its edible filling.

Abé saw my scissors in the first-aid box. She asked for them, and Douté cut her hair. Then she cut Namkwa's hair, and before long several other girls joined in to make a social event round the scissors. Eventually I, too, was drawn in, and asked to shave the lower portion of the girls' necks. They liked to have their necks shaved very high, and the line extended round to the front of the face to give the appearance of a very high forehead. Nkasi came out with a page-boy look, and everyone seemed pleased with what they saw. Then Abé recognized soap in my shaving kit. She was quick to ask for this as well, and together with Namkwa hurried off to the borehole to make the most of it.

During this activity I was amused by Douté. He turned his attention to his overalls, the only pair among the Bushmen, and searched its seams and folds for lice. Nearby, older women lay, heads on each other's laps, and dozed off while fingers probed for nits. De-lousing brings content, like back-tickling.

While Abé and Namkwa were away, Thamae gave me a crash course in the obligations of a Bushman son-in-law, and the behaviour expected of me. He told me that I would have to work for my father-in-law for a 'limited period'. In later years this led to considerable conflict between Gruxa and me, for my father-in-law was inclined to see no end to the duty.

Generally I had to provide him with meat, and when there were lions about, help collect large amounts of firewood to keep them at bay. All that I provided had to be passed through Namkwa,

who, in return, would receive foodstuffs, berries or bush-
potatoes from her mother. It was also customary that I should
'find' Namkwa in the village of her parents, and only when the
work period, generally two or three years, had expired, could I
take her to my people.

Both Xamxua, who took on the task of teaching me the Bushmen manner and customs, and Douté said that the parents'
influence over their daughter should stop on her marriage. It was
not so in our case, for it took years to break Gruxa's hold over
Namkwa. He was a particularly obdurate man, whose stubborn-
ness provided me with much cause for complaint. It was a frustration I shared with my brother-in-law, Thxale, who married
Nkasi. We had many sessions moaning about the old man.

I was also taught that I must not speak directly to either of my
in-laws. Anything I had to say should be addressed to Namkwa.

Nor could my father-in-law, and particularly not my mother-
in-law, sit at our fire. If they should come to our place, I had to
ensure that firewood was available for them on one side away
from our fire, but within hearing distance. I was expected to show
the greatest respect to my mother-in-law, and avoid her completely, for after all was she not the one who gave Namkwa to
me?

Nkasi, on the other hand, was my 'little wife'. As Namkwa's
sister she stood very close to me. Should she marry and her
husband die, I would be obliged to marry her so that she would
not suffer from want.

'But what would Namkwa say to this?' I asked in surprise.

'That is a matter for the sisters to decide,' said Thamae, 'but
she will accept Nkasi for she came from the same womb.'

In theory this was right and proper, but I learnt that the
actuality of any such situation could lead to violent disputes
between a wife and her widowed sister, especially when the
husband paid more than a casual interest in his sister-in-law.
Jealousy knows few boundaries, and it also hovers around the
Bushman life. It even hovered, I was to discover, menacingly over
my marriage.

Namkwa eventually returned after midday. With no ceremony,
and quite unconcerned, she lay down in our hut. I was sleepy, and
crawled in next to her and tried to sleep. Flies followed us in to

threaten our comfort. So I took off Namkwa's doek, covered both our faces with it, and we slept in peace.

Towards evening a number of Bushmen came to our fire. This time it was the 'younger set'. Thxale, Guanaci and her husband, Kesi and her husband Nxabase, Shucre, Tkose and a few others. I had brought with me a quantity of the powder base for a nutritious drink, Puzemandle, which is popular among Africans in the South African gold mines. I asked someone to prepare some. It was Namkwa who rose and mixed the powder with water and brought it to me. I offered her the first drink, which she accepted, and quickly passed on to her mother. On subsequent rounds I was always the first to receive, then Thamae, and the elders, and then finally the younger ones. Each waited his turn, and if the drink did not get all the way round there was no sense of ill-feeling. For my part the feeling I had was one of growing optimism; somehow it seemed to me that Namkwa, though she still sat off to one side, had begun to participate in her role as my mate.

I looked forward to the evening fire, for these sessions helped me get to know the various members of the village, particularly those in Namkwa's age-group. One evening when the younger ones had gathered again, Nxabase's eldest daughter, Tkose, began a hand-clapping game. A lively, life-and-soul-of-the-party girl, she clapped her hands, then hit her mouth with the right, clapped again and hit her forehead. She did this quickly, and without losing rhythm or missing a beat. It prompted Shucre to start singing; a melody that then and other times reminded me of Schubert's *Trout*. Picking up a stick Shucre hit the ground at the same time as Tkose clapped, and when she lifted the stick Tkose in turn hit the ground with her hand.

The action and split-second timing was governed by the rhythm in the song, and I was fascinated. Soon Namkwa moved alongside Shucre and joined in. Later I learned how strict is the discipline of the beat – if Tkose had missed a beat she would have received a crack across her hand.

Unnoticed I got out my tape recorder, and recorded their performance. When I played it back the reaction was dramatic. They clapped their hands in delight and disbelief. I had to play the tape again and again, and again, while they tried to identify each voice.

The older women near our fire were not to be outdone. In the centre of the little settlement they made a fire, sat round it and began clapping and singing. One after the other they rose to dance their own improvisations of the Bushman shuffle, and then returned to their places around the ring. The women watched each solo with amusement, and the more imaginative the innovations the louder was their delight.

All this roused the men, who put on their rattles and began shuffling in rhythm towards the women. So the whole village came to the dance, swaying and turning, singing and clapping, simply because it was there.

As easily as it started, so did the dance quieten, and dissolve into the night. I sat and watched the shuffling forms retreat, watched them in silhouette moving and bending to their bedtime chores. At this time of night firelogs are rearranged, and drowsy embers kindled for the nightwatch.

There a little figure stretched and yawned. Another squatted in a ball, stared in blank communion with his flame. And over there, smoke puffed silently, out of the day's last pipe. When you looked again, they had gone, crawling under the outline of their huts and into sleep.

It was quiet. You could almost hear the lion on the prowl, leaning stealthily on every pad, pausing stiff on every step. Until quite unexpectedly, jackals howled, and tiny creatures flurried in the sand. Gradually I became attuned to the irregular rhythms of the night, snuggled up against my mate, as the whole became melodious, melding in a flow of sleep.

In the days that followed I became more and more preoccupied with my food experiment. When I undertook to live and eat like a Bushman, I had little idea what it would involve. I found myself becoming almost obsessed with my stomach, and the thought of food. It was not simply a matter of hunger, the long hours without a meal or the irregularity with which meals came around. I also suffered from the stringiness and bitter taste of some of the veldfoods I had to eat. I could barely swallow them.

The stoic scientist, however, pressed on regardless, and interest drove me out with Namkwa and her friends, Tkose, Shucre, Kwé Kwé and her sister, on one of their daily harvests.

Each was equipped with a three-foot wooden digging stick hardened in the fire and sharpened like a chisel. Two of the girls took along shoulder-bags into which all put their pipes and tobacco.

At first the girls hunted for the *n'tch'am*, or bush-potato, a long stringy tuber I'd already met. It is the root of a ground creeper and grows some 20 inches down. It is juicy and can be eaten raw, but is better roasted. The girls straddled the creepers they found, and used their digging sticks like canoe paddles, throwing up sand behind them. As they dug deeper they loosened the roots until they could pull them out with their hands. Not all bush-potatoes have a descending root, nor are all of them as bitter as those I'd sampled. Some are pleasant to taste, and the older women are, it seems, more adept at finding these than the younger girls who had been feeding me.

As we wandered along we came on a clump of grewia bushes. The girls fell into a scramble to pick their small brown berries. An acacia bush also caught their fancy because of the lumps of resin sticking to its bark. These were devoured as readily as if they were candies. Tkose found a large green caterpillar. She tore off its head and rear end, squeezed out the intestinal contents and offered me the body. I declined politely, and gave it to her. But she shook her head. Later I learnt that these are only eaten when there is no other food available. A hairy caterpillar I saw was also firmly rejected by the girls, and I was warned not to touch it because its hairs were poisonous.

We changed direction and headed for a large open patch where there was an abundance of tsama melons. It was now clear to me that the girls knew exactly where to find each type of available food. They hunted as a casual pack, straying apart but remaining within calling distance. Repeatedly they came together to share a pipe between them.

Some of the melons were cleaved open on the spot with a digging stick. They were sampled, and if not bitter were mashed and eaten. In between the tsamas we also found numerous gemsbok melons. Most of these are very bitter, and only those with no blemishes were thrown into the bags.

I was anxious to witness the preparation of our haul. During our absence Abé had cooked some of the left-over meat. Now she placed the pieces in a wooden stamper, and pounded them to a mince-like consistency. Then she added stock to make the

Namkwa

Douté with Dr Heinz's first jeep

Dr Heinz with Gruxa, his father-in-law (left)

mixture richer before replacing it in an iron pot to keep warm.

Namkwa and Shucre dextrously removed all the seeds from the tsamas and gemsbok melons and roasted them in a bed of hot sand and coals. When done they were sifted out with a reed sieve and mixed with the grewia berries before being pounded to a meal in the stamper. Meanwhile the insides of the melons were cooking, the tsamas looking something like cooked cucumber. Finally everything was poured into the stamper and mashed together into a greyish mass. It didn't look very appetizing. I was fond of Abé's mince, but the tastiness of the melon dish came as a surprise and a much-needed booster for my flagging stomach. I knew I would survive my experiment.

My parasitological work was progressing satisfactorily enough, but I was still faced with the collection of soil samples for study. Namkwa showed a singular lack of interest in this, although when I asked Tkose she jumped to my assistance. Round our hut, however, Namkwa became more co-operative, and visibly at ease with me. She no longer sat off to one side, and her laughter sounded relaxed and carefree. When the others had left our fire she would remain for some time with me, smoking and sharing a cup of tea. She took to the canned beer I had brought, now and again asking for some, and when I asked for a drink of Puze-mandle she was enthusiastic about mixing it.

For all that, her concern for my comfort didn't go very deep. And certainly not as far as a scorpion bite. One evening I carelessly picked up a piece of firewood, and with it a scorpion's sting. I yelped and she sprang up and killed the thing, but did nothing more. She just sat back and watched while I panicked and ran for my medicine box. There was a syringe, serum and needles, but I found to my horror that the needles didn't fit. There I was with poison accelerating through my bloodstream and I couldn't inject an antidote. I thought I was beginning to die, and the bloody woman was just sitting there.

With an effort I pulled myself together, told myself to stop acting the ninny and accept the inevitable. I must say I didn't feel like waiting for that, especially since I'd read once of the agonizing thirst that might accompany the dying.

Angry, I asked Namkwa for a pot of water, just in case. Then

I swallowed a sleeping tablet and lay down trusting to luck. Despite my pain, the pill was effective, and I slept. When I awoke, I realized somewhat petulantly that I was alive, the water untouched and Namkwa still unconcerned.

Looking back I'm embarrassed by my behaviour, and even need some convincing that it actually happened that way. Southern Africa, of course, has no deadly scorpions, and Namkwa knew that I had been stung by the less painful of the two species in the Kalahari. I realize now that my pain then was more from panic than anything else, and nothing like the stings I've had subsequently from the other species. Those were dreadfully painful, but then Namkwa showed more concern.

The most violent reaction I got from Namkwa that first time arose out of my work. For days I'd procrastinated over the task of obtaining vaginal swabs from the Bushwomen, and didn't know how to begin. In view of my reasonably satisfactory relations with Namkwa I decided that I could risk getting her co-operation. For a Bushwoman to expose her genitalia to a man was quite out of the question. This much I had learnt. The solution, I thought, was to teach Namkwa what was required and take the first swab from her. I chose a day when the men had all departed for a hunt. Namkwa had agreed to help, but she became hysterical when I tried to take the swab. She scrambled to her feet and ran screaming through the village to her mother, who pacified her. Strangely, however, my mother-in-law was not angry with me.

This naturally was the end of my experiment. For twelve hours Namkwa avoided me, and I thought it also meant the end for us. That evening in bed I tried my best to restore her confidence in me and convince her of my good faith. I smothered her with apologies and in the end I think she understood how sorry I was, how sincere I was to make amends.

In the village, among the women, I had to turn on all sorts of diplomacy to restore the old atmosphere. They eyed me with suspicion, and I knew clearly that the price to pay for this particular investigation was too high. I didn't want to forfeit the rapport I had found. I didn't want to lose Namkwa.

I've often tried to analyse my early infatuation for Namkwa, and my behaviour towards her. Like the scorpion sting I've sometimes wondered if I really did behave and feel the way I say it happened. Did I really on that first time out become so desperate for a girl who could not read or write or speak with me, who knew nothing about me, my work, Beethoven, Boskop, and all the rest, and cared even less?

The answer is, I did. I was like a scientist with a new discovery, a romantic with a fresh ideal, and Namkwa in her innocence epitomized my passion. Her indifference merely made me keener.

Thamae asked her one day where I should find her when next I came. With a casualness that hurt she said, 'Oh, you'll never find me.'

'Why?' I said.

'Because I'll be somewhere near Manyane,' she replied.

I turned to Thamae, who said this was a pan some 60 miles away. I didn't know then that Manyane was quite outside her territory, and that she would never go there. She said this because she thought her answer would induce me to forget about her and leave her alone.

She didn't know how determinedly I would pursue her, or what changes she would bring to my life. The remarkable thing is that when I'd seen through the wonderful fantasy I'd draped around her, and found the real woman, she remained a thing of inspiration. She instilled in me an energy and drive, call it an inner strength, that would survive all the adversity that lay in wait for us, not only on the outside, but within our own relationship as well. Neither of us was paragon enough to perfect an idyll, and I was too much a creature of my background to give up all for her. I could not lose my appetite for my old life, and I knew that Namkwa couldn't fully satisfy me. But I also came to realize, often pining in the deserts of my academia, that I would return and return again to Takatshwane and to Namkwa.

On my last morning Namkwa lay in my arms with her head on my shoulder, and I watched the sun come in through our door. I looked up at the crude branches around us, the wasps' nest above me and the lizard peering behind a stick. I couldn't stand upright in my hut, but it had been home, cosy and comfortable. In Johannesburg home would be different.

While I packed the Bushmen sat around hoping to pick up any of my discards. But there was not much to leave. I gave Abé and Douté a blanket each and both seemed satisfied. The villagers gathered round to shake my hand, and wave goodbye. I held Namkwa's hand for a long time, and looked into her eyes, but I could detect no echo of the feelings that moved in me. I climbed aboard my jeep, and pulled away through the grass and sand towards the long road.

I had little inkling that even before the sound of my engine had faded Douté would accost Gruxa and demand my chopper. My well-meant gift had become a source of conflict, and Douté's demands were to disrupt the harmony of the group for days. Nor did the ill-feeling abate altogether, for where I was involved tensions invariably reared. Douté had already played a significant role in my Bushman life, and, though I already distrusted him, as I drove back to Johannesburg I was grateful for his help. In time we would come to challenge each other.

SIX

Into the Storm

'Well, here's to a good trip,' said Asbjorn Jensen, the vet, as we toasted each other in the pub at Mafeking. It was a few months later. He had just come in from Ghanzi and I was returning to the Kalahari.

It was quite opportune that we should have met there, for Mafeking was well out of my way. In those days the capital of the Bechuanaland Protectorate was, by strange delineation, outside the Protectorate, in the northern Cape. I had written several letters to the authorities there requesting permission to shoot buck for the pot. But I had no reply, and so went to Mafeking to hustle a pot-licence out of them.

As we drank I noticed a weird darkening of the sky. 'What's happening to the sun, hey? Are we having an eclipse or something?' I said.

Both of us jumped up and went outside. The sky was frightening, rumbling and rolling with the coming of a deluge right out of the Bible.

'Man, let me get out of here,' I said. 'In my open Willys I don't want to be caught in that storm, I'll drown.'

It wasn't a wise decision. Asbjorn went back to his hotel, and comfort, while I got nowhere near to outrunning the storm. A few miles south of Lobatse it caught up with me. It was only five in the afternoon, but so dark that I had to drive with lights. And they weren't much good, for the rain came down in curtains. Only lightning flashes showed me the road, which had swirled into a stream.

I picked up the turn off to Ghanzi, and splashed on. There are numerous dips in this road, and for 364½ days of the year they are bone dry. This day had to be different. I navigated several of the dips but then plunged into one that carried the torrent of a river. My engine spluttered, faltered and stopped. I was stuck.

Logs crashed against the jeep, which creaked in two minds whether to stand or deliver itself to the current. It was pitch-dark, and the water was still rising. Soon it was washing over the floor of the jeep, and out the other side. I hastily tried to rearrange my load, putting all the perishables on top. Then I decided to disconnect the electrical system, and ventured toes into the water. To my consternation I couldn't touch ground. The car began to lean downstream. I mounted the bonnet and sat there like a baboon in the Kruger National Park. I tried to pick out sturdy trees, thinking that I might make them swimming if the jeep went.

When I saw jagged tree-stumps crashing by I became less optimistic, and as the night wore on and our list increased I became decidedly pessimistic. The rain poured on, down my neck in a rush to my feet. This is my last day, I muttered. What irony, I thought. Drowning in the driest country in southern Africa.

Somehow the wobble in my wheels never took off. By 2 a.m. the rain had subsided, and hope appeared again as headlights approached me. A large car stopped, and in its beam I was staggered to see how widely the stream had spread.

It was just as well it had, for that volume of water down a narrower channel would have borne me away hours ago. I tried shouting at the car. In the din they couldn't hear. I saw some activity, and then the car moved. Bloody fools! I thought, they're going through. They did too, although for a number of yards their lights were under water.

When they saw my dilemma they threw me a rope with which we were able to anchor the jeep until the water subsided. This it did almost as quickly as it had risen, but I still couldn't budge. My petrol tank had been completely submerged.

We spoke about my problem, and waited. I didn't know my helpers but discovered they were friends of the Indian Trader at Kang, and they told me they had managed to get through by disconnecting their fan-belt. Then we heard the put-put-put of a tractor. A young Tswana man jumped off, and agreed that I had a serious problem.

'But first we must get you back on the road,' he said.

Once pulled clear by his tractor we decided it was essential to drain the petrol and separate the water. During this process I spilled a considerable amount on the ground, and a quantity seeped into my trousers. For the next two hours I could not sit still for more than a few seconds. Despite our efforts the engine refused to start.

'Never mind, put her into second gear, and I'll pull you,' said the young Tswana.

For more than 20 miles to the outskirts of Kanye he pulled me, before the engine showed any sign of revival. It spluttered, spat and coughed and then caught.

'How can I repay you?' I said. 'What do I owe you?'

'Not a shilling,' he replied. 'I'm just glad she's running again.'

'But you've had considerable expense. Surely you must let me compensate you for the petrol you've used,' I insisted.

'One day you'll find me on the road. Then you can give me a lift,' he said, and smiled. We shook hands and parted, not expecting to see each other again. Years later I was to meet him once more, not in need on the road, but in high office in independent Botswana.

I drove on with considerable relief, singing in the sunrise. But now the sand was wet and firm, and I made rapid progress. Soon I would be back in Takatshwane. At once the familiar doubts rose in my mind. Would Namkwa be there, or would she be at Manyane? Would I find her at all? I would find her, I told myself, even if it took weeks to do so. This resolve didn't convince me. And should I find her, what would she be like? Would she treat our union seriously? How would she behave? Apprehension crept all over me, and the more I thought of her, the more afraid I became of our meeting.

At Kang Store I was distracted from my fears by the aftermath of the storm. On the way it had occurred to me that the storm had been widespread, but I could hardly credit such far-flung ferocity.

A large rainwater tank had been torn from its base, and sent rolling some 300 yards, through two steel-wire fences. Not a single window-pane in the shop was unbroken, and though the roof had not yielded, there were large cracks everywhere.

'We had hail the size of chicken eggs,' said Osman, the trader. I could almost believe him.

On the last 92-mile leg to Takatshwane there was hardly a tree with its bark intact. Bushes had been battered and stripped. I was sure I would never have survived the storm here without crawling under my jeep. Its canvas roof would have been torn to shreds.

In such a storm numerous buck and other animals that cannot retreat into some sort of warren are slaughtered. Some are killed by hail, others by lightning, which is a killer even on clear days in the Kalahari. Nor do human beings escape the onslaught.

In all my time in Botswana this was the only storm covering the entire country that I experienced. General rains are rare, and then rather mild. Rain over the Kalahari is usually sporadic, and its fall quite arbitrary. A heavy cloud will come up, inundate a strip of land, and leave immediately adjacent stretches brown and barren. The wet veld is remarkably responsive, and within days it is green with grass and budding with foods.

Nature has another way of refreshing the desert flora; by fire. Although the Tswana and Bushmen are responsible for some bush fires, the majority are nature's own product. They are kindled by lightning, and can rage through hundreds of miles of dry bush. After the fire, as after the rain, comes the green, and a flora peculiarly adapted to extreme forces.

As I neared Takatshwane I noticed an abundance of tsama and gemsbok melons. It was obvious that the veldfood crop had been a good one. This didn't please me, for I knew that at such times the Bushmen move far from the government waterholes to places where they can get enough water from the melons. My fears were realized at the Takatshwane borehole, where the government pumper told me that he had not seen any Bushmen for some time.

On my own, I knew I wasn't equipped to locate my band of Bushmen. I therefore unloaded my heavy baggage and hurried up to Ghanzi to find Thamae. Once again I was assailed by doubts. Had I come all this way in vain? Had Namkwa been right when she said I would never find her again? Man, I told myself, you have to find her.

In Ghanzi there was no time for social calls. I picked up Thamae, promising his schoolteacher that I would help him with his arithmetic in the bush, and rushed straight back to Takatshwane. I should have been worn out, I hadn't slept for ages. But my anxiety and the urgency I felt overwhelmed the fatigue that was there. It has always been like that, the adrenalin driving me on as I near Takatshwane.

If this was something to wonder at, the uncanny knack the Bushmen have of sensing the arrival of strangers in their territory has never ceased to amaze me. I know that the Bushmen recognized the tyre-spoor of my vehicle as distinct from any other: and that they have heard and distinguished the sound of my jeep at a distance of fully 4 miles. But this hardly explains the extra sense of their perception. News seems to travel on vibrations like radio waves, and it goes right over my head.

Their curiosity is more understandable. They appear round friendly visitors like ants at a picnic, to see what is going on. We had hardly arrived at Takatshwane when a few of my friends materialized. They had heard that I was near. By noon the next day Douté and Abé walked into our camp because, as Douté put it: 'I saw you pass along the road.'

The one family I was anxious to see was not there. My heart sank, but I tried to look relaxed and not show my anxiety. The following day I asked Douté whether he knew where Gruxa and his family were.

'They can be anywhere,' said Douté. 'He often goes off on his own with his family.'

'But have you no idea?' I was pleading.

'He has various places where he keeps his things. I don't know where he is today,' he said.

Then he and Nxabase clattered away together without coming up with any answers. Thamae explained to me that Gruxa was a quarrelsome, bad-tempered man who often took his wife and daughters off on their own to a 'place'. He could be at any one of several such places, where he kept a cache of food and other possessions.

I said, 'Tell Douté that we will just have to look for him. I'd like to start in the morning, and would Douté please come with me?'

Douté looked at me. Yes, he would come.

I thought it strange that Gruxa, an old man, should take off alone into dangerous bush with his three females. My experience was that XKo groups were small entities living in the closest proximity, sharing each other's virtues and vices, and most private affairs. Their ties were those of kinship, companionship and interdependence, and these can be very binding. I learnt, however, that no tie is strong enough to prevent periodic outbreaks of friction, the intensity of which depends on the individuals involved and the mood of the year. When the signs are particularly threatening wise XKo will see the necessity of avoiding otherwise inevitable physical conflict, and will part company until moods have improved.

My father-in-law was rather notorious for such break-ups, but I never did find out why he had gone off on this occasion, and it was unlikely that his reasons were climatic.

The Bushmen are so close to their environment that they have an instinct for survival in their blood. They know that when times are bad the group can only live together by breaking up. To save the fabric of their small society, they must sometimes take it apart.

One testing time is before the summer rains break, when the Kalahari is incredibly hot. The heat increases day by day and regularly reaches 120° Fahrenheit. The land is parched – it has been for a year – and the bush is bare. Last year's melons have all been eaten. Tubers are hard to find because their tell-tale runners have been burnt by fire, eaten by buck or withered away. The animals are dispersed and game is scarce. What there is must be hunted with snares and traps, for even the supply of beetle larvae which provide the Bushmen's arrow poison dwindles away in the dust.

The people are hungry, thirsty and baked on their vast earth oven. They grow tetchier and more irritable daily; they laugh no more. Instead they grow covetous, mean and threatening, and it is no wonder. It is at such times that each family might turn inward and go its own way. But old Gruxa, it seemed, went out on a whim.

The next day we set out. For me the trip was exhausting, but I kept going on anticipation and the stimulation of observing the Bushmen. They walked in a flow of limb and sinew. It looked so easy and unhurried, but I had to stretch my stride to keep up.

On and on they went, swaying round bushes that tugged and tore at my clothes without ever touching their bodies. Every so often, without breaking their rhythm, they would snap off branches to clear an easier path for me. The worst stretches were the patches heavily ploughed and undermined by field rodents. Like plumping through soft snow under a brittle crust, it was laborious going, and annoying too.

Douté hardly noticed the difference, and seemed to ski across the sand and undulations as though he were on even ground. Occasionally we crossed parts rife with 'devilkies', tiny spiked seeds that cling like mad and pierce the soles of the hardest feet. Douté simply went into light gear, barely pressing on each step before flitting on to the next. Rarely did he have to lift a foot to remove a thorn, and then he did it in mid-stride.

I had my shotgun with me, and once Douté stopped to indicate the presence of a steenbuck. He did not point, but with outstretched arms and upturned palms — a gesture full of poetry — he 'presented' the buck to me. He saw and heard far more than he thought worth while pointing out to me, but when we crossed a track he indicated with a graceful motion once again the direction in which the animal had walked.

We crossed the spoor of two people. He said something about Geitchei and Theugei, and I understood that the two women had passed that way while collecting food.

After some time we saw the spoor of an entire column of Bushmen. I asked, but he said none of Gruxa's family was among them. I hesitated, unconvinced. He walked ahead some distance, studying the footprints carefully. He then came back to me with a string of names, none of which sounded like Namkwa. I insisted we should follow the spoor. He said, 'Namkwa,' and shook his head. With a shrug he went my way.

About one and a half hours later we could hear stamping in the distance, and soon entered a small village where a woman was pounding tsama melon seeds. Douté, needless to say, had been right. There was no trace of Namkwa and her family. We stayed long enough for a tsama drink, and for Douté to ask after Gruxa. Then we pushed on.

It was now clear to me that Douté knew exactly where to find Gruxa. I had long ago lost the direction in which I thought our camp lay, and I followed him blind and gladly. For him every nondescript bush held a signpost, it seemed as though each branch arrowed the way. He indicated by the sun when we should be there, and I knew that he'd be right.

We walked into a small clearing, and there found the mother preparing something at the fire. Her daughters sat nearby smoking and chatting. Just off-stage Gruxa was chopping wood.

The women heard us, and Nkasi and Namkwa jumped up. There she was, as I'd left her. She laughed and turned around. I took her hand in greeting, and she held mine while she bent her head away and went on laughing. I tried to put my arm around her, and she pulled away, turned around again and laughed and clapped, as Bushmen do to show surprise. I was relieved. The laugh was warm. Her eyes were clear. And she wore my bright red doek. We could start from there.

Nkasi laughed like her sister, spontaneous and welcoming. Namkwa's mother beamed, and made the meeting even warmer. Gruxa came up on cue and greeted me with 'morning', the only word of English he had picked up from me.

When Douté, on my suggestion, said we should all return to the village site of the main band, Gruxa grumbled unhappily and showed his displeasure at the thought. The abundance of food about, the melons and meat, was reason enough to remain. The girls however needed no urging. They were already rolling up their few belongings and ramming them into their shoulder-bags. Packing took seconds.

I got the old man to understand I'd fetch the meat with the jeep, and reluctantly he got ready too. With swinging strides the two sisters set off, *xobbi* over their shoulders. The blanket I had given Namkwa was tied bag-like and filled with odds and ends. She carried it over her shoulder with her digging stick balanced on the horizontal by the pull of both hands.

I hurried after them while Douté and my in-laws, starting later, followed some way behind. It was clear the girls were happy to see me. They laughed and chatted non-stop. Then Namkwa ran back to me, and asked for some *thauntcha*, which is XKo for tobacco. After a few puffs the girls set off again. This caused me to wonder whether the prospect of material gain had anything to do with Namkwa's pleasure at my arrival. She wasn't really delighted to see *me*. After all, wasn't she a Bushwoman, whose whole life had been subject to economic dictates?

I let tiredness dull my doubts, and plodded on. The way home was longer than I had anticipated, and we were going direct. I struggled to get my legs to go forward with some semblance of harmony.

On the light side of nightfall we arrived back at the jeep. I'd walked the whole way, and it felt like it in every muscle. Thamae, the lover, had flirted the day away with the girls, and prepared nothing for our return. I was ready to slump, but perked up at once when Namkwa without a word from me began organizing things. Now I knew she was my mate.

She took my bedding off to a more private place (we were not at the same site of my previous trip) and built a windbreak. While I stretched my aches I watched her work. She moved with self-assurance and obvious competence. She sent Nkasi off for firewood, and quickly had a fire going at the foot of our nest. Then she made tea and prepared our meal. I grew impatient lying there, admiring her, and tried to draw her down to me. But she pulled away each time to do something else. Even when all was done she insisted on sitting alone by the fire and smoking her pipe. Finally she rose, and without a word stripped off her duiker-skin, dropped her loin cloth and slipped under the blankets next to me. She nestled up against my chest, covered by my arms. She was so small she seemed to cuddle right inside me. Gently I kissed her and tentatively felt my way to where we had left off. It had taken hours on different nights before she let my tongue play on her lips. Now she responded, more relaxed, and squirmed in answer to the sensuous feeling wakening in her.

Life with Namkwa settled down to the routine of a normal Bushman marriage. Abé no longer was required to look after me, for Namkwa did it all. She cooked and fed me, brought me tea and gave me attention. She resented others intruding on her household duties, and only occasionally asked one of the young boys to help in the most basic of the cooking chores.

Though by nature not an early riser, Namkwa would get up first thing to make us coffee. We made a game of the ordeal. I wouldn't let her go without a kiss, or let her get dressed without a romp. It was as much her fun as it was mine, for she laughed and teased me too.

The game over, Namkwa would set to clearing the previous night's pots and dishes. Like her Western sisters she would invariably leave them overnight. Being male I'd lie on for an extra nap until she came back with a kick and a cup to wake me up.

Most mornings, Namkwa a had to cook second time, because her mother and Nkasi, and sometimes other women, would come round for a social chat. These visits are a common occurrence in a Bushwoman's life, and often before I'd dragged myself up Namkwa might have gone off visiting another fire. Sometimes if there was something special to see or hear she'd come and call me. More often I'd follow on my own to squat and listen, for at that time I hadn't learnt the chat.

Though I was gradually picking up the clicks, I still relied on Thamae to help me communicate, and during the morning he and I would settle down to work on my conversation. In turn I would help him as promised with his arithmetic.

For all his willingness Thamae wasn't much of a teacher. After all, he was still learning XKo himself. In the end I turned to Ntumka, a bright young man, who seemed to know my problems. Namkwa was no help whatsoever, and only in later years did she show any interest in correcting me, teaching me, or answering any of my specific queries. Had she been more co-operative, I'm sure I would have learnt the language far more rapidly.

As it was, I had a long and mostly single battle with a language that had nothing in common with the Indo-Germanic languages of my experience. Besides, I wasn't a linguist, and had no idea how to work out the grammar. If the theory was difficult, the different clicks were equally hard to make out. I could only distinguish two of XKo's five clicks, and came nowhere close to pronouncing them.

I tried. I clacked and clocked and clucked and contorted my tongue in every possible way. Then when I found a click I was delighted. But I still didn't know where to put it.

It was only after much hardship and study that I improved. My greatest breakthrough however came when I managed to free myself from the grip of English and German constructions. I had been trying to fit XKo into a mould of our own rules. But XKo into English forms wouldn't go. It was, I discovered, a language on its own.

While I worked at my language frustrations, and my research, Namkwa would stamp berries, sometimes for an hour and a half non-stop. This labour was worth the effort, for we discovered that the berry mash mixed with Puzemandle powder made a pleasant porridge. Occasionally she would come over and listen to us, or sit stringing beads until the midday sun grew too hot. Then we would retire to our shelter, and lie down in togetherness, her head pillowed on my thigh.

Fetching drinking water from the borehole and having a wash became part of the afternoon pattern. Namkwa wouldn't miss this interlude, and each day sprang to her rightful position beside me in the jeep.

Back at the village I buried myself in my work, while Namkwa cleaned around our hearth, carried away old ashes, raked the sand with a branch and brought back our bedding which had been airing all day.

Round about five o'clock, Namkwa would join a number of other girls setting off to collect firewood for the night. Then I was forced to stop whatever I was doing to listen as they chatted away in tune, and wove light songs around their heavy bundles. I listened particularly to catch the sound of Namkwa's laughter or perhaps some joke that she might toss across the fields. Each happy note would reassure me.

At this time activity stirs around the settlement. The girls come back, and so do the hunters and women who have been out collecting food. They return with their stories of the day's events, talk of lion spoor, new food beds or a meeting with some other Bushmen.

Once the sun set, Namkwa, I learnt, was not supposed to leave my fire, even if I were away. So while she could she went off to make last calls and hear the news. When it darkened she came back to me.

Life with Namkwa was not, however, all berries and Bushmen victuals. One incident gave us a foretaste of our many outbreaks of misunderstanding in the years to come. We were sitting together at our fire finishing a pot of tea when Nkanaki passed by. In those days she was very pretty, and I called to her. Nkanaki stopped, and allowed herself to be amused at the jokes I offered.

Other girls joined us, and I suggested that Namkwa should make a new pot of tea. She did this readily, and passed round cups to all the girls except Nkanaki. I thought this was uncalled for, and insisted she should give Nkanaki tea. Namkwa blithely pretended not to hear. She bent over the fire, fished out a hot coal, rolled it quickly in the palm of her hand and proceeded to light her pipe.

I rose, brewed some more tea, poured a cup and sugared it for Nkanaki. Namkwa said nothing. She got up and went over to her mother's fire, the only place after dark that she was allowed to go on her own. The other girls, sensing tension, left rather suddenly, leaving me alone with Nkanaki, who was waiting for her tea to cool. Now she drank it quickly, and left as well.

Namkwa did not return, so I went to bed. After a considerable time she came back and sat at the fire. I called to her but she didn't reply, nor come to bed. I called her several times, but she just sat in silence. So I got up and pulled her into our nest. I nearly regretted it, for one would have thought I'd caught a wild cat. With spitting ferocity she kicked and hit at me until her rage petered out. Then she returned and slipped into bed, as usual with her back to me.

For a while I lay in two minds, but then began to slip off her duiker-skin, beads and loincloth. She didn't resist. Nor did she draw away when I put my arm around her. This became the pattern whenever we 'made up'.

The next day was one of those when all activity ceases at 10 a.m. Not only is the heat unbearable at 115° Fahrenheit, but the sand is so hot that no one can walk on it with bare feet. Most people therefore sleep through the heat under trees. The Bushman finds it very easy to sleep.

Suddenly the village tore into action. From several directions men came running carrying sticks. I don't think I have ever seen them move so quickly and with such precision. I heard someone shout 'si'isa'. The next moment a Bushman was holding up a 5-foot mamba, Africa's deadliest snake, and so poisonous that anyone bitten by it might just as well measure his lifespan in minutes. The man threw the snake into the bush, and the village settled down to doze again.

Water time: Dr Heinz rations the flow for Namkwa (left) and Thxale, his brother-in-la[w]

Ntumka, Dr Heinz's young 'teacher'

Tkose digging up a bush potato

*Nkasi, Namkwa's sister, washing
herself with melon pulp*

Namkwa with her dog Sibi

Bushmen are ever wary of snakes. Only few eat them, and all are ready to kill them. As with other things, they seem to know intuitively when a snake is near. Thanks largely to Namkwa's watchful eye I've been fortunate in my experiences with snakes. Except, I should say, on those occasions when she has made me feel a fool in public for not recognizing the obvious signs that a snake was among us.

I'm afraid there must have been many occasions when my Bushmen friends wondered at my stupidity. There was one evening, however, when I acted with intuition. Weary after hunting all day, I went to our hut to lie down. But before I did, for some inexplicable reason, I picked up my torch and shone it on my pillow. There, stretched in lethal comfort, was an 18-inch snake. '*Si'isa*,' I exclaimed. There were a few people nearby, and their reaction was instant. Namkwa was the quickest and before I could move had killed it with her digging stick. By now she had come to regard my personal safety as her responsibility.

Snakes were one experience. But in my early days as a freshly fledged Bushman, there were countless others. Each little happening I notched up as something new, and the only thing I took for granted was my constant fascination with the life around me. Because of my language problems, my other inadequacies, and the disadvantage I felt at being so different physically, I was still very much the observing stranger. But gradually through my relationship with Namkwa and its reciprocal obligations, I came to recognize my need to identify more closely with these chosen people, to absorb their values and actually live as one of them. To do so I needed to know where I belonged. For this would govern much of my behaviour. Up to then I had casually spoken of Bushmen bands without knowing what really constituted a band. I assumed it encompassed a village group, but this was a loose assumption for I discerned that individual band allegiances did not stretch right around the village. Behaviour patterns were the clue, and by watching them, particularly the interaction between my in-laws and others, I slowly put my band together.

Even then there were so many subtleties in everyday exchanges that my circle had a very vague circumference. I was a long way from a meaningful genealogical table that told me exactly where I stood. To play safe I decided to confine myself largely to those people who, in the normal course of a day, had most to do with us. I also relied on Namkwa to give the lead in my relationships with others, and so enable me to compile a list of 'dos' and 'don'ts' of Bushman etiquette.

To some extent all this was hobbling for my scientific curiosity but it paid dividends and I have no doubt that by acting within the norms of the Bushmen behaviour patterns, I learnt far more than I could have as a detached and purely objective anthropologist.

For one thing I was most eager to visit other Bushmen in their nests, or huts, to see just how they lived at home. Mindful of my ignorance of the social conventions, I waited for Namkwa to suggest when we should go visiting. Only when I was certain that I wasn't transgressing the code did I initiate visits. Fortunately Namkwa often invited me to join her because she wished to show me something that she knew would interest me.

I was able to see Douté make a new bow on one such social visit. I went to his place not as an observer, but as Namkwa's husband; a fact which evoked from Abé the response, required by custom, of a gift of berries.

I sat with several other men around the operation. They were not there simply as spectators either, but proffered advice and from time to time also participated in the task. This way work becomes itself a strong social factor, causing the men to gather, talk and help each other.

Douté's bow came from a grewia branch about 3 feet long. He held one end with his toes while he tapered the other. His instrument was an ordinary penknife which he sharpened frequently by lifting sand on its blade on to a log and using the sand as an abrasive. When he'd tapered both ends (I noticed he had cut no notches) he held the bow briefly over his fire and bent it straight. Round the middle of the bow he wrapped moist animal tendon, tucking the ends under the coil. The tendon, which contracts hard on drying, gives the bow a very secure grip. He then strung the bow with strong string made of spun sinew, wrapping it tightly round the tapered wood and once more tucking away the moist ends.

While this was going on Tasa brought along a dried duiker-skin. He'd dried it by cutting tiny slits about 3 inches apart round and just inside the edges, then stretching the skin on numerous pegs inserted through the slits and hammered into a shady place. He set to scraping it, removing all the hair except a clump which hung as a decorative tassel. His tool was a piece of sharpened flat iron jammed into the end of a gemsbok horn and every ten or fifteen strokes he stopped to restore its edge on his awl.

After his scraping Tasa chattered awhile, then went off to finish his cure. I learnt that the skin is buried overnight with a covering of fat and water. The next day it is kneaded, stretched and worked until it is soft and dry. This process does no more than break the fibre of the skin, and is not a chemical tanning process.

I came to regard my father-in-law as an expert in this activity, and always asked him to prepare the skins I obtained for Namkwa. This was not just son-in-law diplomacy. His expertise showed, particularly in the quality of the pretty tassel that he left.

Although there was a sameness to the pattern of our nights, a number were packed with incident. There was the night Namkwa lay laughing on my shoulder at the repartee that criss-crossed from skerm to skerm between the men of the village, and carried on until nearly midnight. Hardly had this died down when screams galvanized the village into action. They came from the spinster hut, where flames rose to show it was on fire. Quickly its burning grass was stripped off and the fire brought under control.

In the uproar everybody began abusing Kwé Kwé, the *enfant terrible*, who had for sound reasons withdrawn from the mob to Douté's hut. Apparently she had been responsible, and had set fire to the hut out of sheer spite.

Kwé Kwé shared the spinster hut with Shucre and Tkose, who were considerably older than she. That night they had hoped to entertain some visitors (I should think boyfriends), and tried to get Kwé Kwé out of the way. But Kwé Kwé wouldn't budge. As the older girls' insistence grew, so did Kwé Kwé's anger, and eventually she picked a faggot from the fire and just shoved it into the grass of the hut.

Such destructive behaviour would probably have been rewarded with a good hiding in other societies, but not among the

Bushmen. Douté gave her a thorough scolding, and made no impression whatsoever – Kwé Kwé continued to scowl angrily. She was an aggressive little creature with a charming side to her personality; I often saw her trying to provoke the older children, putting her little fists in their faces and daring them to retaliate. Usually they managed to ignore her.

On another evening Thamae's impetuosity gave rise to another incident. For some time he'd been bent on the seduction of Nkanaki, who was a friend of Namkwa's sister Nkasi, and who often sat at our fire. With Nkasi around, he couldn't get very far, but this evening Nkasi hadn't returned from collecting veldkos, and Thamae literally seized his opportunity.

He tried to joke and charm Nkanaki to his skerm, but when this failed he tried to drag her off by force. He pulled her along struggling, and wouldn't let go even when Nkanaki's mother intervened. The struggle attracted the attention of the other Bushmen, but none moved an inch to interfere. I didn't know what to do, but took my cue from the other men, and did nothing except sit back and await the outcome.

After some time Nkanaki's mother began crying, and I heard Nkanaki remonstrating. Thamae only then let her go. This didn't stop the mother's wailing. She went on crying, but her distress hardly raised an eyebrow. The next day a few of the men joked with Nkanaki about the near-rape, and even her mother showed no ill-feeling towards Thamae.

I was the only one who seemed upset by the incident, for I was sensitive about doing the right thing, and Thamae I felt was my responsibility. I was the reason for his being there, and I wanted him to behave, but no amount of admonition seemed to have any effect. When it came to women he was incorrigible. On the other hand he was practically indispensable, and although I was his employer, and he regarded me as his superior, we were also companions. He was also my closest confidant.

He knew all about my feelings for Namkwa, and my relationship with her. He shared my secret, and I must say this for him, he kept it loyally, even in the face of a number of inquisitions that he was to suffer at the hands of a fellow scientist and police officers.

As the days wore on I sensed a tension creeping into our lives. Day after day the hunters came back empty-handed, and Thamae and I had no more luck with my shotgun. If this were not enough, Gruxa, my father-in-law, started his grumbling again and worried me continually for some of my food, which by then was also running low.

Thamae told me that Gruxa wanted to take his family and return to the place where I had found them. The other men strongly opposed his leaving, and Namkwa, who initially was prepared to follow her father, decided on staying. This angered old Gruxa, who tried to justify his bad temper by insisting that his daughter did not want him any more, and blamed me.

Meanwhile, my mother-in-law was disturbed by the controversy around her family, and wanted to stop the gossip round the other fires. She too opposed her husband, and as a public sign of her goodwill towards me she wore a doek which I had given to Namkwa for her. She also sent me via Namkwa a handful of bush potatoes; a gesture that prompted Thamae to comment, 'Now you know she accepts you as her son-in-law.'

Fortified by all this, I told Thamae to make it perfectly clear to Gruxa that he could not just go off with his daughter without my consent. This upset the old man all the more, but he stifled any outburst, and for a while the antagonisms, at least their outward signs, were hidden. Namkwa appeared unconcerned.

The uneasy peace was broken by the arrival of a herd of cattle at the Takatshwane borehole. As was usual, the herd was accompanied by a number of Tswana, as well as Nharo Bushmen cattle-drovers from Ghanzi and two white farmers. Gruxa, at the borehole to fetch water, sat down with the drovers to hear the latest news about Ghanzi.

In the course of his chat he complained vehemently about 'that white man who married my daughter, and now, when I want to go back to the bush, he refuses to allow my daughter to leave'. Letting off steam was one thing. Telling the outside world, and it was bound by its taboos to be hostile, that his daughter was consorting with a white man, was another.

The disclosure disturbed my mother-in-law, who had accompanied Gruxa to the borehole. The next thing, Namkwa was in a state, and wondering what dreadful consequences would follow. By evening the matter had become the subject of discussion among all the Bushmen of the band. They were not only concerned about Namkwa, but indeed were now worried about the entire band.

They buzzed with anxiety, and I soon found out what had happened. Now I was worried. How far would the disclosure go? Back to Ghanzi? To Johannesburg? The following day I decided to go down to the borehole to cultivate the confidence of the two white farmers, and with luck forestall any reports of my marriage to Namkwa getting back to officialdom.

I had hoped that the Nharo drovers would have kept the information to themselves, but apparently they hadn't been able to wait before passing it on to their white 'masters'. I knew that Ghanzi farmers weren't surprised by this sort of thing. It went on all the time, and indeed one of the men was quite amused. His comment to one of the drovers amounted to a philosophical shrug: this European was a man, and in the bush a man needed a woman. It was just possible I could establish some rapport with these two, and get them to understand that my work would be placed in jeopardy if my liaison became public knowledge.

I spoke to them about my food experiment, and my need to have someone to collect and cook food for me. I spoke about the stool examinations I had carried out on behalf of the children at the Ghanzi school. I tried small talk, I tried bonhomie. But I got nowhere. I could detect no understanding of what I was talking about. I therefore resigned myself to the worst.

Soon afterwards the worst was realized. By one means or another the news reached the District Commissioner's Office in Ghanzi.

Two days later Namkwa told me she was leaving with her family the next day. She gave no reason, just said she was going. I blew up. She knew I would be leaving myself in a few days, and I felt she had no good cause to leave before my departure. What had decided her to go? Surely it couldn't be that she wanted to leave me? After all, didn't her display of jealousy show that she had acquired some feeling for me? Didn't she take me everywhere with her? That evening I sulked. I did not sleep with my arms around her.

The next day the young girls, Shucre, Nkasi, Nkanaki, Tkose, Kwé Kwé and Namkwa, asked me to give them a lift to the Takatchu valley 5 miles away, where they wished to collect some

veldkos. They needed a lift because they wanted to take the small
children along. I took them over, and promised to fetch them at
noon. Back at the village Thamae and I packed quickly and
loaded the jeep. I was doing exactly what any wise Bushman
would do in the charged circumstances: I was leaving.

All the people, mostly the older ones, who had stayed behind
in the village, knew there was something wrong. They sat at their
fires or near their huts eyeing me. It was most unpleasant. When
I was ready I tried saying goodbye. No one rose. No one said a
word. I tried to shake hands with some of them, but my white
hand, all I had to offer them, was rejected. My mother-in-law and
father-in-law looked at me, and turned away. 'Come on, let's get
out of here quickly,' I said to Thamae. We jumped into the jeep
and left Takatshwane.

I had intended spending a few days at Lone Tree Pan, but it
was only the hearty welcome we received there that induced me
to stop over at all. A small boy with a fungus infection of the head
took my interest. His name was Bolo Bolo, and he attached himself to me. Without being asked he served me like a slave. The
following afternoon his sister, Kamka, came to our fire. A pretty
girl, she played her dongo and sang demurely. In the evening she
helped with the cooking, and sat about until it was time to turn in.
In the morning she was back early, and helped Thamae prepare
coffee.

Watching Kamka it was inevitable that I would compare her
with Namkwa. I saw none of the self-assurance and independent
spirit that moved Namkwa. She spoke with me, and laughed
easily. She tried to teach me her language, and gave me no feeling
that I was something to be kept at bay. She had the sort of
personality that would offer no traumas.

The last few days at Takatshwane, Namkwa's sudden cooling,
my leaving, had been nothing if not traumatic. I had been angered,
but now my pride was hurt. I thought of Namkwa's indifference,
her reticence, her unco-operativeness, and the little things that, in
my mood, erased the signs that we were coming together. I
thought of the troubles with her father, and the troubles to come
in Ghanzi.

The sum total was depressing. On the other hand, here was
Kamka, obliging, sweet and obviously companionable. And there

was Kamka's father, Duce, a far different proposition to the grumbling Gruxa. We were easy in each other's company, and he seemed happy to please me.

If I were to pursue my aim of becoming one of a Bushman family, then Duce's band appeared to offer all the benefits and none of the hassle. When I came to leave I gave Kamka a doek, and Duce a present. I told him that I would return in three months and look for him. Then I would like to speak to him about his daughter.

On the way home I had ample time to review what had happened, and ponder the possibilities of the future. I knew deep down that I was acting the part of the wounded lover, self-pitying and pumping myself up with sulky pride. I knew too, that I had been unfair, and was rationalizing the relationship from my own selfish angle. After all, what did I know of Namkwa's real feelings? If only it had been possible to communicate properly, our parting might have been quite different. I would already be planning to return to her, instead of thinking up alternatives and reassuring myself that if there were to be an end to Namkwa, this was the time to make the break.

By the time I got to Johannesburg, I had one question firmly fixed in my mind: did I really want it to end?

SEVEN

Back to the Wall

'The sort of thing that you are doing in the Kalahari ... ', or words to that effect, were all I needed from one scientist to convince me that the story was out. What shook me, however, was the rapidity with which my secret had travelled to Johannesburg. Within two months of my return the news had obviously leaked to the Kalahari Research Committee and Heaven knows who else. If my university colleagues had learnt of my activities, then the South African government authorities and police could hardly remain ignorant.

I should probably not have discovered so soon that my secret was out, were it not for the fact that I was once again concentrating on planning and financing another trip to the Kalahari. In view of my association with Philip Tobias, the K.R.C. chairman, and his enthusiasm for the Kalahari, it was inevitable that I should discuss my plans with him.

The Kalahari Research Committee had established itself as a body of some influence with an exclusive membership virtually confined to the University of the Witwatersrand and more or less associated bodies and institutes. Part of its function was to endorse for the British Bechuanaland authorities all research projects related to the Bushmen – at least so I was told.

In doing this they screened projects and applicants, and passed their recommendations on to the Bechuanaland authorities, who would then rubber-stamp each particular project in or out. Without the endorsement of the K.R.C. it was just about impossible to do work in Bechuanaland.

They soon made it clear that I was not one of the worthy ones. I received a curt note from the committee informing me that they could and would no longer endorse my expeditions to the Kalahari. Somewhat desperately, I tried to lobby the few members that I knew on the K.R.C. But I simply bumped into a wall of disapproval. I couldn't help but feel that no matter how sincerely they tried to justify their bias, the underlying reason was that I had broken some sort of academic faith, and transgressed the rules of propriety. I suspected they thought the motives behind my expeditions were more sexual than seriously scientific, that I had taken a Bushwoman in a sordid affair.

The chairman pulled no punches. In the first place he did not believe in one-man expeditions. He maintained that serious research, of an anthropological nature or otherwise, in the Kalahari could best be carried out by teamwork, and that in terms of money invested this would bring the greatest return. Even if I didn't have my intimate relationship with Namkwa at the back of my mind, I would have opposed this view. I'd experienced the inefficiency of what I called 'circus expeditions', and my view had support from other scientists.

The chairman made it perfectly clear that I was unqualified for ethnological field work, and accused me of lacking scientific humility for wishing to include social anthropological studies in my programme of work. He said I should stick to my last. I knew only too well my limitations, but I also knew the force of the drive behind my affair with the Kalahari.

Tobias was a formidable adversary. A brilliant scientist, he has earned his fame, and the glamour that accompanies it. As Professor of Anatomy (he succeeded Raymond Dart) he held an influential post at Wits University, which allied to his prestige made him the sort of man you would prefer to have on your side.

In retrospect I believe that George Silberbauer was at the core of my opposition. He was more directly concerned with the Bushmen than the others, and because of his official status could hardly be disinterested in my association with the XKo. He was also in a position to place all sorts of practical obstacles in my way. He was still a man whom I regarded with awe. I was impressed at that time by his knowledge, the quality of his research, and his ability to express himself so readably. I was also impressed by his official title. It was, therefore, not surprising that I was anxious to cultivate his help and co-operation, and possibly his friendship.

Unfortunately this basis for our friendship proved fragile. My intense interest in the Bushmen, who were never far from our conversation, must have convinced him that I had more than a passing fancy for these people. He came to my office, and in a talk that lasted nearly two hours, he tried to persuade me to give up my ethnological interest in the Kalahari Bushmen. Nothing I could say would satisfy him that I had no intention of infringing on his territory. I pointed out that in his capacity as Bushman Survey Officer he was obliged to obtain qualified information from all Bushmen, including my XKo. I understood the practical difficulties in doing this, and knew that further spreading of his research would keep him from his main interest – the Gwi. Couldn't we co-operate?

I could supply him with any information he required, and be a help to him. I pointed out that his people and my XKo had contact at a place called Lone Tree. Wouldn't it be worth while to sit together and compare how their two cultures were fertilizing each other? Apparently not. He suggested various alternative projects, but refused to compromise on his main aim, to get me away from the study I had set for myself. Nor would I surrender what progress I had made.

I couldn't understand why he was so opposed to my befriending the XKo. If he'd said that I would end up doing them more harm than good; that my relationship with Namkwa – and I assumed he knew about it – was foolhardy and sordid, it might have made sense. I was left with the impression that George Silberbauer was jealous of his preserve, and the exclusive nature of his knowledge.

Opposition also came from the Colonial Office types in Mafeking. Time and again I bumped up against the bland face of British 'Old Boydom'. Even if they had nothing against me personally other than the fact that I wasn't one of them, their early lack of co-operation convinced me that they had. For me, Botswana Independence came as a relief. I found dealing with Tswana government officials far more satisfying. They proved friendlier, more helpful, and, surprisingly, even more efficient in some departments than their British teachers, whose special knack I decided was that of making life difficult for me.

I confided in a close associate of Professor Raymond Dart. His advice was brief and to the point: 'Go to Dart. If there is one man who's on the side of the underdog, it's him.'

I was hesitant. Professor Dart was a man with a reputation and personality that made me feel puny, and I couldn't see why he should bother himself with my problems. There was no saying he would support me; on the contrary, I ran the risk that he might listen, even sympathetically, then, in all his wisdom, turn me down. I went to him.

Dart did listen sympathetically; then, and on many other occasions. He was always accessible, and the awe-filled respect I had for him grew to affection. I was privileged to have him take an interest in my affair, and even more honoured to have his advice. His encouragement was the ballast I needed.

He threw me out of his office only once, when I was particularly despondent, and ready to give up.

'Go out and fight!' he said. 'And then talk to me.'

Dart paved my way to another strong ally – Glynn Thomas, the Assistant Vice-Chancellor of the University. A completely different man, he had none of Dart's ebullience; he was a quiet, polite and gentle man who knew his mind and saw to it that things were done. The solution he offered was his imprimatur on my work. Although the Bechuanaland government had almost bound itself to accept the suggestions of the K.R.C., it could hardly ignore any recommendation coming from the University itself, or a man who ranked above the Chairman of the K.R.C. in the academic hierarchy.

This made beautiful sense, and further helped to strengthen my resolve. It did not end there. Glynn Thomas saw me through my difficulties for a period of years, and took a real interest in the progress of my work among the Bushmen; my debt to him is enormous. I simply could not have managed without this sort of help.

I also needed money. Expeditions were costly, and I could not afford to set out on my own resources. Dr Folli had helped subsidize my first trip, but couldn't be expected to stake me again, so I looked around for likely benefactors. To my considerable joy and relief, the Sir Ernest Oppenheimer Memorial Trust made me a research grant, which I was determined to repay in results.

I also got money from other varied sources; from individuals, medical and business firms, and even from the Du Pont Corporation in America, for whom I carried out some investigations. I begged for donations, for petrol, tobacco, foods and beverages, and anything which would reduce my expenses. I even took to collecting wild animal fat, especially lion, and selling it to African medicine men for their *muti's*, or medicament.

Despite my success at scrounging, my financial situation was still precarious, and it became obvious that I needed a firmer academic deck to stand on. I was at a disadvantage because I was not a qualified anthropologist. As much as money and friendly support I needed to add theory to my work, and to match my adversaries in their jargon. I therefore decided to study social anthropology.

The natural university to choose would have been Wits, my place of employment, but my relations with the K.R.C. and the Social Science department were so strained that I decided reluctantly to look to another university: the University of South Africa, which is based in Pretoria.

Professor Myburgh, head of its Department of Anthropology, took an immediate interest in my plans, my work and its problems. He gladly accepted me as a B.A. student, and despite the fact that I was not yet qualified, went all out to help me secure research grants for field work.

Naturally Social Anthropology was my major, and I chose German as an auxiliary major. The curriculum required a Bantu language, but I succeeded in convincing the University that a Bushman language would be of much greater use to me. I chose the five-click XKo, and so perhaps became the first student in the world to submit as a language credit an unwritten Bushman language.

The years that followed were among the most strenuous of my life. German I had hoped would be an easy credit, but I got bogged down in ancient literature, and all the required reading the course entailed. This, together with my anthropological study and my Medical School work brought me to the brink of mental exhaustion. I was also depressed by the fact that I neglected my linguistic studies. During my field work I had assembled a large vocabulary, and battled with XKo grammar, but back in Johannesburg I had no time to review, let alone study, my notes.

There were many times when I felt like packing it up. But at the back of my mind there was always Namkwa.

In 1962 I obtained my B.A. in anthropology, and went on to a B.A. honours course. I was getting on top, but my difficulties weren't over. One of my critics told me that neither a B.A. nor a B.A.Hons degree from the University of South Africa qualified anyone for serious anthropological research.

It was clear that the vehemence of my adversaries was not lessening. The infighting was carried further to the Medical School, where I worked. The head of my department was approached to prevail upon me to stop going to the Kalahari.

I'm sure I was a source of much concern to him and this move gave him the opportunity to call me in and discuss my Kalahari ventures and my work in his department. He suggested I was unwise to antagonize such influential men, but he did not insist that I stop my expeditions. He merely said I should reconsider what I was doing, and then do what I thought was right.

I knew that no amount of reconsideration would compel me to drop the Kalahari, and to reassure my senior I told him that I would do everything in my power during my time at the Medical School to justify my standing as parasitologist. This would make it easier for him to give me permission to leave during term vacations. My promise secured, I believe, a working agreement between us, and thereafter the professor never stood in my way.

It was at this time that I decided it would be politic to embark upon certain research experiments which had been in my mind for some time.

I was interested in the biology of the two species of human tapeworm found in southern Africa: *Taenia solium* and *Taenia saginata*. In particular the pork tapeworm, *Taenia solium*, interested me. This parasite I knew was common in pigs but in southern Africa extremely rare in man. I suspected that we were misdiagnosing *T. solium* in humans, and that it might be more prevalent than we thought. Otherwise, where were all the adult tapeworms?

I decided to infect myself with the larval stage of this tapeworm from a pig, on the assumption that the adult which grew in my system would surely be the *Taenia solium*, no matter what it looked like. As a result, my experiments showed that there were considerable superficial similarities, enough to confuse diagnosis, between the two tapeworm types.

More than that, the experiments proved, at least for me, how dedicated I was to carrying on with my Kalahari love. Harbouring a tapeworm is not only unpleasant but risky, because of the danger that its larval stages may get into the muscle system where they produce considerable pain, or into the brain, where in later years they may lead to a form of epilepsy. My parasitological enthusiasm was not strong enough to undertake the danger. But my enthusiasm for Namkwa and her people was.

Only by producing results at home could I parry the argument that I was not fulfilling my duties as a parasitologist, teacher and researcher. This would enable me to go to the Kalahari with a clean slate, and enable the head of my department to let me go with a clear conscience.

It was also part of my strategy to go to the Kalahari as often as possible. Establishing a presence there would make it increasingly difficult to keep me out, provided I kept my slate clean. This meant briefing my Bushmen friends on the threats that existed, and the need for the utmost discretion in talking about my life in the bush. I was emphatic that nothing incriminating should get out. Today I wish I hadn't been so obsessed with keeping a secret life, for had I not been, some things might have turned out differently. The tactic was two-edged.

Above all, my cardinal aim was to vindicate my expeditions with sound results. No one would assist me, no one would back me if I did not prove my worth. As a result, I tried to develop long-term research projects which were both imaginative and significant. I also solicited a small corps of close friends to whom I could entrust my secret, so that in collaboration we could carry out projects for which I alone was not sufficiently qualified.

I took them to Takatshwane with me, and if I had any fears they were soon dispelled. My friends were impressed by my relationship with Namkwa, and her personality. To my pride, they also found her extremely useful in the pursuance of our work.

As far as I was concerned it was an understatement to say that Namkwa was useful. Her value to me was immense, not only in terms of inspiration, but in the part she played in my understanding of the Bushmen.

More than anyone she was responsible for my academic progress, and without her I could have hardly rushed through my preliminary degrees to an M.A. I obtained this degree in 1965 with a thesis entitled *The Social Organization of the XKo Bushmen.*

I don't know how they found out, but not long after I'd received the Master's degree I received another short note from the K.R.C. informing me that it would have no objections to endorsing my research work in the future. Subsequently I learnt that all the members of the committee, with the exception of one, voted in my favour.

In 1970 I was awarded the Simon Biesheuvel Medal for my research among the Bushmen of the Kalahari. This was good, but the seal came with the first letter of congratulation to reach me. It was signed by Philip Tobias!

EIGHT

Return to Namkwa

Back in the Kalahari my early difficulties were of a different kind, but no less acute. I had left the Bushmen in bad temper and a state of mind that drew a question mark on my future with them. In fact I can now appreciate how ironic it was that at a time when I was desperate to convince people that it was right that I should return to the Kalahari, the Bushmen themselves were probably hoping they'd seen the last of me. I took them gifts, but it also seemed I brought them bother in abundance. I went charging back to Takatshwane when others less stubborn and more sensitive might have stayed away.

The next time I set off (after Gruxa's disclosure to the cattle-drovers and my meeting with Duce and his daughter Kamka), I sang, as usual, in the escape from Johannesburg. Behind me I had the security of an Oppenheimer Foundation grant, and the satisfaction of knowing that I was a *bona fide* student of social anthropology recently enrolled at the University of South Africa. But as I got closer to Takatshwane, doubts again began to erode my eager anticipation.

To my apprehensiveness was added the irritant of my unpredictable and incorrigible vehicle. The engine began to boil, and I couldn't diagnose the fault. My supply of water was limited and I faced the prospect of breaking down at least miles short of Takatshwane, with nobody to help me. I had little choice but to drive as far as I dared without losing water, stop, and wait for the temperature to drop again. I drove this way through an agonizing night. At last, in daylight, I reached the borehole at Lone Tree, and replenished my water tanks. I saw no Bushmen and no sign of Duce and Kamka. I was told they were 'in the bushes'.

Late that evening, tired and irritable, I arrived at the Takat-shwane borehole, where I stopped at the house of Solomon, the pumper. In this mood I asked Solomon to send someone to the village and call Nxabase, my Bushman 'brother'. In due course he arrived with several youngsters. We greeted each other heartily, shaking hands, clasping thumbs and shaking hands again. I asked Solomon to make it very clear to Nxabase and the others that I had no intention of returning to their band unless the nonsense with my father-in-law Gruxa and also Namkwa stopped. I said I was spending the night at the borehole because there was some-thing wrong with the 'nolli' – pidgin for 'lorry', and the name for any jeep and the vehicles that followed it.

Nxabase promised to run all the way. He said he would tell Namkwa to come to me. After an age he came back alone. He moved up to the fire, pulled out his pipe, searched through his shoulder-bag for some tobacco, casually picked up a small piece of glowing coal in his bare fingers, flicked it into the palm of his hand, and shook it a few times before dropping it into his pipe. He drew on it deeply, spat out some tobacco juice and drew again. Eventually he turned to Solomon and gave a sigh. It was pain-fully slow.

'Namkwa says her husband must come to the village,' he said.

That was all. No reply from Gruxa, no assurance from Namkwa. Just 'come'. I was furious and sent Nxabase off again.

'Tell them I want a straight answer to my question. And I want it from her, and from him.'

Nxabase had a sip of the tea which I had left in the cup for him, and melted once more into the night. This time he was quicker, and again he returned alone: 'Namkwa says come to the village.'

There was nothing I could do except fume and go to the village. I felt completely outplayed. Reluctantly I got into the jeep and drove off with Nxabase. Once at the village he directed me towards one of its fires. I stopped and in a moment I was crowded by my old friends, surrounding me with their musk-like smell. Each one ran up eager to shake my hand. I felt none of the animosity that induced several of them to snub my goodbye on my previous visit.

It seemed as though all was forgotten. I was warmed by this reception, but I kept looking beyond the firelight, trying to penetrate the darkness. Perhaps she was standing back, shy, waiting for me to come to her. But I saw no one.

I had been long enough with the Bushmen to know that it is not done to show impatience, so I acted as though all was well. Gruxa came up and greeted me; my mother-in-law stood off to one side as was proper. Some younger Bushmen began unloading the jeep, and I tried directing their efforts but they simply put everything in a pile.

There was still no sign of Namkwa. I busied myself with other things; pulled out some tea and asked someone to brew a pot. I stood with folded arms and stared philosophically into the fire. Suddenly Namkwa was there, and I turned around. She looked beautiful and her silent expression was unmistakable. 'Here I am,' it said.

Months later when we spoke of that evening she told me she had wanted to go to meet me at Solomon's. But her father resented my return and harped on the worthlessness of an absentee son-in-law who did nothing to provide for him. The other members of the band had tried to point out to him the advantages that accompanied me, such as the tobacco I always brought, the maize meal, the presents, and the meat my gun could shoot. Although Namkwa knew what the outcome of the argument would be, she was determined not to run after me. She would not tell me; she would show me how she felt.

Now she stood there. To emphasize her feelings she had decorated herself. Small triangular bead pendants hung from the hair on her forehead, a broad colourful belt girdled her hips. She wore her duiker-skin over one shoulder, bright bracelets about her arms and red ribbons of beads round her calves. Her skin was light and clean, and it shone and glowed with the Nivea cream I had once given her. It was the Nivea smell that had made me turn round.

While we stood looking at each other, Thxale picked up my sleeping-bag and groundsheet and two others lifted my tin trunk. I followed them to a small hut where Namkwa spread out the groundsheet, laid out our bedding and rolled her woollen blanket into a pillow.

Discreetly the others disappeared and once alone I could no longer hold on. I reached out and pulled her to me. She made a feeble show of resisting but she didn't turn her head when I kissed her. For a short while I held her, then told her to look in my trunk for some gifts I had brought her. Eagerly she broke away and scrabbled in my trunk. Within seconds she came up with the things she knew were for her: more Nivea cream, some shortbread biscuits, beads and a jar of honey which Bushmen regard as a special present for their wives. A tin of talcum powder puzzled her but I spread a little on her hand and explained as well as I could what it was for. She liked the smell and in the nights that followed never failed to put some on.

She did not always take so easily to the things I brought her. She was exceedingly chary of new foods. She would ask if they were good and only got round to trying them some time later and usually when I wasn't looking. It took years for her to taste the chocolate I brought.

Tobacco was something else again. On this occasion she continued to rummage through my things until she finally found her special tobacco that I'd hidden at the bottom of my trunk. When I brought out a cigarette lighter it lit her face with delight and she clapped her hands for the joy of a new toy. I then pulled out a bottle of Marsala and we sipped the sweet wine from my mug, and ate a biscuit each. A simple act, but it somehow meant a great deal. It became a ritual that lasted for years: the sip of wine and a biscuit before we went to bed. As important as our kiss in the morning when Namkwa was getting up.

We took off our clothing and crept together under our cover. I lay on my side holding her, and she fitted, this tiny creature of the bush, snugly above my tucked-up knees. Gently I took her hand and guided it between my legs. I could feel her apprehension and her whole body trembled, but she didn't pull her hand away. An act of such intimacy between a man and woman is unknown in Bushman culture and later I learned that such contact is in fact resented by the Bushmen. That night Namkwa disregarded the taboos and she lay in my arms and I in her hand through a blissful night. She didn't break away and when Bushmen noises rising with the dawn broke into our sleep, we still lay with limbs entwined.

Namkwa and I slipped once more into an easy relationship. She spent most of her time around our hut, and much of it singing.

She was clearly happy, and I basked in the harmony we had found. More than ever I felt I belonged to Namkwa and her band and in this security I was better able to approach my anthropological field work with a level head.

During my last visit I had tried to define the extent of my band. Now I saw how the jigsaw pieces fitted together, and for the first time understood what role each played in the structure.

Gruxa, my father-in-law, was the oldest male in the group. He was what could loosely be called a headman (a very volatile concept in Bushman culture) and as such was vested with a certain degree of authority. Some said that Gruxa had handed authority over to Nxabase, but if this were so he continued to make his opinions known and it was clearly evident that they were respected. In an XKo band any other senior male might also influence its affairs, but the only one in our group to exert a similar influence was Tasa, whose mother was Gruxa's sister. Tasa also happened to be Nxabase's brother-in-law. He thus stood in a special relationship with Namkwa, whose respect for him was characterized by her insistence that Tasa, as well as her parents, should have given his consent to our marriage.

There were several old men in the band, including the father of Thxale (who had become my brother-in-law when he married Namkwa's sister, Nkasi). But senility ruled out whatever influence their senior age might have commanded. Xauko and his brother Ntchumka, however, were two older members whose views were not ignored. Xauko was married with several children and Ntchumka, twice widowed, was the father of young Shucre, who had attracted Thamae on the night of our first visit.

Group leadership then did not run on any well-defined pattern except that it became clear to me that both authority and responsibility were shared by the elders of the band and the extent of one's influence depended as much on one's intelligence, initiative and example as on one's age.

Although there is little work leadership in a band, it is usually the 'headman' who initiates group undertakings. Places of rest and villages are arranged by him, and since the headman is generally the best hunter, he will provide for many of the band. For this reason he will take preference at the fireside over others in receiving food from a young couple. In negotiations with other peoples, the headman is the main representative of the band. He may also be, but need not be, the religious leader. In our band this latter role belonged to Tasa.

A rich headman such as Douté is expected to share his wealth with his band. Consequently Douté's band all profited from his donkeys and dogs and most had blankets. There are no strict rules of succession to 'headman', and a son is not necessarily heir to the leadership. The headman could, as Gruxa was supposed to have done, simply hand over his authority to another.

Another reflection of a headman's position is the prestige of his wife. Provided she is not too young, the headman's wife will enjoy considerable respect and will exert a positive influence in decisions. This explained the influential roles played by Nxabase's wife, Kesi, and Tasa's wife, Geitchei. They were the leading females in our band, and probably more important than Gruxa's wife, my mother-in-law, who was of the same age-group as Geitchei and her tetchy elder sister, Theugei. In the next age-group there was Xauko's wife, Guanaci, and Nxabase's wife, Kesi. They were followed in the age hierarchy by the young girls such as Namkwa and Nkasi, Shucre, Nxabase's daughter Tkose, and Nkanaki, daughter of Theugei.

To this generation also belonged Thxale; Tchallo, Tasa's youngest brother; Gathua, an orphan; and Thomate, Nkanaki's husband. Then there were the small children.

Another important individual was Xamxua, with his wife and children. He was the ceremonial oldest and had band membership with both Douté and Gruxa. Because of this he was not always with us, but he nevertheless was to play a very important role in my Bushman life.

This was all there was to the band I had joined. These were 'our people'. Douté's band, 20 miles to the north, also fell in the category of 'our people'. The link lay in strong kinship ties and manifested itself in the character of our social relationships which enabled the two bands to 'visit' each other.

There were three other bands with close ties, but not as close as Douté's band. Just east of us were old Midum's people. They shared the Takatshwane borehole with us, but somewhat surprisingly our two bands shared no kin. Twenty-two miles to the south-east was the area where the Lone Tree people hunted.

During periods of drought they shared their borehole water with Domadjasi's band, who lived just south-west of us and west of them. My band knew of other XKo bands further afield, but there were no ties with them. No one went there to seek a wife, nor even to visit. As opposed to 'ours' these were 'those people'.

Such a group of people, or group of three or four bands, I later called a nexus of bands, a concept which, I was to learn, caused raised eyebrows among colleagues working with Bushmen. In those days I was not particularly concerned by this nexus complex, and unquestioningly accepted what Xamxua, Nxabase and others told me. Years later I returned to the subject, and not only found confirmation of my earlier information but also established the nexus boundaries and the names of each nexus. However, acculturative changes had so overtaken the XKo Bushmen generally that the younger generation no longer knew anything about these matters. I felt that the band nexus was the largest social unit within which there were ties and bonds which made its members aware that they were one people. But later I received irrefutable proof that, at least as far as the male initiations are concerned, lines of communication go far beyond the nexus. The XKo unknowingly taught me that no elder can or should conduct an initiation for the boys of a band or nexus without first informing the neighbouring people of another nexus. And in warning a youngster about his duties and obligation of secrecy they state that they do not want the people of the neighbouring nexus to come and fight with them because they have failed to instruct him properly. It became clear to me that certain lines of communication go further than anyone had ever anticipated. Furthermore I think that the nexus complex could be found among other Bushmen as well, if proper investigation were carried out.

With my growing understanding of such things other patterns of Bushman life emerged more clearly. Without having noticed before I saw how the huts or sleeping nests were arranged in close family groupings. Parents were never far away from their married children, so that Gruxa and my mother-in-law, Thxale and Nkasi, Namkwa and I, were within easy borrowing reach of one another. However, we didn't live on top of each other, for privacy is a respected commodity among Bushmen. Indeed when my in-laws had built their hut so that it slightly faced ours, the others

took them to task: 'Why must you face your hut to look into that
of your children?' they said. 'Do you want to watch your son-in-
law sleeping with your daughter?'

There were similar groupings among the married throughout
the village. The unmarried young boys, however, all slept together in a nest of their own. Even in the bitter winter they slept
around their fire, completely naked, without any covers. This was,
I assumed, part of their hardening process, which was impressively
Spartan.

The young girls also lived together in a spinster hut. They
were expected to leave their parents' home and build their own
hut when they were 'old enough to see'.

One afternoon four Lone Tree Bushmen arrived at the village
while we were all seated round a fire. They deposited their
weapons on one side and settled themselves some six feet away
from us. They saluted us and shook hands with some of our older
men. They had come 22 miles through heavy sand, but they gave
no indication that they were in the least fatigued or thirsty. Nor
did we rush to give them water. Thxale offered them tobacco, and
only after they'd been there some thirty minutes did Shucre fetch
and hand them an ostrich-eggshell filled with water which they
sipped and shared.

Out of the lively conversation it transpired that they had come
to trade tobacco with our people, but their talk also told of large
herds of wildebeest migrating just south of Lone Tree. An
animated exchange went on for several hours, and gradually,
almost without my noticing, the visitors moved into our circle.
Normally they would not have been so forward.

Then Nxabase came and sat down next to me. We smoked,
and he chatted to Thamae for a while. Finally he came to the point.

'You know Maloi at Lone Tree?' he asked.

'Yes, he used to be pumper here, didn't he?' I replied.

'That was before Solomon came. But Maloi and I are good
friends. We want to go and see him.'

'Well, that's good,' I said. 'Why don't you go?'

'No, we all want to go and visit. I think we should go and move
there for a while.'

'Nxabase!' I exclaimed laughing. 'Why don't you say so; you
want to go to hunt wildebeest.'

Then he also laughed: 'That is so,' he said.

Bushmen do not usually hunt in the territory of another band. But the Lone Tree Bushmen probably felt they had something to gain in this instance. They knew, from my stay with Duce and Kamka, that I was rich in tobacco, and if they wanted me to visit them, they would also have to induce the whole band as well. The wildebeest were effective temptation for someone like the perpetually hungry Nxabase, and hunting wildebeest would hardly deplete the band's game resources. These animals were on the move and would be gone tomorrow anyway. Antelope such as steenbok and duiker were a different matter. They do not migrate and no one would think of allowing neighbours to hunt them.

We discussed Nxabase's plans at length, and decided we would leave the next day. I would take Namkwa, Nkasi, Thamae and some baggage in the jeep, and the others would all foot it out.

At Lone Tree the following day we called on Maloi and told him all our people were coming to visit. He suggested we seek a camping place a few miles to the east near one of the large pans. Here Geisa, the headman of the locals, and his wife, Thekwe, organized their womenfolk into helping us get our huts built. The older women went off and collected dry branches for the hut ribs while the younger women brought back masses of grass on their backs. By nightfall our hut was finished, so was Nkasi's, and a skerm had been built for Thamae.

I was at the borehole fetching water when the rest of our band came into view, a long line of them carrying all their belongings, hartebeest skins and shoulder-bags, bows and arrows and digging sticks. The old men carried their 20-foot hooked sticks with which they catch the underground springhare in its warren, and the children rode piggyback or chattered up and down the line. Bushmen don't expect the little ones to keep up on the march, and will carry them if necessary. Here the obligation to carry a child rests on the mother's brother's shoulders. He is the one who will lift and carry a child when it is tired, and consequently he is a most important crutch in a little person's life.

I noticed that Nxabase wasn't in the line, and then I saw him walking with Tasa some distance from the main body. Later they explained that it is customary for the hunting men to walk parallel to the main file but off to one side where they might chance upon game undisturbed by the procession.

Within two days our village was established. Its area had been cleared of grass, all projecting tree roots, thorns and anything that could possibly harbour scorpions or snakes. Any belongings likely to attract ants were hung from the trees. The individual dwelling places varied in design. Some were simply sleeping hollows cleared under the trees, others were protected by almost semi-circular windbreaks about five feet high and covered with grass. There were also a few more substantial shelters, roofed and shaped something like a quarter of a coconut shell. For security against the marauding lions which follow the wildebeest the dwelling places nestled close together, some back to back, but never facing each other. This rule was particularly pertinent, as I had discovered, when a young couple were close to their older dependants, or when one's immediate neighbour was a relative with whom one had a formal relationship, such as one's husband's married sister, or one's wife's brother and his spouse. 'It is bad to hear them fart or having intercourse,' explained Thamae.

He also pointed out that we might have made camp nearer to the big pan which held some water, but that would have stopped the wildebeest going there to drink. These animals, of course, were the reason for our move, and in the days of hunting that followed we made our stay worth while. Both Thamae and I shot several wildebeest, and the community was well supplied with meat. These were days of plenty, and village life was suffused with contentment.

For me, family life acquired more meaning. Although breakfast was still an erratic event and I grew not to expect any, Namkwa was a good housewife who cooked adequately and who swept around our hut and fire methodically. (This was not only motivated by a tidy mind, but was also a sound precaution against snakes, whose trails would mark smooth sand as clearly as white chalk on a slate.) Namkwa made an ingenious little platform for plates, cups, saucers and cutlery, which was washed regularly. Evening dishes however were always left overnight, not that they ever needed much washing, for they were usually scraped and licked clean by the youngsters. Sand, ashes and the barest amount of water were enough to requalify them for the shelf.

Bushman households invariably have a fire going, and ours was no exception. Namkwa's had meat stewing most of the day. Each afternoon she would extinguish the old fire, remove the ashes and food refuse to an ash pile some yards away, replenish the firewood and build a fresh fire.

The fire has special significance for the Bushmen. It is vested with a personality, and it is not just a source of warmth, of light, a means of preparing food, a safeguard against lions, or a pipe-lighter. It is an object of considerable respect, and the taboos associated with it are designed to guard against it being demeaned. Namkwa violently objected on one occasion when I threw a pus-soiled bandage on the fire, and pandemonium broke out when I carelessly tossed a steenbok bone (steenbok are taboo for a young woman like her) into the coals. Whatever else it is, the fire is not an aid for the disposal of those objects considered dirty or harmful. These are buried.

Night emphasizes the social significance of the fire. In the Kalahari black its dome of light is many things; eating-house, smoking-room, dance-hall, debating-chamber. To step outside its reach is to step into the dark, cold and danger.

One evening I decided I wanted to go for a walk in the pan. It was one of those beautiful nights, full of the moonlight that customarily lures out Western lovers. It certainly brought out the romantic in me. Gone was the enervating heat of the sunbaked day. The white-hot sand had been polished soft silver, and I could picture the pan, a pewter lake lying cool and unfevered there. I wanted Namkwa to share it with me.

Namkwa looked at me as though I were out of my mind.

'How can you go out walking now?' she exclaimed. 'This is the time the snakes are about. Do you want to die?'

'You can watch out for the snakes,' I said. 'We can take a stick along. You will see them.'

'I'm not going, and you're not going either.'

'Well, then I must go alone.'

She didn't say anything. She got up and held me. Stubborn, I coaxed her along, and we walked to the pan. All along the spoor she chatted loudly and sang snatches of song while she swatted at the bushes with her stick. She was making her noises to scare off any snaky creatures in the vicinity, and if I had any illusions of two lovers walking along arm-in-arm all starry-eyed, they were sadly dispelled.

At the pan I found my pewter illusion; a moonlit lake of sand. But the bush creature alongside me twitched. As alert as an antelope ewe with her lamb, she pitched her senses to the sounds, assessing each for danger. Not until she succeeded in getting me home did she relax and laugh again at the stupid white man, for only a stupid white man could think up such a ridiculous and unnecessary thing to do.

Generally, I realized, the Bushmen thought me incapable of looking after myself, and they were patently paternal about my inferiority. It was true my magic instruments gave me a certain power, and my 'nolli' was very handy to lift and carry and bring to camp the meat we killed. But when nollis broke down, white men died in the veld. Even my gun impressed them little.

I can pinpoint a change in their attitude to the day I was forced to run with the hunt. I had taken Thamae to one of the pans intending to work in the shade of a tree while Thamae went off to do the shooting. As they had done before, the Bushmen left a couple of their fellows to look after me. For a while I looked at my work. Then suddenly one Bushman pointed out a small herd of hartebeest. We watched it for a while, and soon picked out an old buck. My companions made it clear that we could catch him if we tried.

I knew that Bushmen in teams of three or four run down buck in early summer before the rains break, when the animals are poorly nourished. The hunters take advantage of the fact that a ruminant, prevented from chewing its cud on the chase, develops indigestion which eventually slows it down and enables the hunters to come close enough to throw their spears.

I did not feel at this time and place that such nature was on our side, and I saw little gain in exerting myself. But my companions were insistent, and setting our sights on the old buck we took after the herd, me lumbering along behind. For some reason the hartebeest fled rather nonchalantly, hardly taking us seriously. Although they were often out of sight they seemed to dally until we caught up with them again. As we jogged the sweat poured from me, but as I slogged on excitement came like a second wind to contain my weakness and lend stamina to my failing limbs. I smelled the kill.

It became apparent that it was the old buck that was holding the herd back, for he was obviously tiring and could barely respond to the others encouraging him along. My two Bushmen then made a determined sprint and separated our prey from the herd. For a while, the herd bothered itself about the old buck. They coaxed and cajoled it and often stopped to wait for it. But the old buck needed more than encouragement, and when the herd decided there was no hope they fled on and disappeared altogether.

Eventually the old buck sank panting to the ground. It eyed us wearily but the Bushmen pointed at his hoofs and horns. They were still formidable weapons. It was decided that my companions would hold its attention while I stole round behind it and stabbed it with my sheath knife, and that was what I did. I walked up to the animal and plunged my knife deep into the kill. It made an effort to stand, but the Bushmen were on it in a flash.

We walked back to our place under the tree. When Thamae returned empty-handed, I said casually: 'Now we must collect our meat.'

Talk of the hunt buzzed all evening round the camp. Each moment was rerun a dozen times. Each gasp for breath was turned into a guffaw. It wasn't my imagination (although I probably had an inflated idea about my heroism on the hunt) but after this they spoke to me differently. There was a note of equality in their tones and even Gruxa looked more respectfully on his son-in-law, especially after I had given him a large hunk of the hartebeest's hindquarters. Namkwa's mother also softened, and although she still sat at her little fire next to ours she took a much more active part in the conversation, laughing and clapping her hands in approval.

I found all this very satisfying, and was still preening myself on my prowess as a Bushman when another deflating incident occurred that once more reminded me that I still could not consider myself one of the men. We sat round our fire one evening when suddenly a weird whining sound, rising and falling, came out of the dark bush. Everyone froze to attention.

'*Gausi kxa*,' said someone. 'Gausi is crying.'

The women got up, rushed a few paces into the dark, hurled obscenities at the bush and just as quickly returned to the safety of the fire circle. All I could gather was that there was this horrible thing in the bush insulting the women and calling the men. In the excitement I did not notice all the men steal away, leaving Thamae and me the only males among the women. Nor could we follow them for we had no idea where they had gone. I sat there, my curiosity smarting, feeling very much the odd man out. Thamae's presence was no consolation. Whatever was going on I had no part in it.

In almost incoherent bits and pieces, Thamae and I gleaned from the women that Gausi was a horrible creature intent on licking your blood with a hard cold tongue. He could see in all directions for he had eyes both in the front and the back of his head. He usually came to visit the men late in winter, and the noises we heard were his method of calling his 'boys'.

That night I went to bed with Namkwa curled snugly alongside me, but I stayed awake thinking of what had happened. I was depressed that I should have been so totally ignored by the men.

I must have fallen asleep for the next thing I knew, I was being woken by the women chanting an unfamiliar song. I sat up and saw that Namkwa had gone. My first thought was that all this had something to do with Gausi.

Otherwise unsuspecting I got up, dressed, and followed the song to its source. I found all the womenfolk sitting or standing about the spinster hut. Inside I saw Tkose sitting on grass with her back to the entrance. Old Geitchei was busy removing all Tkose's beads and decorations, while Theugei placed a leather cap on the young girl's head and a hartebeest skin on her back.

Again I had no idea what was going on, and when I saw Namkwa and a few of the girls wandering off into the veld I thought that whatever was happening couldn't be very significant. I didn't know that the girls had gone off with the set purpose of building a new hut outside the village. Some while later Nkanaki lifted Tkose piggy-back, and I, still puzzled, followed them to the newly completed hut where she was made to sit down on grass, again with her back to the entrance. Nkanaki and Shucre seated themselves outside on either side of the opening.

Thamae explained that Tkose had suddenly begun to menstruate for the first time during the night, and all the chanting, the new hut and the ceremony around Tkose were all part of the band's female puberty rites.

I saw no men anywhere near Tkose's hut, and decided it was no place for me. Reluctantly I moved away and tried to keep my anthropological eye on events from a distance. In the late afternoon, however, Namkwa came and actually led me back to Tkose's hut, where I spent most of the next few days satisfying my curiosity.

Through Namkwa I came to understand the full significance of the unfolding ritual. This was the most important moment in a girl's life, for when her first menses appeared the child became woman. Now she had to assume the responsibilities of womanhood, and be instructed in how she should conduct her adult life.

Few girls anticipated the actual event, but if one did, she would inform her grandmother or some older woman such as Geitchei, who would immediately organize the others and see to it that an isolation hut, like the one built for Tkose, was prepared. In her own case, Namkwa told me, her menses appeared while she was out collecting veldfood.

'My mother,' she said, 'carried me part of the way home, for I was not to touch the ground with my bare feet. I was too heavy for her and so they sat me down and gave me sandals to wear home.'

Thereafter the procedure followed the same pattern as the ceremony I was witnessing. Each morning before going out to collect veldfood, and in the late afternoon when they returned, the womenfolk gathered at Tkose's hut. They clapped and sang and most of them marched around the hut with their diggingsticks horizontal over their shoulders, chanting and exposing their backsides.

While this went on, Geitchei and Theugei sat with Tkose. Geitchei spoke to her much of the time, instructing her in the ways of their bush life, its laws and norms of behaviour, her duties towards the elders of the band, her relationship with other members, her duties to her husband and what she ought to know about marriage and childbearing.

Namkwa assured me, when we spoke later, that although sex

was discussed no stress was placed on its erotic aspects during these instruction sessions. In fact, she said, what she knew about sex, she had learnt from me. The intimacy we enjoyed she believed, did not exist between married Bushmen. She qualified this, though, by saying she did not really know, as she had not been married to a Bushman.

On the fifth day of Tkose's isolation and instruction, she was turned around. Her face was painted to resemble the markings of a gemsbok brow, and a similarly patterned piece of gemsbok skin was hung at the back of her hut. I had seen Gruxa and Xamxua each carving long, thin, straight grewia sticks and decorating them with a hot knife. These were suspended from Tkose's neck down her back. 'To make her grow straight,' said Namkwa.

Old Geitchei sat next to Tkose. She massaged Tkose with sweat from under her armpits, and gave her various bits of food and a pipe to pull on. Each item given to Tkose was first blown on as if to bless it. Then the old woman called for a bow and arrow, and, guiding Tkose by holding her arms, aimed an arrow at the gemsbok skin. As the arrow hit its mark the women ululated. Normally Bushwomen are forbidden to handle the men's weapons, but this act, it is believed, brought the weapons luck.

Meanwhile the dance of the eland which had been going on outside became more intense, and when it was at its highest, some men appeared with horns of springbok, wildebeest and hartebeest tied to their heads. They joined the circle and butted the bottoms of the women as they danced around the hut. Unlike the other occasions when the women showed bare buttocks, each now had a string of beads suspended over the anal fold to conceal the erotic appeal of their exposed behinds.

Soon Geitchei emerged from the hut with Tkose clinging to her and standing on the older woman's feet. Not until they had joined the dancing was Tkose allowed to touch the ground. Tkose was now learning to walk.

When the dance subsided, Tkose was led back to her hut. Later Nkanaki and Shucre ushered her out again, and led her round all the huts to 'meet the people of her village'. Shucre held grass in front of Tkose's eyes so that she would always be able to 'see them nicely'. At each hut, Tkose poked the fire with a grewia stick and pointed to the various objects in and around the dwelling place. This brought good fortune to the occupants, who, mindful of the special powers she possessed, returned her gesture with a present.

Tkose's tour of the village ended the ceremony, but for many weeks after this she wore her leather cap until the final act of the ritual was completed. Then cuts were made on her cheeks and forehead and a tattoo paste, made from the coal of the sticks she'd carried on her back mixed with eland fat, was rubbed into them.

She was now fully woman. Gone was the spontaneous, playful girl, the little leader among children with her life-and-soul-of-the-party zest. Instead she bore herself more seriously, more maturely. It was a quite remarkable transformation which could only be put down to the deep significance of her experience. From a child she had come to puberty, and rebirth as a woman, and in this context each act in the ritual became significant. As a new person she had to be reincorporated into the life around her, and reintroduced to the people, the food and anything which might be of importance to her. She had to be guided, taught to walk again and made to grow up straight. At no other time of her life would she have the same experience.

For the anthropologist in me the experience was of considerable fascination and significance but it also had a bearing on my pursuit of the Bushman way. How was it, I asked Namkwa, that she had called me to Tkose's hut, and I was the only man allowed to witness Tkose's change?

Her reply left me stunned.

'You are a child, for you have not gone through the ceremony of men,' she said. 'There is no harm, for a child, even a boy-child, watching Tkose.'

It wasn't a gesture to my scientific interest that had enabled me to get so close to the ritual. I was just a boy-child. It didn't matter, because I wasn't a man.

As if to drive the point home, Gausi cried again a few nights later, and when the men spoke to me, they said I puzzled them.

'We have seen the marks of the enemy on your skin (I assumed they meant my wounds from the war), and no child can have such marks. You are a man, yet you are a child.'

If they were puzzled, I was unhappily put out. I tried to rationalize the contradiction and convince myself that I was being stupid to worry about my paradoxical state. But it didn't help, nor did I think it amusing that a man who had gone through war and marriages and nearly fifty years of living should still be regarded as a child, and particularly by people whose respect he wanted so badly. I even drew little security from my relationship with Namkwa. For all my physical bulk, my status as a white man, husband and provider, did it perhaps bother her that she was married to one who couldn't claim proper manhood? Who was as ignorant as a child? Who hadn't been initiated as a fully fledged Bushman?

Of course, as a scientist I was curious to know about the male initiation rites, but my main consideration was my need to become a recognized member of the male society. Determined to do something about it, Thamae and I had a long talk with Nxabase. I told him what I wanted, using every persuasion I could think of. I was married to Namkwa. I was one of them. But I wasn't one of them. Namkwa was a woman, I was a child. Nxabase was my Bushman 'brother' but I wasn't a man like him. Did he think it right that I should continue to live with the band and still be different?

Reluctantly Nxabase agreed to help me, and with his assurance I relaxed again. More than ever I felt at home with these people, and at night I slept the sleep of the relaxed. But each morning I awoke brought me closer to my departure. Once more I had to head east for the city and its sophisticated deceits. The evening of my going I once again packed my things aboard the jeep and handed out what gifts I wished to distribute, including one to little Gathua, the orphan whose father had been stabbed through the arm by another Bushman with a poisoned arrow. His was a special gift, a woollen blanket, by which I wanted to show my respect and affection for the whole band.

By 3 a.m. I was ready to leave. All the Bushmen awake to see me go stood on one side of my nolli. Suddenly Namkwa crossed in front of the vehicle and came to my side. She held her hands cupped and stood in the dark looking at me. I didn't know what to expect, for she hadn't done this before. I reached out to touch her goodbye, and into my hand she dropped a string of ostrich-eggshell beads. Before I could react she was gone. Confused, I looked at the beads and felt their quality. They were special.

I looked out into the darkness where she had disappeared, and longed to get out and run after her. Instead I started my engine and drove off.

I don't recall reaching the main road, nor driving down it. I turned over the miles, my mind reeling with the range of emotions that it felt. I carried with me the illusion of the Eve I'd first sought. A woman free of the cunning, the superficiality and insincerity one would find in the sophisticated 'civilized' kind.

Here was fundamental woman in a sort of simple splendour, a basic creature whose femininity bared her emotions, sometimes fierce, mostly gentle, genuine and good. And I, so worldly and corrupt, so cultured by degrees and academia, so happy, had won her heart.

NINE

The Initiation

'You are a man and yet you are a child': the paradox haunted me back in Johannesburg. I became engrossed in initiation rites, and read widely about varying practices in different societies. I read about the tortures to which young Australian Aborigines are exposed during their initiation ceremonies. I looked at pictures of boys rolling on their backs on beds of glowing coals and persevering until the old men released them from their torture. I saw films and read accounts of Sotho and Xhosa circumcision schools in Lesotho and the Transkei where the ordeal was sufficient to drive many young men to hospitals to have their foreskins removed, rather than suffer the traditional custom.

I searched for information on Bushman initiation rites, and struck a complete blank. I had no idea what was in store for me. I'd never seen a Bushman naked, so didn't know if circumcision was part of the ritual. I greatly feared anything like this, for a Bushman's knowledge of sterility, I knew, amounted to nil. Only the intense ultraviolet radiation of the sun seems to reduce the incidence of sepsis among them.

I weighed up all my trepidation against my possible gains, and came to the conclusion that I had to accept whatever hardship or risk the transition ceremony entailed. I convinced myself with increasingly effective scientific reasoning. There was simply nothing I could find that described Bushman puberty rites, and even such a noted authority as George Silberbauer, relying on Bushman descriptions, was inclined to shrug off the boys' ceremony as not particularly significant.

While this might have been true about the Gwi whom he knew, I was curious about the XKo. Then there was Namkwa. I tried to see our relationship from her angle. I decided it mattered to her, and that if I wanted her love and respect I should not expose her to the indignity of being married to a child.

Nxabase had made it clear that such ceremonies could only be conducted during the winter. This was because for some reason Gausi would never consent to appear during the summer. So as winter came south, I prepared for another expedition which I felt would be the most significant of my bush experience. I wasn't travelling alone this time, for my son Ralph was visiting me from Germany, and I had decided to take him along. He had never been to the Kalahari, and knew little of my life there. He certainly knew nothing about Namkwa, nor did I think it opportune to tell him. I anticipated no embarrassment, for this particular safari could easily be carried out without my having anything to do with Namkwa. She would understand, and in any event I suspected that I would probably be isolated from her.

Ralph was agog about the whole trip.

'But how do you know that they will initiate you?' he asked.

'Well, Nxabase told me that he could do nothing without speaking to the old men. But later he came back and said that the old men had agreed provided I come back in June or July. He said that I would find him at Lone Tree when I returned.'

We didn't find Nxabase at Lone Tree, nor any of the others in our band. Only Maloi and Thamae, whom I had sent for, were there to greet us.

'I don't know what to tell you, doctor,' said Maloi. 'Nxabase and the entire band were here for a long time after you left. He knew you were returning for I frequently spoke to him about your plans. I often gave them rations of mielie meal, and even lent them Blackie [his fox terrier] telling them they could hunt with him, but they must return often because Blackie is not used to eating tsama melons. One day they disappeared, and no one has seen them since.'

This news disturbed me, but thinking we'd find the band at Takatshwane, we set off again with two of the local Bushmen. Takatshwane was almost deserted. Solomon the pumper said there were a few of Midum's group nearby, and suggested he might help us. Ten miles on through the bush we found Midum, talked him and his son-in-law into accompanying us, and long after midnight returned to Solomon's house.

Early in the morning we set off on the old road towards Lehututu, looking for a place where Nxabase's group had camped the year before. We asked our companions to search for tracks, but when they returned after several hours, they only reported seeing the spoor of Douté's band heading north towards Okwa. There was no sign of Nxabase or Gruxa.

North along the Ghanzi road we stopped near the Okwa valley where Thamae remembered having heard a dog bark on his way down to Lone Tree. Our calls brought no reply, so we went on into the valley. Here we found Douté's spoor, as well as fresh donkey droppings. Again we called, positive Douté's band had to be near. But we raised nothing except hopes for finding Douté in the morning. It was too dark to follow any tracks.

We made camp and for the first time since Johannesburg forced ourselves to relax. We could do nothing more.

Round the fire I began to badger Midum. I told him what had happened during my last visit, and my eagerness to become a member of the male society. Could not Midum and his men lead me through the rites? If I were unable to find Nxabase, the opportunity would have passed.

Midum wasn't to be persuaded. His replies were classically negative: he didn't know how to do this. Only the old men could do this. He did not have grey hair, he was only a small Bushman, not one of the big men, therefore he could not do what I asked of him. If he were to initiate me, he would surely die. Besides, he did not know how. If Nxabase had said he could do it, then that was it. Only Nxabase could do it.

I gave up, and we all slept round the fire.

Next morning we followed the tracks we'd found, and after nearly 2½ miles met one of Douté's men who took us to their camp. To my surprise I found a few of the Takatshwane Bushmen there, Ntchumka, Xauko and their wives, and Thxale my brother-in-law. We exchanged greetings and as soon as I could I took Douté aside to let him know what I was after and win his help.

'I'm happy to see you, Douté, for you were not with us last time,' I said, hoping to warm the Bushman on to my side.

'I know,' he said coldly. 'In Takatshwane they told me that you had thrown me away.'

'That is not true. Thamae and I looked for you in Ghanzi, but I had no vehicle and when the Public Works Department offered us a lift to Takatshwane we had to take it.'

Douté wasn't convinced. 'How do I know that you did not throw me away? Did you bring me and Abé a present?'

'Did I ever leave here without giving you a present?' I said, and with this bait Douté allowed himself to listen to my problem. I told him I couldn't find Nxabase, but wouldn't Douté, as an old friend, help me. Could not he, a strong headman, and his men take me into the male society?

Douté might have been studying Midum's script in this drama. His answers were just as negative: he did not know how. Only Nxabase could do it. He would like to be initiated with me because he also was only a child. But the time was already past, the time was too short, there were no old men ...

Well, could he help me find Nxabase? Yes, Douté would help me find Nxabase but only after I'd promised him £1. Then he held back until I'd added a blanket for Abé. Finally he insisted that Thxale must accompany him for only he would know where his own band was. Douté was a shrewd headman.

We returned to Takatshwane on Thxale's suggestion, and settled down to wait while Douté, Thxale and one of Midum's men set off. We waited until the next afternoon, when Douté returned saying he had travelled most of the night, waiting only for the moon to rise. With him were Nxabase, Nkanaki, and Thomate, Nkasi and her older sister, Namkwa. My wife. The rest would follow the next day.

Namkwa and I looked at each other. I spoke longing with my eyes, and the subtlest smile touched and fled her face. She didn't know Ralph so was careful to keep our secret at a neutral distance. For me the effort was painful.

When the camp had settled down, Thamae, Solomon and I invited Nxabase and Tasa of Okwa to talk about my initiation. Nxabase was cagey and came up with much the same arguments I'd heard from Midum and Douté. The time had passed, he siad. There wereno old men present. I would tell the white men what they had done.

Halfway through the night we came to terms, and he told me to sleep at his fire that night. Tomorrow they would clear a place of seclusion for me where I would have to spend several days. They would also tell me in the morning what I could and could not eat. Towards evening they would lead me to their secret hiding place.

The next day nothing happened. Fearing the worst I taxed Nxabase who said he had been prepared to go through with the ceremony but the old men had refused. He could not continue on his own. This was a serious blow, but I made a last effort to change their minds. Solomon and I called all the elders, including Nxabase, the two Tasas, Gruxa and Douté to a round-fire last-ditch discussion. We hammered at them all afternoon without getting anywhere.

Gruxa was totally opposed to the idea, warning that if they took me into seclusion they would all surely die. I tried to counter this by pointing out that I was a great doctor, and didn't they know my medicine would be strong enough to protect them all from harm?

'Yes, but you will go home and tell all the white men about this,' they answered. This was obviously a big worry. That I couldn't keep their ceremony secret.

The arguments went round and round in circles until all were fed up. One by one they got up to leave, and Thamae and I sensed we had lost. Desperate I aimed my last argument at the Bushman stomach.

'We have been talking now for hours,' I said. 'We must rest and eat. I shall give mielie meal and a leg of goat.'

The goat leg was a gift from Solomon the pumper, who, realizing it was a good time to pull rank as the government's official representative at Takatshwane, ordered the Bushmen back to his fire. One by one they all reseated themselves except Tasa of Okwa, who sat by his fire making a rope. This angered Solomon who exploded saying he was the big boss at Takatshwane, and when *he* called Tasa, Tasa must come. Tasa did come across then. With splendid dignity he sat down among us.

The meal was good, and the atmosphere grew more congenial. It soon became clear that Douté was the only force holding back. Although he was not the headman of this band, his was the most powerful personality among all the bands, and while he wavered, no one dared give his consent.

He told me later that he did not like Gruxa, and that he did not wish to assist Gruxa's or Nxabase's band in any of their enterprises. He didn't say why he disliked Gruxa, and it took years for me to discover the deep-seated reasons for his animosity.

To my relief, after dark Douté finally came round. Again I was instructed to stay at the fire until the elders came to take me away. They explained that the time I could spare to be with them really was too short (I knew that argument!); they could not give me all the necessary lessons. Nevertheless they had decided to introduce me to the male society, and when I returned they would complete the initiation. They felt they could justify this because I would not be in touch with or look upon any Bushwoman while I was away from Takatshwane.

This settled, the Bushmen left, leaving only Douté, who sat with Thamae and me and called Namkwa to make tea. Apropos of nothing he began to talk about his life.

'My mother, Domku, was a Naharo-speaking XKo woman. She was very intelligent, and kind, and everyone liked her. She came from the farms by Ghanzi and taught me about keeping donkeys and goats. My father, Musomo, knew nothing about these things. He merely sold skins and ostrich feathers to the Kgalagadis. I felt that I could do better by also selling to these people, but I bought donkeys with my goods. I have often told the other Bushmen to sell their things in Ghanzi, not in the bush. But they don't listen to me. Only if they sell in Ghanzi will they get a good price.

'When I come here with my animals, I do this so that all these people can see what I have. I don't want to teach them by nagging, but if they see what I have acquired, perhaps they will also learn.'

I understood the soundness of his argument. But I asked, 'Why are you always fighting with Gruxa then?'

Douté evaded the question and carried on: 'Gruxa married my mother after my father, Musomo, was shot by the police. They had one son. When Domku died he married the woman who is your mother-in-law.'

'Then Namkwa and Nkasi were born from Gruxa's second wife?'

'Yes, that's right.'

'Then they are your step-sisters?'

'Yes,' said Douté and changed the subject.

Soon Nxabase came, and Namkwa withdrew. I was undressed down to my shorts and told to follow. I was led to a place I will never be able to find again. I came to it not as excited as I might have been. I was too weary, exhausted by my travels, troubles and lack of sleep. They could do with me what they would. As long as they got it over with.

What transpired certainly amounted to one of the more remarkable experiences of my life, and I have often been tempted to disclose all the details. As a scientist, others have argued, I am obliged to reveal all. But as a man, anthropologist or Bushman, I don't feel free to break my vows of secrecy unless released from them. I do feel at liberty, however, to compromise my strict pledge and describe what I would call the insignificant highlights of my isolation. They do, at least, give some idea of the nature and the rigours of the ritual.

I was taken to a spot near a large pile of wood, which was lit on our arrival. I was instructed not to look at anyone, but keep my eyes on the ground. Nor was I to ask any questions.

Two men came and washed me from head to foot with water from an ostrich-eggshell, after which I was allowed to curl round the fire and sleep if I wished. This was my first night, in winter or summer, without either a blanket or a shirt or something to lie upon.

Using a small log as a cushion I tried to get comfortable, and in Bushman fashion I rolled from side to side in front of the fire to warm my whole body. Each part furthest from the fire drew the cold into my blood until I ached for sun-up. The men cooked and ate but offered me nothing. Somehow the night passed. With morning the firewood had been exhausted and I was numbed by the cold and the ritual of the night. Calmly the others awoke and carried on with their meal. No one paid any attention to me.

Back from our unsuccessful hunting in the afternoon I was told to send someone to fetch some of my mielie meal, but none of it came to me. All I was allowed was something to drink.

I was then told to strip completely and stand on my shorts to prevent my feet touching the ground. I was given certain pieces of wood, and taught how to hand them from person to person. Then

I was encouraged to place them in the fire. When they were sufficiently carbonized I was told to remove them and give them to old Tasa in the proper manner. He mixed the charcoal with fat, I think eland fat, in a tortoiseshell. Then I had to sit on my trousers while he made a series of cuts on my back into which he rubbed the paste. The men began to dance, and I was instructed to join them.

My second night, again on an empty stomach, was excruciating and quite the most miserable I ever spent in the Kalahari. A cold wind had sprung up, I was hungry and tired and naked and freezing. I suffered every minute, and was just doubting dawn would ever come again when the light came to relieve me. For the time being my ordeal was over. Nxabase made it clear that they had only 'started' me. I would have to return and next time stay longer and learn the laws. I also had to face Gausi.

Back at the village the womenfolk avoided me and I was told what food I should not eat until my initiation was complete. Fortunately mielie meal didn't feature among the taboo foods, and Namkwa prepared me a good helping, which was served not by her but by one of the men. This was the nearest I got to Namkwa, who, like the others, kept away from me.

The following day, Ralph (who'd stayed with Solomon) and I left Takatshwane for Maun. I left satisfied that I'd achieved something and in this knowledge resigned myself to the year I would have to wait before returning. Because I was now completely taboo to the women I could hardly return before the year was up. It had to be next winter, for only then would Gausi appear again to call his sons.

The following July I had no difficulty in relocating the band, and Nxabase did not delay taking me into the final phase of my initiation. I would have to prove myself he said, as a hunter and provider of meat. I had to show I could support a wife.

'We know that you can go and buy food for Namkwa at Ghanzi,' he said. 'But you say you want to become a Bushman. Now you must show that you can provide for her as we provide for our wives. Otherwise you are not right to have married her.'

Though I had been hunting before, I was now faced with a final examination. Part of the test was stalking and running down an animal. Together we headed in the direction of a small pan about 5 miles from the village. Near it Nxabase stopped me and silently raised his index and middle fingers, bending them to indicate hartebeest. Then slowly he raised and lowered his sign to tell me that they were walking calmly.

Quickly we reached the edge of the pan. As I'd been taught in the army, I wormed my way across and nearer without disturbing our prey. Resting a few moments to regain my breath, I took aim at one and fired. The hartebeest leapt with the shot and made off. The chase that followed was more exhausting than the time I ran down the old buck, for although I'd hit it in the leg this was a young strong buck, which despite his wound had several miles left in him. Finally he stood and I dropped him.

We fetched the other men and each of us carried home a large piece of the carcass. Nothing was left behind. Even the blood was carefully scooped into one of the antelope's stomachs and tied.

When we got back to camp I was told that we would go that evening to the 'men's place'. Now the women approached me, jeering and trying to frighten me by telling me about a 'big thing' which would come, which would cut me, particularly on my forehead, and lick my blood with its hard tongue. I would have terrible experiences, they insisted. Much worse than last year, for this time Gausi would surely come to see me.

The men had just told me to strip off my shirt when Douté, looking like trouble, arrived in the village. He came straight to me. 'I will see to it that you are not initiated,' he said. 'You must leave this place tomorrow, and be gone. You have thrown me away because you exclude me from all the things you are sharing. Even this meat is not for me!'

I grew angry. He knew this was not true, and I counted all the things he had received from me. Looking around me, Nxabase and the other men seemed unconcerned by Douté's attack. For some reason they didn't appear as intimidated by him as they might have been on my last visit. This also gave me heart, and soon we picked up our meat and left him standing.

I was led to a place similar to the one I'd been in before. What happened was also much the same as before, but a far more bloody affair. Some things done were different, and they employed instruments I hadn't seen before. As in the female initiation, I was introduced to small bits of vegetable food as well as tobacco, but no meat was given to me. Just as Geitchei had done with Tkose, Xamxua sat down with me and told me many things including the entire fable of Gausi.

He taught me much concerning my relations with others. I was to pick my friends only from among the initiated, and to discuss my problems only with those who were there to help me. Moreover I must show respect for the elders of the male organization. Again and again Xamxua stressed the difference now between myself and those not yet initiated, and especially the difference between us men and the women who bleed periodically. This blood harboured the greatest danger to me, and I must sleep well apart from Namkwa during her period. But the most powerful blood is that which flows during delivery, and I therefore must neglect neither her ritual washing nor mine. He then discussed Namkwa herself; he told me that she was not just anyone, but a girl given to me by her parents. I must therefore respect and listen to her advice, for she was more than a wife, she also looked after me, much as my mother did. 'A married man can't do just as he likes. He can have a girlfriend, but he must not leave his wife for her,' Xamxua said. It was my duty to feed Namkwa, and when she had a child to feed that as well. I must not be too jealous of her, otherwise I would destroy what I had at home – indeed, I must bridle sexual jealousy of any kind. 'Can you,' Xamxua asked, 'cut out and put into your pocket the sexual pleasures that she gives you?' On the other hand, he warned, 'You must not be sexually greedy with her. Don't take her more than once a night or again in the morning. With the girlfriend you can fornicate the whole night, but be careful lest you lose weight. If you wish to marry a second wife, you must wait at least six years.'

Turning again to girlfriends, he said, 'Don't forget the difference between the two women, your wife and a friend. Guard well against those who can cause you to bring illness into your home. If you should have a child with the girlfriend it is your duty to feed it until it can leave its mother and you can bring it home. Remember, no man is complete until he has reproduced himself. Today it is terrible, young men fornicate with their wives all the time, thus killing the baby inside the mother. They show no responsibility towards their children.

'Of course you must look after your mother, but you must

reduce your association with her, and don't go to her for advice any longer. We old men are here to advise you. In fact, you must cut your ties with anyone, of whatever sex, if that person has not been initiated.'

Then Xamxua turned to the dangers that faced me in the future, especially from food offered to me by strangers. 'Take an old man when you go visiting, he will tell you what you can eat. You cannot know where danger lurks in the next several weeks, even with your wife, so don't fornicate with her for at least a month.'

We spoke about all the food taboos and how I could be released from them, and then Xamxua gave me numerous basic rules of conduct while hunting in the bush. I was not to go hunting alone until the elders allowed me to do so. I was advised to recognize the days when Guthe was against me; rather than waste my energy, I should return home and try again another day. 'When you hunt, your mind must be completely on the job, otherwise stay at home, but never forget to keep an eye on the weather. Don't try to force it home, rather prepare a shelter where you are. Once you have shot and wounded an animal, never drink until the buck has dropped, otherwise part of the water will go to strengthen it, and you will be the first to tire, and lose it. Never eat of the meat in the bush except some of the inner organs.

'This school is not made by man,' Xamxua continued. 'Guthe gave it to us just as he gave us all the instruments used here. He gave us the "laws", and as such they are his laws, which have been handed down from the time of the first people. They are laws respected by all people everywhere. That is why such a school can be found anywhere. When the old man (the one the women call Gausi) calls, it is your duty to go out and greet him. He is our uncle.'

Xamxua then turned again to the necessity of keeping the secrets of the school. I must not communicate them to anyone not initiated, to no woman or child, not even to my uninitiated age-mates. 'You have seen a number of things done and also implements used. If a girl were to hear of these, were she to walk into our midst, or even were she to discover the implements used here in a man's bag, she would have to be killed instantly, even though she might be the sister or wife of one of us. We have had big troubles with our neighbours in the past, they came to fight us because they said we did not teach our youngsters well, that they were talkative. Such troubles can come again, from the Gwi, the Balalas, or even from the Kgalagadis, if we are not careful. We have many ways of punishing the boys, we give them a very deep painful scratch on the back, or we beat them senseless, or we take them into school a second time, perhaps even send them to the school of our neighbours. I remember when we had to kill a boy, because he just didn't grow up.

'Today the boys are dancing for you, tomorrow you will dance for others. This school which Guthe gave us must be carried on. But one thing you must never forget, you are now a man and you must conduct yourself as such. What is more, you are much closer to us now, as close to a Bushman as you will ever get, this you must always remember. We cannot expect you to throw away your people, just as we expect our boys to remember that they are Bushmen and that they must not assume the manners or habits of the Kgalagadis or of any other people.'

When the meat was ready the men settled down to eat while I was given leave to sleep. Then while some were eating, others danced and employed 'the thing'. The hours wore on, and again the day couldn't break quickly enough for me. When it eventually came it brought a new tension. The men stiffened to the alert and someone said, 'Douté!' Then I saw their kinsman approaching with a group of his men. They carried their bows and spears at the ready, and there was no mistaking their hostility. And for the first and only time among these people I felt truly afraid. Douté was dangerous.

It was old Xamxua who rose to confront the danger. He went out to meet Douté and stopped him. I could hear them talking; Douté angry and demanding, and the old diplomat fatherly and firm. Gradually Douté calmed, and Xamxua led Douté and his men up to our fire. Silently they placed their weapons on the ground, walked over to the pot and, placated, pulled out pieces of meat which they ate sitting down.

We stayed there for most of the day and left for home towards evening. This move, I think, was earlier than scheduled. I had thought we would stay longer. But Douté's men had finished the meat, and this probably prompted the Bushmen back to the village. Before leaving, both Xamxua and Douté, who I assumed was hurt by not being invited to participate in my initiation, warned me against speaking to any woman or child about what had transpired. I was also told that since we'd left the village none of the younger girls or women had eaten a thing.

'When you get back,' said Xamxua, 'you must give them medicine so that they can eat once more. However, when you enter the village you must not look at a single person, and certainly not at a girl.'

This admonition proved no hardship. In the village all the women withdrew from me completely. Then Nxabase held straw over my eyes, and one by one each woman, including Namkwa, came up to me laughing and joking so that I should recognize her 'nicely'. Tasa gave me some meat he'd cooked, on to which he sprinkled tiny fragments of bark from a piece of wood. Into each woman's mouth I put a morsel of his potion.

This done, the ceremony of my return seemed over, and everyone was free to eat again. Except for me, the hungriest of all. I was now subject to all the meat taboos and could only be released from them one by one. I asked Tasa whether I could eat as I was hungry. He nodded, and called Namkwa: 'Go and ask Geitchei to give you some more of the duiker.'

He picked up our pot to see there was no other meat in it, and told Namkwa to cut the duiker meat into the pot. He took a strip and placed it on the fire. Groping in his shoulder-bag he brought out a number of small sticks strung on some thong. He selected one of these, and scraped some shavings on to the palm of his hand. Carefully he sprinkled the shavings over the meat, and fed me with it. Then he rubbed his armpits and hair with the palms of his hands, and massaged both my throat and abdomen.

'You can eat this meat your wife is cooking,' he said. 'You need fear no pain in the stomach. Any other meat will make you violently ill unless you first come to me and I will give you the right medicine.'

I was very impressed by the zealousness of my teachers in this matter of my initiation. I think they were likewise impressed by the co-operation of their pupil. But the extent of the meat restrictions began to bother me. I knew that boys were only

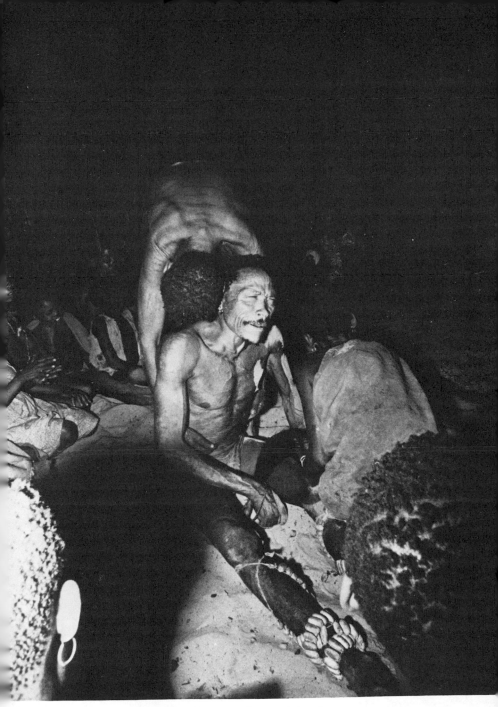

Douté in a trance at the exorcizing dance

Skinning the kill

Namkwa (foreground) assists at the trance dance

released over a number of years, and I didn't relish the prospect of being unable to eat half the things I shot for the pot.

I explained my fears to Nxabase who assured me it wouldn't be that bad. The taboos would be stretched to make allowances for me and my age.

'If you had been a Bushman amongst us, you and I would have gone through the ceremony together because we are of one age. You and I are like brothers. You can eat all the things that I can eat, but we must first give you medicine for anything that is permitted in your age.'

It was therefore only a matter of time before I was as free as I had been before the ceremony. In fact I soon discovered that I was considerably freer than Namkwa who, because of her youth, was still subject to many taboos, especially the steenbok taboo.

As for my experience, my scientific curiosity had been satisfied. I could understand and rationalize each moment in its context as a rite of passage. I could see from the heights of my Western background that some aspects of my initiation, the symbolism and taboos, were rather quaint and primitive. I knew too that it could never have been as meaningful for me as it might have been for a Bushman, whose involvement lent drama to the ceremony, whose beliefs were of another world.

Yet I also knew that the ceremony had not left me unmoved. The whole thing had a veracity my scientific side would hardly have credited. I went into the initiation a wide-eyed white man, and came out of it a Bushman.

This wasn't just a superficial thing, an additional qualification to add to my name. The transition, metamorphosis, call it what you like, went much deeper. I think I felt it in my thoughts, my speech, and in my behaviour. I felt it in the attitudes of those around me. It overflowed on to Namkwa and changed her too. She became more extrovert, the most loquacious woman round the fire, confident and eager to demonstrate her pride in me.

She held on to me when we watched some activity or other in the village. She pleased me with much personal attention; the unsolicited cup of tea, the duiker tongue begged of Geitchei, the cigarette she lit for me, and the Marsala we sipped at bedtime.

There were other side-benefits as well. Naturally, I was now one of Gausi's boys, and when he called, we men would all rise crying out to him that we were coming while the women shouted abuse at him. When queer noises emanated from the dark, the women said these were Gausi's wives coming to insult them.

'They only want to sleep with our men,' they said, and shouted, 'You shits, go fuck your own husband! Leave our men alone.'

Meanwhile we would be out of sight of the village, round a fire of our own and roasting some delicacy or other that one of us had provided. Gausi was a good excuse for a night out 'with the boys', and we thoroughly enjoyed our hidden meetings, the illicit feasting, the dancing and the joking that went with them.

More than sixteen years have passed since my initiation. I have observed and participated in many initiations. No two have been alike, though certain basic elements were present in all of them. Indeed, I have often been amused to hear the old man say that they must think what they are to do. Looking back, I am all the more impressed by the flexibility and adaptability of the Bushmen in dealing with my particular case. There were many problems which confronted them, and which they mastered. I was a white man, my language ability at the time was very limited, more suited to expressing my simple wishes than to understanding complicated discourse, though Thamae helped me tremendously. My foods and my cultural background were different, I hunted with a gun, not with a bow and arrow; my stays with my friends were limited, so that they were unable to keep me under their guard or tutelage; there were those who were violently opposed to my being initiated. It is not surprising therefore that some of the initiation elements were either omitted or abbreviated.

There appear to be no rigid rules concerning the sequence of events before, during and after an initiation. Nor is there any set period during which the 'school' is run. Some say one week, others one month. The size of the class also varies. Bolo Bolo says that he was initiated with twenty-five other boys, some of whom were Kgalagadis.

There is always considerable excitement and consultation before any boy is taken to school. There are his grandfather and uncles to plead his case, and the father who doubts his suitability and maturity. Not to be outdone, the youngster lobbies among his own older friends. Delegates are sent to consult with the neighbouring bands and inform them of the intention to conduct a 'school'. I learnt that it is considered improper to hold more than one initiation during the same winter among neighbouring bands. When I thought of my problems with Douté I understood the significance of the fact that there must be no dissenting voice among the neighbouring people, and I learnt that the validity of such dissent goes far beyond the immediate neighbourhood. Balalas, Gwi or even Kgalagadis can express their opposition, and the latter, as Bolo Bolo showed me, may even send their boys to XKo initiations, and vice versa. I am surprised to learn that today there appears to be a strange love–hate relationship between these people, each resenting the authority of the other in matters of the male initiation.

Once the preliminaries have been settled the elders decide on a 'place' and time. The 'school' must be conducted during the winter months because Gausi can neither appear nor be heard at any other time of the year. Food is plentiful in the winter and is made available by the villagers to the men for the period of their seclusion. When the place has been cleaned, kraaled in and sufficient firewood collected, when the food has been properly stored, when the initiate's place of rest and his 'pillow' (an ordinary log) have been prepared, when the special fire-sticks have been trimmed, and when the elders there feel at home, the initiates are collected from the village. Meanwhile the women have had ample time to instil them with all sorts of fearsome stories concerning their immediate fate. A dance of the entire village precedes the departure of the young men, and is held for them while they are huddled together with their younger play-mates. Repeated prayers are sung over the little group of boys and young men. When this ritual has been completed the little boys scuttle back into darkness, while the candidates are either carried to the place, or together with the other men dance the entire way. Sandals prevent their feet from touching the ground.

Humility of the initiates is achieved by making them keep their eyes downcast, by restraining their dancing or by forbidding them to sing. I saw them being abused, insulted, intimidated and even beaten. At the place of the 'school' numerous dances are conducted by the men on their behalf, while they are ritually washed, instructed and tattooed. Above all, they are made to face up to Gausi.

They are released from various food taboos. As their state is considered to be of the highest vulnerability they are led, helped and also extensively warned of impending dangers. To assist their physical development they are given medicine sticks to wear about their necks and made to wear a cap. The successful execution of their profession as hunters is ensured by ritually shooting a shield (the brow-skin of a gemsbok), which represents an animal. Finally the young men are returned to the village as new-born adults and as such capable of bringing good fortune to each of the households there. This is done by an initiate lighting a stick in each of the fires, the light given to him to see the dangers which beset him at night. Finally their eyes are 'opened' with a piece of straw held against them so that they can recognize each member of the community.

But this does not complete the youngster's training. Before him lies a period of continued learning and vulnerability. He has joined the 'club', but very much more learning from adult men is required to make him a fully fledged member. He has a say in the club, but others, according to their age, have a much greater say, and this he must learn to accept.

To satisfy the curiosity of the reader I have disclosed much of the male initiation, not because I was prepared to betray the faith placed in me by my friends, but because I have noticed a vast deterioration in the elements of the initiation, or even a complete rejection of it, in the past two or three years. I was permitted by my teacher Xamxua to discuss what I have written, but I must ask the reader to respect my pledge and to probe no further. For me to violate my pledge completely would be to disown my teacher and friend, Xamxua. As his pupil, I often sat with him. He had taught me much, but I felt that I still had much to learn, and I wanted to know it all.

'Tell me, Xamxua,' I said on one occasion, 'what is this I read about the mantis? The white people believe that the mantis is a Bushman god.'

'No, we don't believe that. Only the people up north say so. But we do not kill it,' he replied.

'Why?'

'Because the Old People said so.'

'Do you have songs about it?'

'No, we don't have songs like the Nharo or the XKung, we just play the dongo to ourselves.'

'But do you believe in someone who made all the things around us? Who made us and the animals and trees?'

'Of course,' said Xamxua. 'Guthe made all these things. No one will ever know where Guthe came from, but he created Thoa, the evil spirit, as well. He even created his own wife and children.'

'Where is Guthe? Does he stay somewhere?'

'He may live in the sky. The sky is wide and in it he can live anywhere. Why, he may even live far beyond the sky,' the Bushman said. 'But he can also live in the mountains to the east or anywhere else on earth. The Old People said that it is good if he does not live close by, for when he gets angry, he might kill the people.'

'But, Xamxua, you said he has children, what do they do?'

'They lead the Bushman to an antelope, but their big job is to collect the spirits of the people when they die. He has many children to do this.'

'Does Guthe often kill people?'

'No, why should he? Didn't he create them all, and all the plants and animals? You know, he likes people, all people are the same to him.'

Old Gocholu, a visiting hermit, now joined in: 'Sometimes I don't know whether all people are the same to Guthe, because if you look around, there are those who give out jobs, and those who do the jobs.'

'Yes, you are right,' said Xamxua. 'Guthe first made all people the same. Then he divided them into different types of people. I know why we are small. Guthe first made the white man, and then the black ones, and with the pot scrapings he had left, he made the Bushman. Guthe did the same when he made animals.'

'How do you know when Guthe is angry with you?'

'Oh, you know, because now you are going to die, you can't escape Guthe's wish,' said Gocholu. 'A person can be surrounded by lions, they may even sit by his fire, but if Guthe does not want it, not one lion will come forth to kill him.'

Midum nodded assent. 'I know where a lion came into a place

and stepped over three sleeping people before killing the fourth. That was Guthe's work.'

'Yes, and sometimes a snake lives with you for a year before killing you. Why? Because now it was sent by Guthe.'

I continued to probe: 'What do Guthe's children do with the spirits of the dead after they have collected them?'

'They work for Guthe,' said Midum. 'If the spirit is that of a small child, it may work for him for a long time before Guthe makes another person of him. The spirit of a grown-up will work for Guthe much shorter before he uses it again.'

'But what is Thoa, the other spirit of which you spoke?'

Xamxua answered, 'He lives at the same place as Guthe. He is usually bad, but he can be good as well. He usually causes a person's sickness or even death, but sometimes he takes a liking to a person, and then he intercedes with Guthe for his life. You must know, when a dying Bushman recovers, that was probably Thoa's work. Why, he can even lead a hunter to water or towards an antelope.'

Gocholu interrupted: 'Those two get into some terribly big fights, one wanting a person's death, the other objecting. Guthe gets very angry when Thoa interferes. Then the Bushman whom the fight is about is really sick.'

Gruxa joined in: 'Look at that drought we had two years ago. That was Thoa's work.' (They called it '*kulli Thoa*' – Thoa's year.) 'And when Gathua's father was murdered, or a person kills himself, only Thoa can put such evil thoughts into a man's head. No wonder Guthe fights with him.'

'Do many people kill themselves?'

'No,' said Midum, 'it doesn't happen often, and it is a terrible thing, because the spirit of that man will never have rest.'

'What do you mean, it will never have rest?'

'Haven't you seen these whirlwinds that pass every once in a while? Those are the spirits of such dead. When they killed themselves Guthe was not ready for them, he did not call for them, and send his children. Now they must roam forever over the veld.'

We were in the middle of this conversation when everyone stopped dead. 'Lion,' said someone. Try as I did, I could hear nothing. It was the second time this had happened. One night a sleeping village awoke at the cry of a lion whose spoor we discovered next day to be about 4 miles away.

The Bushmen fear the lion for obvious reasons. Their attitude is to avoid any conflict and keep the beast at a respectful distance, so we broke off our talk and returned to the village.

Namkwa was rather agitated, because she thought we might not have sufficient firewood. When we had built up our protective pile, I said, 'You know, Namkwa, when I drive home I usually sleep somewhere near Sukuma, and there are many lions there. Do you ever worry about me?'

'I always worry and I speak to Guthe so that he looks after you.'

'You pray for me? How do you do that?' My mind was still with Guthe.

'Oh, I just sit down wherever I am, in the house or in the bush while I am collecting, and then I just tell him he must see to it that you return safely.'

She continued, 'This time I shall speak to Gruxa so that he must give you medicine to protect you from lions.'

Namkwa's concern for me manifested itself openly in other ways. Her emotions invariably showed. If she were happy she laughed and sang. When sad she became mute, often lying close by my side as I worked, her blanket covering her completely. These moods increased as my departure approached. I decided not to tell her when I was leaving to forestall too much grey creeping into our last days together. But intuitively she sensed the vibrations of my going, and wouldn't leave my side.

The day before I left I decided to shoot some meat for Namkwa before my home trip, and told Nxabase that I would prepare a hide on a bushy island in one of the pans, work during the day (I had a lot to catch up on) and wait for the animals that came down to lick in the afternoon.

As I was about to leave, Namkwa ran up and insisted she come.

'But, Namkwa, you can't come along. Hunting is man's work. A woman will only bring a man bad luck. You know the Bushman law.'

'No, I'm going with you. I don't care.'

Nxabase tried reasoning with her, but she only became more stubborn and climbed into the jeep. Nxabase became angry, and tried to pull her out, but she fought with a ferocity I'd seen before. She screamed and cried until I gave in: 'Leave her, Nxabase, let her come.'

'How can you allow this?' said Nxabase. 'You will never shoot a thing. There is no such thing as a woman going along to hunt.'

'No, Nxabase, look at her crying. Leave her. She can come.'

We prepared my blind on the island, and I settled down to work with Namkwa rolled up in her blanket at my feet. Until the afternoon she lay there, then she stretched and like a cat rose from her lair. All her senses were tuned to the alert. She sat behind me, and pointed to a spot in the bush where I could expect buck to emerge. 'There,' she whispered. '*Tcham.*' (Gemsbok.) Through my fieldglasses I could detect no movement. Then four beautiful rams appeared, 300 yards away, and stood. Namkwa pointed out the best shot, and I didn't doubt it. I took my time and made no mistake.

'In the heart,' said Namkwa, and with an impressive casualness led me straight to the kill. This was the daughter of the man who periodically hived off only with his females. I had thought it strange. Now I knew. When your daughter can hunt like Namkwa who needs men?

TEN

The Jealous Lover

Another time, another trip, I stopped on my way to Takatshwane, just before the road reaches Lone Tree. I had, as always, been huffing and puffing along the heavy road, and was delighted to come upon a section of hard, recently gravelled road. I noticed a tent standing where the roadworkers' camp had been, and I pulled up, partly curious, partly to be sociable. I saw an old Tswana, whom I knew, come out. He was followed by a lovely Bushgirl, well dressed, with hair combed and stretched. We greeted each other. He had a deep and kindly sonorous voice.

'Come in,' he said, and to the girl, his wife, 'Go and make us some tea.'

'Can you eat some meat?' he asked, offering me boiled wildebeest from the large pot on his fire. We ate and spoke and I complimented him upon his choice of woman, how pretty and neat she was. He told me he wanted her to be that way. He always brought nice dresses for her.

'You know, all the people only throw rags to the Bushmen. I don't want my wife to look like that.'

'Whatever made you marry a Bushgirl?' I asked.

He laughed. 'Do you ask me that, when you are married to one yourself? There is no other woman so faithful, so true as a Bushgirl. I can go to Ghanzi or even to Lobatse for several months and she will remain here and look after my things. No one will come close to her.'

'Is it true what the people say, that you are an "inyanga", a doctor?'

'Yes,' he said, 'but so are you a doctor because I've heard that you bring medicine to many of the Bushmen.'

'Well, I'm not a real doctor,' I explained, 'but I know a little about medicine.'

'That is good,' the old man said. 'Then when I'm away and my wife needs you, you can help her and when you are not here I will also look after your wife.'

I didn't hesitate to agree with this and went on to ask him whether his wife came from Ghanzi.

'Oh no! How can you marry one of those from the farms? You can't trust them. They have many boyfriends. No, I met Si'iki when we were working the other side of Lone Tree towards Kang. Her people are from the bushes. She was very wild. Now look at her! And she is good to me even though I am an old man.'

I nodded, for I felt I understood what he was talking about. We knew better than most others who only 'played' with Bush-girls.

We finished our tea and I said my goodbyes. I wanted to get to Takatshwane by sunset. I knew where to find the village, for the old 'inyanga' had told me where it would be. Everyone ran out excitedly to greet me, including Gruxa, who offered his hand and the now customary 'good morning'. But no Namkwa. It was soon clear she wasn't there, and finally I asked Nxabase, 'Where is Namkwa? I see her mother and sister are here, why is she not here?'

'Namkwa has gone to Lone Tree. Did you not stop there?'

'No, I did not know she was there.'

'Well, we will send for her in the morning if she is not back tonight. Then you can expect her in the evening,' said Nxabase.

This reassured me, but then I realized I hadn't seen Thamae.

'Where is Thamae? He should have been here.'

'Oh, Thamae, he is here. He came yesterday with the lorry. He went hunting with Solomon this morning.'

That also set my mind at ease. After we'd unpacked the jeep I called Nkasi, my 'little wife', Namkwa's sister, and asked her to prepare something for me to eat. She seemed subdued. Then I asked her where Thxale was, since he hadn't greeted me yet either.

Her reply came quietly: 'Thxale has gone with Namkwa to Lone Tree.'

For a moment I thought that odd. Why should he have gone

to Lone Tree and left Nkasi behind? Why didn't they all go together? Then I forgot about the unanswered questions, and dipped into the fried bullybeef and roasted onions that Nkasi had prepared.

I talked with some of my friends, but weariness soon took me to bed. To clear my brain of the unending road that wound and wound through it after a long haul, I sipped at vodka mixed with orange. But still I couldn't relax. Why did she go with Thxale to Lone Tree? Was there anything to worry about? Surely not. But why then had she so often left her place in the jeep up front with me, and sat behind with Thxale when we went down to the borehole? Was there anything in the way they laughed and talked? Why, come to think of it, were they so often engaged in horse-play and teasing each other?

Thxale was just a great tease, but Namkwa never fled the teasing like the other girls did. She'd hit back or chase Thxale, and when she'd caught him she fought him like a tomboy. Thamae had once told me that teasing and wrestling were the first signs that Bushmen loved each other. They can't hug and kiss in the open, he had said, and it is bad to have other people watch you cuddle a girl. But 'playing' was permissible.

The chatter of Bushmen at my fire woke me in the morning. I lifted my head and there sat Namkwa, and, nearby, Nkasi and Thxale. She laughed when she saw me awake, and the sound scattered the nightmares that had crawled around my sleep. She laughed and came over to greet me. Then Thxale came and shook my hand and said, 'Good morning.'

I liked this Thxale, my brother-in-law. We suffered under the same father-in-law, old grouchy Gruxa, and with this bond stood very close to each other. He was intelligent and articulate, and could give such an animated account of a hunt that even a stranger to XKo could understand his story. Although I often went hunting with my 'brother' Nxabase, I preferred to go with Thxale. He was a bright companion, and unfailingly entertaining with his splendid sense of humour. But his eye was also keener, his reflexes much faster, his movements quicker. And few could match the aesthetic proportions of his athletic physique. No wonder Nkasi was proud of him. After all, hadn't other girls thought him eligible?

He might even have been a choice for Namkwa but I had reached her first. It didn't bother me, this. I could even think of it objectively. And now that he was back and she was back from Lone Tree, I need not worry at all.

Soon I was raring to get going. Namkwa, however, was tired, and fell asleep. I cracked a beer and exchanged news with Thamae and Solomon, who had come back from their hunt. They told me they had shot two wildebeest and asked if I would fetch them with the nolli. They were up the Takatchu valley, quite a long way away, and I was amazed by the distance Thamae and Solomon had covered on the hunt.

On the way back the vehicle was full of wildebeest, and so as not to weigh us down too much Thamae and Xauko trailed the jeep through the bush. The sun had started its dip, but the late afternoon simmered on the boil. I lurched along in the heat, concentrating on retracing my spoor to Takatshwane. Suddenly I became aware that something was radically wrong with the vehicle.

Thamae ran up and told me that the rear wheels were not in line with the front ones. The centre bolt of the rear spring was gone, causing the rear axle to move forward on this spring. We were at least 12 miles from camp, and the place was full of lion spoor.

'We can camp here,' said Thamae, 'and go home in the early morning when it's not so hot.'

'Yes, but we have no water. We don't even have any matches,' I said, already telling myself that I would never be caught short like that again.

'The matches are nothing. But the water!' said Thamae.

'Well, let me see if I can repair the spring.'

'All right, but I think we should try and fetch some water. If we go straight through the bush it's not as long as if we go down the valley until we reach the road, and then double back,' said Thamae.

I heard that, but by then was too engrossed searching through my spares to give Thamae sufficient attention. When I did turn round to say something both Bushmen had gone. I was alone, I was thirsty – very thirsty – and I was surrounded by fresh lion spoor.

I had masses of meat which I was sure the lions must smell, but had no rifle, no matches, no water and no Bushmen to turn fire out of sticks. I felt utterly abandoned. But fear can be a driving force, and I decided I wasn't going to stay there waiting for Thamae to return.

If I could push on another 4 miles I would almost certainly hit an old spoor of mine, and find my own way to camp. As a parasitologist I have hardly been a creative mechanic over the years. But this was a challenge, and with a jack and a pulley and a few grunts I managed to get things more or less back to normal. I started the engine and moved off, holding my breath. My eyes weren't sharp enough to follow the track I'd made coming. Often I lost it and would have to dismount to locate it again. In the dusk I could do that, but in the dark ... I must abandon the meat! But what good would that do? Damn Thamae, how could he run off and leave me? I could not drive around all night. I could only hope and trust luck would help me find the spoor before dark.

I was just beginning to imagine how I would face the lions, when I hit my old spoor. About 4 miles from home my headlights picked up Thamae and Xauko panting to intercept me.

'Why did you leave me? I had a hell of a time finding my spoor,' I said. Thamae said something about having to get water. He couldn't trust Xauko to understand this so he went too.

'Do you really think Namkwa would have sat in camp knowing that I had no water?'

I was sure she would have moved Heaven and Takatshwane to help me. When we got back she was all over me. Anyone would have thought I had shot the animals myself the way she treated me like a hero, presenting me with a large mug of Puzemandle as a sort of victor's prize.

Her attention didn't falter in the days that followed, a number of which I filled on hunting expeditions with Nxabase and with Thxale. The strength of my rifle made up for a lot of my inexperience, but it could hardly equal the Bushmen's all-round skill. Thxale especially went out of his way to assist me, to interpret spoor for me, and to climb trees to spot our quarry. On several occasions he spotted the buck before Nxabase, and I envied his ability. Still, I was learning and on all our trips I insisted on trying to lead us back to camp. Every hour or so I would stop, look around and point in the direction I thought our camp would lie.

At first, and to their unconcealed amusement, I was often hopelessly off beam. Then I became steadily surer, and once, after a kill, set off for the jeep without bothering to ask where it was. It was a momentous event for me, finding the car. But I nearly spoiled it driving back to the kill. Thxale had anticipated this, and ran to meet me.

When we returned to the village after a successful hunt, the women would run up, dancing around us, stroking our bodies and arms, singing, ululating, and praising us. These were chest-swelling homecomings, when a man was made to feel the value of his efforts. In the city a man might earn his wife's thanks for going to the butcher. In the bush, bringing home the meat is an act for praise and celebration, and it is not only one's wife who comes forward, as Namkwa always did, but one's relatives and friends, who shower one with their appreciation. The reason, of course, is that there, meat is life.

Distribution of the meat is carefully carried out. There is nothing haphazard about which joints go where, and I took some time to learn the rules. Once the animals are skinned and cut into various sections by the old men who have stayed behind, the meat is placed on a large pile. There is no rush to the delivery because each knows he will get his share.

Among the XKo, meat for non-relatives is generally chosen from the upper back, the neck, ribs or head. Choicer cuts go to the family, and to oneself. My preference was for the fillets, and I would give the front or hind legs to Gruxa, Nxabase and Thxale. The actual distribution is performed by the children unless the meat is too heavy or if the cut is a return gift, in which case the hunter hands it to the recipient's wife.

A lot of meat, once it is cooked, is minced in the stamper. This is an economic way of spreading one's meat a little further, and the easiest way of apportioning it between members of the family or visitors. It is common custom for the men to visit other fires when food preparations are on the go, and simply by their presence they coax a little food their way.

The most remarkable self-control in front of food is shown by the youngsters, especially when they are waiting to eat those cuts of meat that the taboos allow; the young Bushmen give no sign of their inner pangs. It is considered improper to show any impatience or that one is anxious to receive the leftovers in the pot. It is also unmannerly to interfere with a visitor who cuts himself a piece of biltong without asking. Nor is it etiquette to complain, no matter what your stomach might say, if your visitor proceeds to dig the only tortoise you have out of its oven of ashes and starts to eat it. In turn, it must be said, few visitors would be so impolite as to go that far.

The day we came back with a gemsbok, a hartebeest and a gift of berries from Domadjasi's women, whom we'd met on the hunt, a combination of ingredients – the meat and food, the lighthearted spirit pervading the village – led to one of those delightful dancing evenings I'd come to enjoy so much. I was sitting with some of the fellows who had been hunting with me. They watched the dance until it moved within them. Up they got and joined the shuffling, clapping crowd. Namkwa had already asked if she could join the fun, and I was left with Thamae.

He rose from where he sat and sat down next to me.

'Doctor, I want to tell you something,' he said.

'You sound worried, Thamae, is it that serious?'

'Yes it is. And I think I must tell you. You remember the evening when you arrived and you did not find Namkwa here?'

'Yes, she had gone to Lone Tree with Thxale, but she returned in the morning.'

'Don't you know why they returned in the morning? Gruxa had sent someone still during the night to fetch them.'

The blood began to rise in my head. Go on Iago, go on. 'But why was that? She could have come next afternoon.'

'Because,' said Thamae, 'Namkwa and Thxale were lovers. Gruxa and all the people had a fight with her and Thxale. That is what I am told. And so they actually ran away to Lone Tree.'

There it was: the simple explanation! I'd avoided it all these days. Now it hit me like a thunderbolt.

'But if this is so, why did Gruxa send for them?'

'Because as your father-in-law he is responsible for your wife while you are away. He is afraid of you. Have you ever seen a Bushman run through the night, especially when there is no moon, if it is not really urgent?'

'And why did Thxale and Namkwa return if they wanted to run away?'

'Thxale became afraid of you, and suddenly Namkwa realized what she had done. That's why they also ran back, still through the night. Didn't you notice how tired she was?'

'Fetch Nkasi,' I whispered.

Nkasi came from the dance and sat down in front of me. We told her what we'd heard. Was it true? Nkasi was silent. She looked at the ground for a long time. Then she denounced her sister. Denounced her husband. Destroyed my hope.

'Just because she's big,' she said, 'Namkwa thinks she can do what she likes.'

Somehow I kept my emotions in check. I told Nkasi to stay with us as I worked out a plan of action. I put it to Thamae and he said, 'Good.' Then I waited for an opportune moment to call the villagers together. When I did so, the dance had waned and Namkwa was curious: 'What is the matter, why are you calling everyone?'

'Go to the house and stay there!' I hissed at her. She looked dumbfounded but went without question. All the others sat down laughing and passing a pipe, unaware I meant serious business until I rose and stood over Gruxa. Then they shut up immediately, for they hadn't seen me act so menacingly before. They didn't know my face of wrath.

'I am told that you, my father-in-law, did nothing to stop your daughter, my wife, from making love with Thxale, nor from running to Lone Tree. What kind of father-in-law are you? You had no power over this man?'

In a stride I reached Thxale, grabbed him, pulled him to his feet and held him tight. In our hut Namkwa began a screeching and a wailing that I'd never heard before. But I didn't let go of Thxale. The action and our closeness let loose my pent-up anger. I wanted to crush him and hurt him. This Thxale! This brother, my friend!

In days gone by a husband might have killed the man and thrown the woman on the fire. Now my impulse was to throw *him* on the coals, but figures sprang to stop me; Thxale's father, Gruxa, and some elders. They held me, not with force, but firmly, gently. Gruxa called me 'Hansie, Hansie' and tried to calm me

Dr Heinz and Namkwa (behind counter) *in Namkwa's first shop*

Dancing children

Namkwa berates Gathua, her helper at the Takatshwane settlement

down, holding my arm. I couldn't throw him off without horrifying every Bushman there, and demeaning all the norms I'd come to live by. I dropped Thxale, and when the men released me, I stood over him and told him to get out, to leave the village and not come back while I was there.

Quickly Thxale got up, ran to his place, picked up his skin, his weapons, and was gone. As it happened I didn't see him again that stay, and Thamae told me that he camped a few miles from the village. Each night he crept back to visit his father and get some food. But he did not go to Nkasi's hut.

My performance done, I began to relax. I pulled out the Marsala and had a cupful. The others dispersed, still excited by the action. They chatted and clicked and it seemed the whole village spoke at once. Suddenly old Geitchei raised her voice: 'What kind of a runner is this that can go off with her sister's husband!' Then I heard her sister, Theugei: 'Yes, she is real rubbish. She thinks because she is married to a white man she is big, she can take any man she pleases.'

And Kesi: 'We better watch out for our husbands, she will also take them.'

'Yes, she can do that, she is that kind,' another voice said. 'She was never brought up properly, the parents are at fault.'

In loud clear tones the comments carried across the village. And had I been the sober scientist at that moment I might have recorded with smug satisfaction the social function in all this. It only occurred to me days later when I had cooled my emotions that this was a classic example of what the Bushmen call 'Big Talk' – a means of expressing their disapproval of the behaviour of one of the band members. It is one of the ways of bringing their wayward into line. It's an outlet too, for getting things that have been bothering them into the open.

In this instance Namkwa, the butt of their abuse, must have flinched with every barb. Several times I got up to go to her and comfort her, but each time pride pulled me back.

Finally I crawled into the hut. She lay trembling, curled up in a corner. I jerked my kaross over to the other side, leaving her uncovered, and tried to find sleep. After a long time I felt a hand, ever so timidly, touch my shoulder. But in my sadistic sulk I shook it off, and she did not try again. In the morning I got up first and left her lying there.

Slowly, bit by bit, we made up. Sleeping with our arms out, resting on each other's bodies. I could feel her anxiety to repair the hurt, but my gestures were not genuine. I could not shake off the shock of what she had done. I suppose I wasn't big enough to forgive.

The rest of my stay now loomed like a hopeless anti-climax, so I decided to cut it short and leave. Once more I handed round my going-away gifts, and was irritated by the way these grasping little Bushmen tried to get from me as much as they could. Namkwa I left with nothing more than a handshake, and a hundred misgivings.

Pangs of mixed emotion rose in me as I drove off, and I tried to outdrive them. Some hundreds of miles on, I came across the new camp of the road gang. They invited me to stay the night. Their boss had given them a lame cow, and they were going to have a party. I could be their honoured guest. Two girls came with a bowl of water, took off my shirt, shoes and socks and washed the dust from my body. With the roasted ribs and beer, the singing, the dancing and the music of a guitar, I drew a curtain on Takatshwane. I even brought out my fiddle, and fed the party with my high spirits. It was a rather manic effort. In the morning I was depressed again. And again over months of mornings.

Years later when preparing this book, I discussed many aspects with Namkwa. She said she had run off into the bush, not as far as Lone Tree, with Thxale, but 'you know that we grew up together so there is nothing wrong with that'.

And ... ?

'We never slept together,' said Namkwa.

Was fundamental woman a basic liar too? Was she only too human?

ELEVEN

The Challenge

When next I took off for Takatshwane my wounded pride and my disappointment in Namkwa had healed, or so I thought. Time, my work and intensive study had taken my mind off her. I had passed my final B.A. examinations, and was preparing for my Master's in the social organization of the XKo Bushmen. I had already collected a fairly impressive pile of information on their daily lives, but there was a lot more to do. My qualification as a Bushman unfortunately did not provide instant knowledge of all XKo customs. I needed to ask a lot more questions and add perspicuity to my literal observations.

Nearing Takatshwane I began to change my mind, at least about going back to Namkwa. Time hadn't healed my hurt at all, it had merely contained it. Now, with the smell of the bush in my nostrils, it all came back to me. It still wasn't too late to make a detour, and take up with Kamka and her kind father Duce again. I could easily do that, for Kamka was a lovely girl, pretty and willing, and I had treated her badly. I had never followed up the doek I had given her, and my promise to return. I could make it up, and she would benefit from the hard lessons I had learnt from Namkwa. What's more, I could get to know a completely new territory, new people, new ways. That would be a great investment for my Master's degree. I'd have an even wider knowledge of Bushman life, for no bands live absolutely identical lives. Yes, I could turn Kamka and Duce to my scientific advantage ...

At Lone Tree, Maloi shook his head. 'No, we haven't seen Duce and Kamka for a long time. I think they are deep in the bush, because there are many tsamas to give them water this year. They don't need the borehole water.'

For some reason this hadn't occurred to me. The news brought me back to earth, deflated. It looked like Takatshwane after all. But I was in no hurry to get there. I stayed overnight with Maloi, and went hunting with him in the morning. In the afternoon there was no further news of Duce, and I got ready to tackle Takatshwane. As I was about to leave, Theutchei, a pretty young girl from Midum's band, came up and asked for a lift to Takatshwane; she wanted to visit Namkwa. I knew Theutchei quite well, particularly as one of Thamae's many passing 'girlfriends'. She would be welcome.

'Where are your things? Are they far?' I asked.

'No,' she replied. 'When you go along the Ghanzi road, you will pass near to my place.'

A shortish way along the road she asked me to stop and wait. She stepped from the jeep and disappeared into the bush, leaving me reflecting on the beauty of her figure and the flow of her movement. How old was she? One really couldn't tell, except that she was young. So many Bushgirls are beautiful, quite unlike the Congo Pygmies, their nearest physiological neighbours. The Pygmy women have something masculine about them, but the Bushgirl is extremely feminine and attractive.

Her beauty, however, is such a fleeting thing. Her subcutaneous elastic connective tissue breaks up completely, whereas with whites and other racial types, age brings a partial breakdown. Old-age wrinkles are a direct result of this process, which explains why Bushmen look so wrinkled, so wizened and so ancient when a white man, for instance, would look middle-aged.

I could easily feel the difference in Namkwa's connective tissue; despite my age, my skin was much firmer than hers, and in relative terms her age was catching me up. One day, too soon, she would be old. What would she look like when she grew old?

I had thought my way back to Namkwa. But where was Theutchei? I should have known Bushmen have no respect for distance or time. 'You will pass near to my place,' she said. That could mean miles.

Forty minutes had passed. The sun was '*Ntcha olu*' – almost inside. I was hungry. Perhaps I should have gone with Theutchei to say hello to old Midum, and scrounge some meat. Now *there* was a Bushman! He was the only Bushman that I know who, it was said, had killed a lion, and killed it with his spear, what is more.

He had a number of strapping sons – in fact many children from several wives, all of whom had died. His band laid claim to the land adjacent to the eastern side of the Ghanzi road, including the profitable Takatchu valley. The Takatshwane people, whose area stretched to the west of the main road, envied Midum his access to the Takatchu valley and, at times, paid him a social visit so that they could hunt there.

Of course both bands shared the same borehole, but because of some long-standing argument there were no kinship ties between them, which in the normal course would have allowed a greater reciprocity in hunting. Consequently I never saw Midum's men hunting in the land of the Takatshwane people unless they were on my vehicle. As one of the Takatshwane people I was their licence.

They did, however, hunt further east where the Gwi lived and where Midum's mother had come from. They could also wander down Lone Tree way, for Midum's eldest daughter, Thekwe, was married to Geisa, the leader of the Lone Tree band. Such kinship links explain away the misconceptions that have arisen, through ignorance, about the Bushman's respect for another's territory. Indeed when it comes to land usage they know all the rules.

It was dark when Theutchei returned, and I had almost fallen asleep waiting for her.

'You know I've been waiting and waiting. I haven't eaten a thing all day. I'm hungry.' I was also complaining.

'*Hau!* Then let me cook something. Have you food?' said Theutchei. I had rice, onions, and bullybeef, and an inclination to stop awhile with this girl. When she had found a suitable spot and got a fire going I pulled out a bottle of Marsala and poured a hefty cup. The wine went down easily, to my gnawing stomach and down to my warming loins. When Theutchei brought the pan with our food, I handed her a fork and said: 'Let's eat together.'

When we had finished I drew her close to me. She did not resist nor pull away even when I brushed aside her little apron. 'No,

Namkwa will fight me,' was all she said. She knew and enjoyed the sex game, but her fear was Namkwa.

'Namkwa has betrayed me with Thxale,' I said. 'She has no grounds to fight you. Besides, how will she know? Are you going to tell her?'

This way I convinced her. I had already convinced myself, and produced good reasons why I should go on. I wouldn't tell Namkwa either, but in my mind I was out to even the score. This was my final retaliation for the hurt and pain she had provided. In its context the hoary old argument worked for me. I don't know how long we lay coupled there, but the fire had waned to a glow before we pushed on. We were about half an hour from Takatshwane and sat close together in the jeep, warmed by the intimacy of our act and reassured by our mutual promise to keep it secret.

Five miles from Takatshwane we saw the camp-fires of the road gang. When I drew up, Thamae emerged and answered my surprise: 'I received your letter to meet you at Takatshwane, but I found no one there, so I decided to stay with the PWD.'

'You mean no one is there?'

'Yes. But Xauko passed here this morning. He is working for a farmer trekking cattle to Lobatse. He said that the people are somewhere near Barachu Pan.'

'Didn't he say where?'

'He said some name I didn't know. He also said someone had been at Takatshwane yesterday. I think it was Thxale and some others.'

'We must start looking for them at once,' I said. 'It is full moon and we should be able to see the spoor. But what about Theutchei?'

'She can stay here until we return.'

Thamae and I reasoned that if they were at Barachu they would have walked along the Lehututu spoor until they had passed the third pan. Our assumption was correct, for we soon picked up the spoor and raced through the chilly night (it was winter again), past the third pan, stopping only to check the tracks. About a mile on we lost the spoor, which all along had indicated the last to go that way; the three men, Thxale, Tchallo and Thomate.

'Somewhere between here and the last pan they turned off,' said Thamae.

'Well, let's just get some sleep and follow in the morning.'

We didn't bother to make a fire, and as a result suffered from the Antarctic wind that had sprung up. Hardly rested, we got up in the early morning dark and began our hunt for the spoor. We found the tracks again about half a mile back.

The wind that had threatened to cover them fortunately dropped as the sun came up and we made a good pace.

'Let me lead, I only want you to correct me if I lose the spoor,' I said to Thamae. I felt good and confident. By ten o'clock the spoor brought us to a pile of ashes under which we found glowing coals.

'They slept here last night,' said Thamae.

Encouraged, we pressed on. I was only carrying my rifle, but it became heavier by the hour. My feet, on the other hand, unconditioned after months in the city, grew heavier by the minute. Worse still, I could feel the blisters growing. They began to hurt as only blisters can.

Why the hell are you following this woman? I asked myself without stopping to answer the question.

My Bushmanship failed over the pans. The ground was so hard I couldn't pick up any spoor. So Thamae took over, interpreting almost indiscernible signs on clumps of grass and plants, and keeping up the pace. Midday came and with it more convincing signs.

'Look,' said Thamae, 'this is where the women are collecting berries. You see the way their tracks go round the grewia bushes.'

A little later: 'Now we can't be too far away because the people came here to dig bush potatoes. You see, here is a hole, there is another. And look, there is a third.'

Then Thamae let out a shout: 'See here! This is a potato which Namkwa dug out only yesterday! It is her spoor, and it is fresh.'

We were very nearly there, and I couldn't feel the pain in my feet for the anticipation, the fear and the relief I felt. We walked towards the 'dum-dum-dum', which is the sound the Bushwomen make stamping their seeds and food in their wooden mortars.

Suddenly we came across the first skerm. A little further on I saw Nxabase stretching a skin in the shade of a tree. In seconds we were in the middle of the village with the village all around us.

Someone sent for Namkwa while I was shown to her sleeping nest. Then she came to me, full of surprise and delight.

Several old women broke into our greeting. 'Stamp him a melon, he is thirsty,' they commanded Namkwa, who ran to roll out her blanket for me to sit on. It was tempting, but I knew that if I sat down I wouldn't want to get up again.

'Are you going to sleep here?' she asked.

'No, Namkwa, my feet are so sore that I should never be able to walk in the morning.' Standing, I pulled off my shoes. Each toe blazed a blister, my heels were raw. I was determined not to stop at this place, but my feet looked serious. Recalling my German army days when we marched in foot rags rather than socks I wrapped my feet in handkerchiefs and thought of giving it a go.

'Namkwa, I've got to return to the nolli. Get your things and let's go.'

She picked up her belongings and called for a few others to accompany us; Thxale and Nkasi, Ntonno (Shucre's husband) and some youngsters. Thxale came cautiously, somewhat apprehensive, but there was no animosity in my greeting. Somehow we all felt relief. It was going to be all right.

Shouldering my rifle and Namkwa's blankets, we began the return trek. For a while my feet gave no trouble, thanks to my Heath Robinson hanky rags. But before long the trek turned into an ordeal by fire. My feet walked in hell, dragging through the car track furrows, stumbling on the banks of the spoor and turning some nightmarish treadmill that got us nowhere.

Bushmen can walk one foot exactly in front of the other, endlessly and easily. So narrow paths worn into furrows do not bother them. I tried walking on the untrammelled middle mound but tripped on grass tufts and caught my feet on roots and bits of bush. So I tried the trough again.

As fatigue took hold I even tried singing. This was another old army trick I remembered which also worked for a while. I plunged along on the strength of *Ein Heller und ein Batsen* or some other incongruous German marching song. Unfortunately the effort wasted valuable breath, and saliva which I couldn't afford to lose. I was becoming steadily more dehydrated, and Namkwa became alarmed at my condition. I must have looked as terrible as I felt. She stopped me, and I leaned against a tree while she stamped a tsama melon and fed me with her hands. Slightly rested I ploughed on with Namkwa mothering my every stride.

Every so often she would scurry off the path and come back with a potato-like tuber. Chewing this quickly restored my saliva. But relief was only temporary. Now my mind was staggering. Feet, pain, arms, rifle, sweat, thirst, head, songs, saliva, all stumbled along in a jumbled incoherent whole. I remember only fragments of the last couple of hours of that blind march. I remember the moon being there and wondering where it had come from. I hadn't noticed the day disappear. I didn't even realize we were getting there until I saw the jeep glowing like the Holy Grail in front of me. Then I allowed myself the luxury of a heartfelt 'phew!' The treadmill had stopped and I could get off.

Gradually I collected my dismembered parts. Put feet and pain together, wriggled my weight-free rifle ache, shrugged my shoulders into place and shuffled my thoughts into order.

Leaning against the jeep I watched the others make camp. Namkwa made up a bed but I didn't hurry to it. Like some sweet torture I anticipated and delayed the moment when I would flop on to it. With the security of my bed awaiting me I began to take a more objective interest in my condition and the activity around me. I pulled out the bathroom scale I used to determine the weight variations of Bushmen throughout the year, and weighed myself. With some satisfaction I noticed I had lost $7\frac{1}{2}$ pounds! It had been quite a march.

The Bushmen, of course, showed no wear, and even Ntonno didn't look fatigued. He had come with us in the hope that I would be able to do something for the large ulcers disfiguring his neck. They looked serious and I suspected glandular tuberculosis which would require proper attention. If I was correct there wasn't much I could do, but I dragged out my medical equipment and gave him an antibiotic injection. That done I succumbed to the temptation to lie down. I think I slept without moving.

In the morning my aches and pains came to life with a vengeance. As I had feared I couldn't get up. I did however call
Ntonno across and I was alarmed by what I saw on close inspec-
tion in daylight. His ulcers were almost 2 inches in diameter and
ugly with neglect. I cleaned them as best I could, knowing that
sooner or later, preferably sooner, he would have to have
hospital treatment.

Over the years I have sent, or taken, a number of Bushmen to
hospital with what I'd diagnosed as TB, but this hasn't won me
any kudos from the medical services in Botswana. On the contrary, the officials have looked askance at my medical activities.
Their doubts I suppose were understandable. I am not a
doctor.

On the other hand, these people had absolutely no access to
Western medicine other than the supplies I carried in my box,
so I had no compunction in acting as a sort of poor man's
Dr Schweitzer. Over many years as a parasitologist, and working
among doctors, I've picked up some knowledge, and have been
able to treat the more superficial ailments, the severe burns, flesh
wounds, coughs, colds and eye infections which the Bushman is
prone to. I don't see how anyone can think I ought to have done
otherwise.

On our second evening round the jeep, the rest of the band
arrived, and established a village round my bed. Quite by the way
Gruxa told Namkwa that we had been followed by a lion for most
of our way. They had seen its spoor. I was told that it was not
uncommon for lions to follow people for miles without thinking
of attacking them. They follow out of curiosity, and only become
dangerous for anyone sitting down exhausted. Then the lion,
thinking the straggler is one of the weak that has fallen by the
wayside, might attack. Out of interest's sake I took the jeep and
we traced the lion's spoor for about 10 miles. From this we were
able to calculate that Thamae and I must have marched a total of
26 miles – 13 out and 13 back. By then I could feel proud of my
achievement. In bush conditions and heavy sand it was a thorough
slog.

Fussed and fed by Namkwa I was soon back to normal, and
once more our relationship blossomed. Nor was it in the slightest
shaken by the arrival of pretty Theutchei, who gave no clue of

our affair. More than ever Namkwa demonstrated her affection, and, just as heartening, she began to assume the role of a conscientious tutor. Her attitude in the past had always been rather casual, even when she guided me to something she knew I'd be interested in. Now she made a point of explaining things and coaching me in my conduct and relations with others.

She also encouraged me to participate more fully in village activities and spontaneous games and dances. One afternoon the girls, Kwé Kwé, Shucre and Nkasi, began a ball game with a tsama melon. Soon the other girls had joined in, singing and laughing as they threw the ball around. They caught with skill and laughed loudly at each dropped pass. The game wandered into lines and circles and the excitement grew as each girl did her own antic dance before letting the ball go.

Soon the melon became a minor factor, and the girls were competing for the most original solo. As the older folk joined in, the children retired to the sidelines to watch and clap the performers. Nxabase was the first man to follow his impulse and jump in to participate. Soon the other men, not to be outdone, began their cricket game, mimicking the cricket's jump. They formed a stamping, grunting circle round a man in the middle. One at a time the others sprang into the ring to leapfrog over the centre man's back. In between such leaps they did other complicated movements until the middle man bent and offered his back again. Then they had to be ready to leap.

The rhythm round the circle governed the action, and the exact moment when the bent back had to be offered. If the other man missed the cue he would be laughed at and made to look foolish. This I know, for I dropped my inhibitions (at Namkwa's behest) to play the game, and succeeded in bringing it to an end with all the players rolling about in tears of laughter.

I was a happy fool, however. I knew my efforts weren't wasted. Such moments I had found were good investments, and eased me further into the society.

We had not been long at our village when Ntumka arrived with some of his people, and his donkeys. Ntumka, who was to become one of my valuable language teachers, was married to Thakum, perhaps the prettiest Bushgirl I've ever seen.

Somehow after three children she had retained a good figure, rare among Bushwomen, whose connective tissue usually disintegrates after the first pregnancy. Now she was pregnant a fourth time, and when she came to us riding on a donkey she was obviously nearly due.

One evening, after she had accompanied us, rattling and bumping, down to the borehole, the baby started to break out. For me this was a stroke of luck. I hadn't been around when a baby was being born before, and the anthropologist was quite excited.

Not so the village, which showed not the slightest interest. Thakum, Geitchei, her mother-in-law and one or two more old women merely withdrew a few yards into the adjoining bushes, where with little or no to-do the baby was born. Unfortunately, unlike Tkose's puberty ceremony, I wasn't allowed to attend the birth, and had to rely on Namkwa's description of what went on.

The expectant mother is usually attended by her mother and any other old women, preferably including the woman who taught her during her initiation. The women wash her hands and body, but not her genitalia. They dig and clear a hole over which the pregnant woman is made to kneel. When the labour pains come more rapidly one of the midwives, who has cleaned her hands with the juice of special roots, squats in front while another, usually the mother-in-law, supports the woman from behind, allowing her to lean backwards in her kneeling position. The midwife woman in front catches the infant and hands it to the other women who dry it with 'woman's grass'.

While Namkwa was describing the procedure and I sat with Ntumka, young Gathua came up to us. He had been sent by Thakum's mother-in-law, who asked whether the baby should live. Apparently Thakum was prepared to let the child die if her husband willed it. Ntumka thought for a few moments and then said it must live. If the child were alive, he wished to see it. I got up and walked towards the birthplace, and met Thakum coming towards me carrying the child. There was no emotion of either pain or joy in her expression. She took the child to Ntumka.

The talk of killing the child bothered me, and later that evening I discussed it with Namkwa and Thamae, who invariably knew exactly what was going on around us. They told me that Thakum was still breast-feeding her little son. Under Kalahari food conditions, and because of the roughage content of veldfood, no woman is capable of feeding two children on the breast at the same time. One infant is sure to die, and all three could be endangered. Ntumka's decision was prompted by the fact that the older infant could now be weaned. Otherwise he would probably have passed sentence on the newborn baby.

'But how is the child killed?' I asked.

'The old woman who catches the baby quickly buries it in the hole before the mother hears its first cry.'

'But don't you worry about having killed a baby?'

'We all worry, it makes us sad, but we know we must save the mother and the older child.'

'What about the placenta and umbilical cord?'

'All blood and water and the afterbirth are caught in the hole beneath the girl, and then they cover it with the sand,' said Namkwa.

'Yes, but you didn't tell me about the umbilical cord. Do you cut it? How do you remove it?'

'We cut it. But never with a knife. We sharpen a grewia stick which we harden in the fire. Only this can cut the cord. It must be buried deep, far beyond the reach of hyenas or dogs, otherwise the child will die. We even cover such holes with thorns and branches.'

'Tell me, Namkwa, suppose Thakum had started to bleed, what would you have done?'

'We would have called you to help. But first the men would have tattooed you with special medicine because they are afraid of the power of this blood.'

Three days later Thamae drew my attention to the animated discussion going on at Ntumka's fire: 'Ntumka's in-laws have arrived, and they are arguing about what name to give the child. Let's go there.'

Thamae explained that the baby was Thakum's first daughter, and according to XKo custom it would have the name of Ntumka's mother. Evidently he objected because it was a common name.

'Then the baby must have my name,' said Thakum's mother.

This suggestion let loose a barrage of words. It went far too fast for me. Only the mother was silent.

'Why all the talk? Don't the others like that?' I asked.

'No, they all agree,' said Thamae. 'They are just talking about it, that's all. Now the baby is named. They've agreed and that's it.'

While I concentrated on this, my fascination slowly moved to Thakum's little boy who had been taken off her breast. For the first time I noticed his swollen neck-gland, and with increasing concern studied his suppurating ear. Oh God, I thought, another case of TB.

Up till then Ntonno had been the only black smudge on my daily life. He hadn't responded to treatment, and I was contemplating sending him to Ghanzi. Poor Ntonno! He was from Douté's band, and had married Shucre. He played the dongo superbly, and when he played to Shucre his musical creativity was astonishing. His reputation went so wide that Bushmen at Lone Tree, hearing a tape recording, needed only a moment: 'Ntonno!' they exclaimed.

Thakum's child doubled my worry, and it was soon apparent that his ear wouldn't respond to antibiotics either. As if this weren't enough, it was clear to me that Xamxua's son, Tanate, was coughing suspiciously and that Ntumka's younger brother, Sureté, was a TB case if ever there was one. He had come with Thakum's parents, and frankly I wished he hadn't.

What frightened me was that Bushmen share everything like cups, pots and pipes, and none of them would understand or appreciate the contagiousness of TB. I had to get these cases out and away from our band before we were all infected.

It would seem that Ntumka's family was very prone to TB. Years later Ntumka's cousin died in the Ghanzi hospital, and I brought his body home. He was not the first to die during the years I had been visiting Namkwa and her people, but it was the first burial that I actually witnessed, and I was impressed. The closest relatives chose a site for the grave only a short distance from the village. They measured up the body and began to dig a grave with an east–west axis. The head was to lie at the western end, for that was the direction in which the spirit would leave the body. The grave was very deep, about 10 feet. At the bottom a cavern was hollowed out in one side into which the body was stretched out with a 'cushion' under the head. The side of the cavern was closed with branches and leaves, so that the dirt would not fall on the body. The people all lined up to throw a handful of dirt each into the grave. Mothers were particularly concerned that their children should also throw a handful of dirt into the grave, which provoked much anxiety and crying on the part of the children. Two vertical sticks of wood which protruded at the top were placed into the grave before the earth was replaced. After the mound had been shaped a horizontal piece of wood connected the two protruding pieces. Then numerous branches were placed over the grave. The men who had dug the grave finally made a small fire next to it and said a prayer in which they bade their comrade farewell and asked Guthe to look after them and to see to it that they were supplied with ample meat and veldfood. It was then necessary for them to wash their hands in medicated water prepared by the father of the deceased.

Bushmen fear graves and rarely return to them, even avoid them. This is easy to do because graves are quickly recognized by their covering branches and protruding sticks.

I took Ntonno to the Ghanzi road with Thamae, and a letter to the hospital setting out my suspicions. A few days later Thamae returned on foot, telling me that a number of Ghanzi farmers had passed, but none would take Ntonno, although he had shown my letter. They all insisted on payment. With two rand Thamae set off again, and Ntonno eventually got to Ghanzi.

Meanwhile Namkwa shocked me with a casual remark in bed one evening.

'You know, Shucre has divorced Ntonno.'

'But why? They were in love! I have never seen any two Bushmen so much in love.'

'Ntchumka, her father, forced her.'

'Why?'

'Because Ntonno is sick.'

'But that's no reason to divorce a husband.'

'Yes, but Ntchumka says that he can never support and feed his daughter, so she had better look for a new husband.'

Poor Ntonno! At least he had a good chance of recovery. I decided I would rather take the three others to the Kanye hospital. I wouldn't be staying much longer, and could deliver them on my way home. It was 350 miles away, but I knew the treatment would be good. It would be worth it.

Shortly before my departure, when sadness at leaving Namkwa was already seeping into my work, I spoke to Thamae about her.

'You know, Thamae, I could never have made it back to the nolli without her help. Perhaps she wanted to make up for what happened last time. She has been so considerate in everything I'm sure it shows she loves me.'

'Doc, I think the time is right for me to tell you something. Today I want to tell you about something that has worried Namkwa, your wife, for years. And which has even worried you, though you did not know it.'

Go on! Go on!

'You didn't know about it. Because you are not able to read the spoor of Bushmen, you did not see. Had you been raised among these people you would have seen Douté's spoor all round her sleeping place at Barachu.' Thamae must have seen my expression. 'Now just listen to me, Doc! For years Douté had wanted to marry Namkwa, but she and Gruxa refused. He has pestered her, and always comes here when you are away. He was at Barachu just before you came. He thought he was in luck because you would never find her there.'

'How do you know all this?' I asked.

Thamae got up and called Xamxua. When the elder sat down he told Namkwa, who had been hovering about, to go to her sister's fire; we wanted to speak as men.

'I am glad you called me, for I am your teacher,' Xamxua started. 'You must always come to me when there is something on your mind. Now listen. Douté is married to Abé. She is an old woman.'

'Yes, I know.'

'Douté is like a step-brother to Namkwa ... '

'Yes, I know that also. He told me on the night of my initiation. He said that Gruxa married Domku, his mother, after Musomo had been killed by the police.'

'Douté still feels young. Younger than Abé his wife. He thinks that he can feed a second wife because he is rich.'

'What does Abé say about this?'

'She refuses, but he pays no attention to her.'

'Go on.'

'Douté is in love with Namkwa, but Namkwa doesn't love him, and Gruxa absolutely refuses him.'

'Why?'

'Because she is like a sister. That is against XKo law. But Douté is the son of Musomo and I knew Musomo well. Douté doesn't care. He wants Gruxa to give her to him. But Gruxa refuses. That is why they are always fighting. This is why Gruxa gives Douté presents, just to put him off. But Douté keeps coming back.'

'But what does Namkwa say?'

'She hates him, but she ... we are all afraid of him. Don't you remember the time you were initiated? He was ready to kill you and fight us.'

'But why?'

'Because he is jealous. Now I must tell you some more. People say Douté told Nkobe, his own brother's wife, to sleep with you. Do you know why? Because he wanted to get hold of you. He is from the farms. He is not stupid. He knows the way white farmers go for pretty Bushgirls. He felt if you fell in love with his brother's wife, he could bleed you with presents to him.'

'But I thought she was ugly.'

'Yes, that is where his plan went wrong. So then, when you spoke to him about another Bushgirl he saw another chance.'

'You mean he introduced me to Namkwa on purpose?'

'Yes! He told Gruxa anything you gave him or Namkwa belonged to him because he introduced Namkwa to you.'

'So what did Gruxa say?'

'They argued and even fought. You remember the chopper you gave Gruxa when he gave you his daughter, well, they even fought about that.'

It was all fitting into place. All the riddles and doubts that had affected my relationship with Douté.

'But Namkwa hasn't told me any of this. How does Namkwa feel?'

'She does not know how to get rid of him because he is so strong.'

'What do you mean, he is so strong?'

'He is Musomo's son. He is the strongest Bushman here. Who would really fight him? Didn't you see your father-in-law give him Nellie, the dog that he really loved? Who would really fight him?'

I had listened to Xamxua, first with fear, then growing anger.

'I, Namkwa's husband, will oppose Douté.'

Only one doubt remained. I must hear what Namkwa had to say: 'Can I call her now?' I asked.

'Yes, call her, ask her how she feels.'

Namkwa came, somewhat apprehensive. She had seen the animated talk, and wondered what we were saying. She answered our questions, and she spoke, eyes downcast at first, then as she relaxed with growing feeling: It was not right that she marry a brother. She would surely be killed by Guthe. She did not want another husband. She could never be a second wife. She wanted me. She hated Douté. She wanted me!

In bed that night we lay close and Namkwa hugged me hard. I said nothing, but played, over and over, the words I had heard. Clearer than ever I saw my duty to help and protect Namkwa; to help my father-in-law; to fight and defeat this Douté who threatened the whole band. Somehow I would have to do it, and do it convincingly. I would think of something.

I left the band with my promise to be back, and said 'auf wiedersehen' to Namkwa. With me I took Thakum and her latest child, her little boy, and the other two TB suspects, Sureté and Tanate. I delivered them to Kanye hospital, a sick little group many miles from home.

Some time later I heard their story from Thakum. While they were there, and before Sureté's course of treatment was complete, Thakum's tuberculine boy died. The death of the boy caused the others to panic, and the same night, Thakum and her baby, Tanate and Sureté, ran away from hospital. Before them lay 350 miles of thirstland, and just the other side of that was home.

Day by day they walked, living off the land. But Sureté was dying, and couldn't keep up with Tanate and Thakum. Thakum told me they would go on ahead, and wait for Sureté to catch them up. Usually by nightfall he would find them, but sometimes they waited another day before he caught up. It must have been ghastly, going all that way, particularly for the failing Bushman. But Sureté was determined to die in his own land. And, shortly after he got there, he did.

On the march there was nothing Thakum and Tanate could do for their companion. They could only move on and on, wait for him to catch up or die along the way.

They were not indifferent, but that is the way life goes in the bush.

TWELVE

The Taming of Douté

'I, Namkwa's husband, will oppose him!' That's what I had said, but my boast in the bush would not be easy to carry out. Back in Johannesburg it haunted me. But I was determined to see the challenge through. Douté must be met.

What bothered me was how? He was no ordinary character. I didn't need the others to tell me of the power that he wielded; I had seen it. He was clever and scheming and could manipulate other men. He was bold and aggressive and ambitious, and not intimidated by custom. In fact he showed little respect for XKo laws, or the dignity of age, otherwise he would have left Gruxa alone and subdued his wish to marry his step-sister. Nor would he have offered me Nkobe, his own brother's wife. Clearly he was not beyond taking the law into his own hands.

Only something extraordinary, I decided, could tame him. I could possibly buy him off or bribe him, but where would that get us? It was unthinkable. So was physical violence.

I couldn't see myself attacking him. Nor could I point a gun at him, for such a threat could backfire and I'd only demean myself. Nor could I beat him in any trial or test of skill and stamina to prove who was the better, stronger Bushman. On his home ground he was unbeatable. But it had to be on his home ground that I had to meet him.

Then it came to me. My greatest strength lay in my power as a medicine man, and the magic of my instruments. I had command of forces far beyond the ken of any Bushman. I had medicine that could heal, needles that could close long festering sores, that hurt like a snakebite when they went in but killed the poison. I knew the secrets of the nolli, the thing that could catch dongo music and everything the Bushmen said and say it back. The Bushman could make fire by rubbing sticks together, but I had brought along a tiny thing that made it even quicker, just with a flick of a thumb.

All these things had at one time or another impressed my Bushman friends, and though they didn't understand them they had come to accept them. Now was the time to bring out all my resources and use them to my advantage, to play on their naivety and put the fear of Guthe in them. Or better still, his evil spirit, Thoa. I had to show I had the power to call up the spirits, and that such power was inaccessible to others.

I began to conjure up a few more elaborate tricks which would reveal my diabolical power. My idea was to project in front of the Bushmen an image of Thoa accompanied by such magical trimmings as smoke and fire and some impressive patter. In a Hillbrow novelty shop I bought a hideous and frightening face mask. I then had a photographic transparency made of the mask propped among startling colour effects. To project the slide I constructed a projector that would work with a 12-volt globe in an inconspicuous, harmless-looking box. Then I bought a green smoke-bomb and equipped myself with a quantity of magnesium powder and an extra supply of beer.

Depending on my timing and performance, I knew that this plan could terrify the Bushmen, and I had to convince myself again that I was justified in exposing my friends to the experience.

For years, I'd now discovered, Namkwa had been tormented by Douté. Not only was she afraid of him, but so was the whole band. He had held the band to ransom ever since he had introduced me, and had assumed a proprietary right in the things I left behind. Gruxa's chopper was only one example. Food and tobacco I had left behind with Namkwa he would claim within days of my departure.

If he were allowed to have his way with Namkwa (Heaven forbid), certainly I would be a loser, but even if I withdrew there was no saying how the existing conflict would be resolved.

Takatshwane had become too much a part of my life for me to contemplate withdrawing to leave the Bushmen to sort out their problems in their own way. In any case, I was an admitted member of the male society, and to abandon them would make my union with Namkwa meaningless. The main problem was to get through to Douté. He was cynical enough to be unimpressed by my little wizard's show.

In April, three months after leaving Takatshwane, I returned and awaited my opportunity. To ensure Douté was available I drove to Okwa to let the people know I had returned, and that I was hoping to see Douté. Within a few days he had arrived at Takatshwane.

I had spent some time polishing up my oratory and preparing a dramatic commentary. What I said would be as important as the mechanics of the plot. On an afternoon when Namkwa was out food-collecting, and the village was practically deserted, I set up my apparatus. My 12-volt battery I placed behind my pillow, not far from where I would sit. I covered the wire leading from it to the light-switch hidden at my side, and placed the projector box innocently a few yards away.

A short distance in front of it I arranged the pile of mielie meal and Puzemandle sacks, and casually draped a groundsheet over them, ensuring that it hung almost vertical and wrinkle-free. This was to be my screen. Into my nolli I placed the magnesium powder, the smoke-bomb and a stack of beer-cans.

That night Nxabase ate with us, and when he had scraped out the pot I said, 'Nxabase, go call the old men. Call Douté, Tasa the elder, Gruxa, Ntchumka, Xauko, Xamxua my teacher, Tasa from Douté's band, and any other old men who are with him. Yes, also call Krei Krei and Krake Tchrau. Tell them that I want to speak to them.'

I chased the children away, telling them that they must scat or else the evil spirit would get them. To Namkwa, I spoke gently: 'Tonight you must not be afraid. You must sit as close to me as possible and hold me, so nothing will happen to you. Trust me, and don't be frightened.'

Curious, she asked me what was going to happen, but I said, 'Don't ask. This is a matter for the men. Women must just sit and listen, otherwise I must send you away.'

One by one the men arrived. Some younger men also turned up, but I sent them away, saying that this was a matter for the old men. Namkwa was the only woman there, and she sat close to me.

As they settled, shuffling into a circle round the fire, I said,

'Tonight I want to discuss with you a matter which makes my heart sore. You are the old men, and some were my teachers. I can speak only to you.'

I felt their attention prick up. So this was business! From the sack of tobacco I gave each a generous helping, and sat down in my place again. They stuffed the tobacco away, and some lit up. All were listening.

'I want you to advise me as my fathers, as my brothers. So let us sit and talk about this matter and drink beer together.'

'Yes, you are right, you are my pupil. You can speak to me,' said Xamxua. The others grunted, clicked and nodded.

I went over to the vehicle and brought out one beer after another, opened them and handed them round.

While we drank we spoke casually, not hurrying on the business of the meeting. But I kept a watch on the time, and when I judged Douté must be affected by the drink, I sprinkled a little magnesium powder on the fire. Immediately Namkwa huddled closer.

'There is nothing ordinary about this fire any more,' I said. 'I have given it power. I have given it particular strength.'

The men sat up, wide-eyed.

'You men listen,' I went on. 'I have called you to speak about what pains me. There is someone in our midst who is not honest with me; someone who knows the Bushman laws which you taught me, but who scorns them; someone who learnt respect for his elders as I learnt it from you but who has fought with his father; someone whose greed is so great that he forces others to give him their goods so that he need not steal them; someone who can marry another man's wife even though she is his sister.'

With this speech a general mumbling broke out, but Xamxua said, 'You speak the truth!' I waited for the mumbling to stop: 'Perhaps this man is rich, for he has donkeys. Perhaps he is powerful, for his father was also powerful, and everyone cringed before Musomo has they now do to him! But I will not cringe. Today this man shall know that I am more powerful than he is.'

I looked straight at Douté, who looked back at me with unsteady eyes. With growing confidence I threw out my challenge:

'Is there one among you who can call Thoa, your spirit of

evil, and make him do what you ask? Is there one here who can ask Thoa to appear to show his face?'

'Never!' exclaimed Xamxua.

'Then know that I alone have the power to do so. I alone can bid him destroy that man who treads in my house when I am gone. I alone can hear from Thoa directly what goes on here when I am far away. Indeed, I know it instantly. Do you believe me?'

Again there was another sound of mumbling. Douté, however, sat staring, not saying a word. Xamxua, the elder, again replied, 'We believe you!'

'Then look!' – as I said that the bomb went off, belching out heavy tails of green smoke. At the same time I flipped the switch and through the cloud a weird and eerie face loomed out of the groundsheet on the sacks. Namkwa screamed and dug her nails into me. The men jumped up in terror, eyes fixed on the apparition. Douté's eyes stood out on stalks. Hardly had they recognized the evil one, Thoa, right in front of them, when I threw a handful of magnesium into the fire. The tremendous flash threw everyone backwards and blinded them. When they looked again, the image of Thoa was gone. Their fear and incredulity showed. At that moment, I, charlatan and amateur magician, was all-powerful.

All that was left was to perform the blessing: 'Now go to your fires,' I said, 'and think about what you have seen and heard. Let this be a warning, and let everyone know that Thoa will be provoked but once. The next time he destroys!'

Muttering, each man drifted off. In the dark I heard old Krei Krei say, 'He is too strong, too strong. He will kill us all!'

I turned to Namkwa, who was sallow with fright. She hung on to my hand. 'It's over now, Namkwa,' I said softly. 'He will never come and worry you again. I know, for I saw his face ... don't be afraid. I said no harm would come to you if you sat close. You did. That is all that mattered.'

She stared into the fire and didn't say a word. I wondered what she was thinking. Almost mechanically I filled her conical tin pipe with tobacco and held it. I held it for some time, unmoving, before I leant forward and pulled out a glowing ember. Without thinking I pushed one end into the sand to cool it. I felt no elation, no particular pride in my performance. It had worked all right. As well as ever I had expected. But what was it going to prove? What would it mean to them? To us? Had my medicine been too strong?

Had it merely served to show, once and for all, that I wasn't one of them? Was someone to be feared, an alien. Could they ever sit again with me, joke and laugh and be at ease? Would their children flee from me as I approached them?

In my conceit that I had become a Bushman, I could vindicate my act, though I knew I would never use such tactics again. But how could I presume to come to this, their land, and interpret what was best for them, and pass judgment on their conduct? I began to think that I was no better than their Douté. I was everything I called him – selfish, aggressive, ambitious, scheming, ruthless, and a manipulator of men. I even held the woman that he wanted.

I had taken advantage of their innocence, their ignorance, their hospitality and their material poverty for my own ends. How could I blame Douté, when it was I, the parasitologist in pursuit of some diversion, who was the cornerstone of all this conflict?

Even as I searched my conscience, I drew the ember from the sand, dipped its glowing tip into our tin pipe and puffed hard until the thing was too hot for me to hold. Mechanically I passed it on to Namkwa, who still had not moved. She rolled it quickly between her palms to cool it. Then she too pulled at it, sucking deep depressions in her cheeks and enveloping her head in smoke.

Neither of us said another word that night.

Namkwa was singing when I awoke, and when she saw my eyes open she came over with a cup of coffee and sat down beside me. Together we spoke about nothing. Then I asked her, 'Where is Douté?'

'He has left long ago,' said Namkwa.

'He, all alone?'

'No, with his people. They left on donkey.'

I felt relief, but once again no real joy. I still had our village to face, and didn't want to talk about the night before. I wanted to get away and hide my anxiety in some concentrated work. I took my typewriter and folding chair over to the shade of a large camelthorn tree. There I attacked a stack of typing that had built up, and there Namkwa joined me with one of the sprinkbok mats Nxabase had stretched for me, and her shoulder-bag. Squatting down, she poured out a mound of beads. From her bag she also took a piece of antelope sinew which she chewed to make soft, then split and spliced and finally rolled into a fine thread. While I worked she strung the beads, leaning close enough for me, once in a while, to stroke her head or slip my hand down over her breast.

Lunch was a mixture of grewia mash and Puzemandle, and afterwards I got off my chair and lay my head on her lap. She started to move her fingers through my hair as though she were delousing me. Then she laughed and stopped.

'But don't stop. I like that ... '

'You don't have lice.'

'Never mind. Just pretend I have.'

So Namkwa scratched through my hair, and as I dozed she suddenly leant down and gently blew into my face. She began on my forehead, blew on my cheeks, lips and ears. This was a true Bushman kiss. And I, whatever I was, was Namkwa's husband.

THIRTEEN

A Confrontation

After the rain the bush vibrates with the verve of its revival. You can feel it tingle in your blood; see it in the joyous tumble of the lilac-breasted roller and hear it in the clap of the clapper lark applauding louder. Our storm had come and thundered, lighting up our trembling littleness with great forks of fire and washing down our wasteland, before it passed on. Now the village ran with energy, practically springing back to life.

Old Xamxua and my 'brother' Nxabase came over to my hut, and taking it for granted I was with them, told Namkwa to gather up my things for the hunt.

'After such a rain, the duiker and the steenbok will be out and if we go now, they will still be "tame",' said Xamxua, scarcely concealing his hunter's itch to be gone.

'Yes, and the pans will have water so animals will come to drink,' said Nxabase, as if I needed extra urging.

We hopped aboard the jeep and were soon revving southwards towards Barachu Pan. About 3 miles on we suddenly saw two ragged figures coming towards us through the bush. An old man and one much younger, they looked as though they had been a long time coming. The young man, his hair unkempt, wore an amulet around his neck, a tattered shirt and equally tattered short trousers. He was walking barefoot. The old man had on a peaked cap, a remnant of some hat. His face was tough and wizened. His old khaki army jacket, its lapels trailing down over each shoulder covered his top half, and a long pair of ragged trousers hung frayed down to his toes. Round his middle he had tied a belt of rope, and he carried a shoulder-bag and a battered ex-army water-bottle. They had no blankets, no skin kaross or canvas, or even a scrap of food as far as I could see. And that water-bottle had to be empty.

The old man's name was Dick Somdakakazi of the Transkei, and he was an inyanga looking for new medicines. His young companion was his pupil, and his patient, and they were searching for the medicines that would cure him, and which only the Bushmen had. Amazingly, they had been on foot for months.

I told him who I was, that I had been with these Bushmen for a long time, that I was their 'doctor' and knew most of their medicines. I didn't think they were the Bushmen to help him because all they knew they picked up from Bushmen further north, the Nharo and Gwi. These were theirt eachers. I turned to Xamxua and said, 'Speak to the old man in Tswana, tell him where to find Bushman medicine.'

Xamxua came out of the conversation with an obvious respect for the inyanga and not a thought for hunting.

'We must look for Nxabase the Elder. We must take him there,' he said.

'But Xamxua, that's miles away, far up the Okwa valley. Besides, do you know where old Nxabase lives? He is always moving around trapping.'

Xamxua was not impressed: 'It makes no difference. I will look for Nxabase and take this doctor to him.'

That settled the matter. We turned round and went back to our village. When Namkwa had fed the travellers and given them drink, we made tracks for Okwa, where we eventually left the odd couple.

On the way back to the Takatshwane valley I was reminded that there was a new pumper at Lone Tree. He was a Kgalagadi who came from somewhere near Lehututu. For a while he had taken up with a Bushgirl, Tchaga, from Ohe, where I had heard Bushgirls were open game for the black man. I had been curious to travel down to Ohe and felt now was as good a time as any. I put it to my passengers that we forget about Barachu and hunt further south, near Manyane, before going on to Ohe where we could see the Bushmen who lived there. There was general agreement and we decided to leave the next day, taking Thomate with us because his people were from there and he knew the land.

In some respects this was one of the most beautiful trips I had been on. We were a spirited group of Bushmen, and I, as ever, revelled in the company of my friends who filled the nolli.

On the way south we shot a wildebeest and camped that night near Manyane Pan, where we watched many animals saunter to and fro. We fed ourselves on roasted wildebeest ribs as beautifully cooked as any meat that the expert Namkwa had ever prepared. The men's appetites, however, were not satisfied, so they scraped a bed of coals into a hole and made an oven of leaves and sand for the animal's head.

All around us the bush was alive. Lions whoofed messages to one another over our heads, jackals had their own loud talk and korhaans cackled angrily at the din. For several hours the Bushmen identified the noises; lion and korhaan, the jackal, the booming ostrich, the springbok rams. While all this went on Namkwa and I lay curled up, unafraid in each other's arms. But we had little sleep. It wasn't the lions that bothered us, but the Bushmen and their blasted wildebeest head. After midnight, they decided the head must be done, so they dug it out and spent the next couple of hours noisily taking out of it all they could.

In the morning, going on to Manyane, we saw a shimmering movement near the horizon. '*Nxei!*' said Thxale, and soon we saw the hartebeest. A mass of them, so many that our imagination could barely credit so many thousands. Barely aiming I shot four, and we left two youngsters to skin and cut them up while we went on to Manyane and then to Ohe, the Kgalagadi village.

We shot another hartebeest to take with us, and soon afterwards drove into another most unusual sight. There in front of us was a migration of ostriches, I guess a few thousand of them galloping southwards at a clip. Apparently, I'm told, such a flock will push on regardless of obstacles like wire fences. Though the leading birds might get crushed against the wire, the others force it down and carry on their way. I can believe it, though until I saw so many of these odd birds in one fell galloping swoop, I wouldn't have believed that either.

On to Ohe with the sun dropping and Thomate guiding. I hardly knew what to expect at the Kgalagadi village. By the time we came to leave it, however, our trip was made more unforgettable by the disgust I felt, and the anger that went with it. I knew the general attitude of white and black to the Bushman:

I had seen paternalism at work, heard white men wonder if they'd ever be human and Bantu call them 'baboons'.

I'd also heard old Xamxua say that Guthe made the Bushman from the scrapings in the pot, and seen them shrug and say, 'Oh well, we are Bushmen, we are stupid.'

In fact many Bushmen have been conditioned to the role that society has assigned to them, to accept with gratitude the rags and discards of the other races and to tolerate their whims. They have been cowed into an attitude of submissiveness that has made the Europeans, I don't exclude myself, and the Tswana think them insensitive to slights.

They are wrong. These are the people who can interpret the slightest quirk in animal behaviour and they are equally quick to pick up the signs and slights in human nature too. I've seen the other side of their submissiveness, round their fires, in their jokes and stories and their mimicry of outsiders who have demeaned themselves as humans. And behind it all, the hurt remains. I've seen it in their eyes. That time, and other times, when Nxabase and I paid a visit to Maloi when he was pumper at Lone Tree. His wife had made us tea and Maloi and I got ours served in cups upon a tray. When we had finished she poured some in an empty tin for my 'brother' Nxabase. He said nothing then. But afterwards he said: 'When you have had your fill, we always eat from your plate and drink from your cup. It was not right to give tea in an old tin can when it would have been better had we shared a half-empty cup. That is customary among the XKo.'

Here in Ohe my hate of the concept of rigid racial superiority and inferiority was intensified. I knew that life in the bush was tough, but by the time I left this place I knew I could never accept miserable subservience and submissiveness as a way of life for my Bushman friends. And if there grew an element of dedication in my Bushman life, it was to bring my friends, not to ask for respect, but to a level of dignity and self-respect that demanded it.

We camped in a small wooded patch outside the Kgalagadi village, and in the morning a man arrived at our fire to tell me it was necessary to introduce myself to the headman.

We pulled up at the headman's kraal, and I went in. There, lying on the ground outside his hut, and leaning against a chair, was a massive man, obviously lame or incapacitated from the hips down. Around him were a bunch of Kgalagadi children and some women, two of whom I gathered were his wives. This man was Molehele, headman of Ohe, for whom something of a living hell had been set aside. A few years later when he was completely incapacitated he was confined under a roof to a cot that reeked of faeces and urine. His only companions then were the two Bush children who had to take him food. What he left they shared with the flies crawling in handfuls around him.

I introduced myself, and he asked me why I had not come to see him the day before. I blamed the lateness of the hour, which was a reasonable excuse. Then he asked for tobacco, medicine and meat. I suggested that his son (he had, I gathered, several grown-up children) should come to our camp for medicine and tobacco, and that he give us permission to hunt for him in the afternoon. He grunted his agreement and we left him.

From where we were, a blind man could have seen that the Bushmen here were held in virtual servitude by their Bantu masters.

In the afternoon of our first day at Ohe, we were surprised by a visit from Tchaga's mother. She sat down and poured out her problems. She told us she and Tchaga had been fetched by Molehele's son, for whom she worked without payment, because he was her 'boss'. Her parents belonged to Molehele and that is why she belonged to his son. Whenever there was work, he would come to fetch them, and would beat them if they refused. She begged me to speak to Molehele and the son about her so that she could return to her husband.

When Molehele's son arrived for the medicine and tobacco, he also complained of being poorly, but I could see nothing wrong with him, and told him so. Then with a gesture that he might have thought amusing, he turned and with a sweeping hand pointed at the Bushgirls, most of whom were married, standing around: 'Well then, I suppose it is too many of these at night,' he said.

We went off hunting, and brought back a hartebeest for Molehele. Before taking it to him we loaded Tchaga and her mother in the nolli, thinking then was as good an opportunity as any to talk to the headman about letting them go.

'It's odd that you should talk to me,' said Molehele, 'for Tchaga's mother has just been here saying that you wished to take her home and that I must protect her. She did not wish to go with you. But speak to my son, he will tell you what you must do.'

I was astounded, and the son, when we approached him, was equally unhelpful, saying, 'How can I let her go when she does not want to leave? Let us go to my father and seek his advice.'

Back to Molehele, the son proceeding to give his father all the reasons why she should not go. We were getting nowhere. While all this was going on, other Kgalagadis had forced both Tchaga and her mother to climb down from the vehicle. When we got to it, they were gone, and we never saw them again. Later we heard they had been taken to some distant cattle-post.

In the meantime, back at the camp, there had been other developments. We had left behind Ntchumka, a pleasant middle-aged man, to act as guard. His had been an unfortunate life, for he had lost two wives. His first wife, the mother of Shucre, had died of TB. His second, a charming playmate of Namkwa's, had died of snake-bite. The other Bushgirls were afraid to marry him, although he was still in the prime of his life. He did, however, enjoy a clandestine affair with Kesi, Nxabase's wife – an affair that developed into virtual polyandry.

It was said that everyone, including Nxabase, knew of this but they turned a blind eye to it. Apparently, in the poor man's circumstances, it was the least they could do. Now at Ohe, Ntchumka had found a way out of his solitary confinement. He had set eyes upon a local lovely who responded eagerly to his advances. Not only did she agree to sleep with him that night, she was also willing and ready to go back to Takatshwane with him. Her brother was her only older relative, and we had no difficulty in obtaining his consent to a marriage with Ntchumka.

Unfortunately, Ntchumka's luck wasn't to last. The next day, when we returned to our camp after saying goodbye to Molehele we found the suspicious Kgalagadis had driven off all the local Bushmen, including Ntchumka's third and one-night bride. Thamae collected the facts. Someone, he was told, had come to warn the girl and any others that several horses had been dispatched to a place somewhere along the road where the sand was heavy. There it was intended to ambush us and remove any local Bushmen or girls we had in the nolli. It wasn't clear if they intended any harm to us, but their Bushmen would be severely beaten.

There was nothing we could do. Thoroughly disillusioned, frustrated and angry, we made for home. The only relief was leaving the oppressive atmosphere which had one other positive aspect. It opened my eyes for the first time to sordid practices in areas far beyond easy access to the Bechuanaland Police. I wouldn't forget about Ohe.

Driving home Xamxua sat up front and elaborated on the hardships of the Bushmen.

'During the drought,' he said, 'they catch our people, they give our people their dogs so that they don't have to feed them, and make the Bushmen hunt and bring back meat or pelts. The women have to hunt for berries. Often they take everything so that there is not enough food for the babies of the Bushwomen. They catch the men when they need someone to plough or harvest, and when they don't need us they send us away again.'

Some months later on another trip, I was surprised to see that Nxabase and his brother-in-law, Tasa, no longer lived near each other as they had always done before. They had fallen out after an incident that made me seethe.

I was told that some of our band had come across a group of Kgalagadi hunters from Ohe, and among them was a man named Mosinini. He saw Kesi, Nxabase's wife (and Tasa's sister) and laid claim to her, saying she must stay with him. These hunters then went poaching eland on Barachu Pan, and made Kesi collect veldfood for them. This went on for some days, with Nxabase and Tasa looking on, until Kesi complained that her children were starving because she was having to give the Kgalagadi all the food she collected.

Tasa proceeded to berate his brother-in-law, and drove him to run away with Kesi. Mosinini, however, had horses, and following the spoor of the runaway pair soon caught up with them. In front of Nxabase he gave Kesi a severe beating, and told the wretched fellow that Kesi was his property as her parents had belonged to his father. It was because Nxabase had just stood there watching his wife being beaten that Tasa broke off relations with his brother-in-law.

Incensed, I went to the police, and Mosinini was arrested. Nxabase then stood up and gave evidence in court, but only when the man was actually imprisoned, unfortunately only for poaching, did Tasa soften and restore his old relationship with Kesi's husband.

On my way back to Johannesburg after this particular trip I decided to stop at Mafeking to pay my respects to the newly appointed Governor-General of Bechuanaland, Sir Peter Fawcus. As usual I received a cool reception from the government officers, but when I had made it clear that I had no personal business to discuss, that I merely wanted to pay my respects, I was offered five minutes with Sir Peter.

I went into his office and found a very receptive man, quite different from the Cerberus that guarded his door. We exchanged protocolish handshakes and some introductory chat, and then he asked me what I thought and knew about relations between the Bushmen and other peoples in the Kalahari.

'Do you really want to know?' I asked, hardly believing I had such an audience for my views.

'Of course, otherwise I should not ask you. You may speak as openly as you wish.'

I then began to tell him of my experiences at Ohe, the affair with Kesi and other information that I had gathered. I didn't mince words. After my formal five minutes had run to three-quarters of an hour, Sir Peter finally let me rise.

'Dr Heinz, I want you to write a full report on what you have just told me. Send it to me personally. If there are any expenses, typing or paper, please send the account to our auditors.'

He thanked me, and we shook hands. Here, at last, was an opportunity I couldn't pass up, a chance, quite accidental, to reiterate the opinions I had been harbouring, and reach the very ears of Government. On the other hand, I knew that a truly candid report might foul the friendship and good relations I had with some government officers, and further antagonize those who disapproved of me. It wouldn't be an easy report to write, for I would be laying myself open to attack, and it might turn out to be a futile exercise anyway. In the end I decided to do as my conscience dictated, and submit a report.

Among the things that I believed fell within my brief was George Silberbauer's plan for a Central Bushman Reserve, an area where Bushmen and animals could be conserved in their natural environment, free from interference or encroachment by other peoples. I was totally opposed to it. Though he recommended educational facilities, year-round waterholes, and the freedom to choose between a traditional hunting/food-gathering role and participation in the socio-economic life of a developing state, I couldn't help but feel he was misguided. Although he said it was not the intention to preserve the Bushmen of the Reserve as 'museum curiosities and pristine primitives', this to me was what conservation meant. I was one of those who saw the Reserve as a human zoo, and a cage for the remains of a stone-age culture. Even if this were an appealing proposition, morally or scientifically, I believed it was impossible to guarantee the integrity of such a reserve. It would be impossible to maintain an unchanged environment, for changes outside the Reserve wouldn't respect its boundaries, and would be bound to affect a people ill-equipped to deal with change.

I felt that Bushmen, with their powers of observation and deduction, could be trained relatively quickly to carry out certain important jobs, and that the general task should be to guide and prepare them for the changes that would be inevitable. I really didn't think the Bushman, for all his natural gifts, could do it on his own.

As for disclosing what amounted to serfdom within a British Protectorate, I wouldn't be theorizing on future intangibles. I had the facts of my own experience, and knew that here was something tangible for the authorities to tackle.

I duly prepared my report, and sent off copies to Sir Peter in Mafeking.

On the Sunday after I dispatched my document, one of the Johannesburg newspapers burst out with a story of slavery in Bechuanaland. I was horrified, for although there was very little fact to connect my report and the newspaper story, I feared it would be construed that I had 'leaked' the story.

In fact the two reports had no common source. My inquiries indicated that the newspaper had picked up their story from the comments made by a Mr Beukes, the head of the South West African Baster Community, on his return from a trip overseas.

His complaint apparently revolved on an incident involving certain Ghanzi farmers who had kidnapped another Baster, Dr Abrahams, and handed him over to the South African police.

(He was subsequently returned to Bechuanaland.) It was Mr Beukes who accused the Ghanzi farmers of conducting slavery on their farms.

Government officers weren't to know this at the time, and the 'leak' was, as I feared, blamed on me. My good faith had already exploded in my face. Worse, however, was to follow.

Sir Peter sent my report to the District Commissioner for Ghanzi who was a young and promising administrative officer. He had had enough unpleasantness over the Abrahams affair, and was now faced with trouble from Heinz. Nevertheless, he proceeded to do the proper official thing, and a police investigation was commissioned. Unfortunately it produced negative results for, according to Thamae, its character was so intimidating that no Bushman would have dared speak absolutely openly. I eventually received a letter rejecting my report. This was the official opinion, and it has never been withdrawn.

Disappointed in my failure and rather bitter, I resolved to be my own police force. At least I would try to protect the Bushmen. Simply as a white man (with, perhaps, a bit of armed coercion) I could pull my racial rank and probably manage to disrupt the machinations of the system in my territory.

My first test came not much later. Returning just after dark from a hunting trip to the southern pans, I walked into a confrontation with some old 'friends'. There were three Kgalagadis in the village.

I asked one of the men who had remained behind about them.

'They want Thomate to show them where the leopard is of which he was speaking.'

'Is Thomate here?'

'Yes.'

'Tell him to come and see me.'

Thomate came and told me that he had already shown them where a leopard stayed. They had promised to pay him with a pot and a shirt. He showed them the place, but they didn't keep their bargain. Now they wanted to know the location of a second leopard's lair, and Thomate was reluctant to tell them.

'You don't have to show them,' I said.

'They are forcing me. They say that they will beat me if I don't go with them,' Thomate replied.

I bristled. This was too much. Right here in my own village. I took my rifle and with Thamae walked over to their fire.

I asked them what they wanted, and they told me that they wanted Thomate to go hunting with them.

'Leopard,' I said.

'Yes,' they replied.

I then reminded them that they had not paid Thomate for the last leopard he had led them to. Yes, they remembered, but they would pay for both now.

I drew myself up and said, 'Look, you have come to this village and it is late. No man shall go from this place hungry or thirsty. I shall give you each a cup of mielie meal, water enough to cook it and to drink, and each a cartridge for your shotgun. You may stay here long enough to cook and eat your food, but then you go. And you go tonight! Furthermore, I never want to see you in my village again.'

They mumbled protesting sounds and I merely told them to take it or leave it. But I wanted them out. Tonight.

I went back to my fire. Namkwa cooked our meal and we ate. By the time we had finished I calculated they would have had time to do the same. Yet I could see no signs that they were leaving. I sent a little boy over to see and report what was going on. He came back and told me that they were preparing to go to sleep.

That was all I needed. I jumped up and shouted for Thamae, loud enough for them to hear.

'Thamae! Load my rifle. Bring plenty of cartridges. Load the shotgun as well. You keep that. We will chase those bastards! If they can't hear what I say, I'll show them. Ntchumka! Come here! You jump on the nolli and take the spotlight. Thamae, wait till I say, but then don't be afraid to shoot.'

Purposefully I made a din, and almost instantly the village was alive to the commotion. We got into the vehicle and I revved the engine hard.

'They are getting on their horses, I can see them,' shouted Ntchumka, and with that we started off, spotlight and shouts and hooting posse after them. We followed until all we could see was their dust thrown up by their gallop across the pan.

The next day we found their new camp. They hadn't stopped

until they had cleared 2 miles between us. They didn't come back, and Thomate, who came from Kgalagadi country, stayed with us.

Several months later I returned once more to Ohe. This time in a brand-new Nissan van, donated by the Datsun-Nissan Organization, and with my friend, Dr O. Martini, a medical officer of the Witwatersrand Native Labour Association.

We found Molehele in a dreadful state. He had deteriorated into a slob, lying among his filth and flies. The stench was revolting, and I had to admire Dr Martini's professional courage, which took him inside Molehele's hut-hole to examine the dying headman. There was little Dr Martini could do, and Molehele, the patron, died shortly afterwards.

I made a point of going to Molehele's son's house. He came out carrying a matlose kaross he was working on. I greeted him from my height, and reminded him of the hospitality which I had shown him when he last visited our village.

'Now we are thirsty and hungry, and we want you to show us the same hospitality,' I said.

He made a few grudging remarks but I stood my ground, and finally, after some more direct coaxing, he went in and came out with a calabash of sour milk.

I returned to Ohe on various occasions, and established something of a presence there, as much as to say, 'I've got my eye on you.'

It wasn't enough to destroy completely a system many years old. But, at least my policing wasn't wasted, for my Bushmen friends have not reported any further nasty incidents or difficulties to me.

FOURTEEN

The Rape of Namkwa

One of the remarkable things that struck me early on about Bushman behaviour was the inordinate lengths to which a Bushman would go to hide his feelings. Whether hungry or thirsty, anxious or impatient, he was required to sit it out with stoic or poker-faced composure. One can see the necessity for this. If they were a volatile lot giving vent to every impulse, life, with all its strains, would be intolerable. This doesn't mean to say that the Bushman is entirely successful in hiding his emotions – in particular jealousy, one of the plagues of bush life.

I only need to think of Douté and Gruxa, and myself. Our jealousies revolved very much around Namkwa (who couldn't contain her jealousy either), for we all wanted a major share in her – each for his different motives. On another level, I unfortunately also became the object of jealousies between the different bands. As my reputation increased, and the benefits I brought became more significant, I found other groups wanted more of my time and largesse. Although I owed my first allegiance to my Takatshwane people, I realized that for the sake of harmony among the bands I had to spread myself somewhat. Otherwise, for instance, the Lone Tree Bushmen would say I had 'thrown them away' for their Takatshwane kin.

Consequently I paid brief visits to Lone Tree, sometimes on my way back to Johannesburg. I was just leaving for one such visit with Thamae (Gruxa's grumbling had induced Namkwa to remain behind) when Shucre ran out in front of us calling me to stop.

'Simmertchei wants to see you,' she said.

Now, this was like a command, for Simmertchei was Namkwa's

mother, my mother-in-law. What on earth did she want?

Not far from where the car stopped was a clump of bushes. I followed Shucre towards it, and there saw my mother-in-law and her sister (to whom I owed an equal amount of respect) and Kesi. Simmertchei looked straight at me and said, 'You are leaving us now, but before you go I want to speak to you. I have been very sick. Then I recovered but now I am sick once more. This time I shall die. When you come back you will not find me here. I want you to look after my child.'

I had never spoken to her directly before. When I visited her hut with Namkwa I never sat close by and she always sat apart at our place. If I collected firewood some would always go to her; if I shot a guineafowl or partridge I would give them to Namkwa to take to her. From this distance I was, I hope, a considerate and respectful son-in-law. After all, hadn't Xamxua told me that she bore the girl who was my wife? There was no one to whom I must show more gratitude or respect. As a conscientious Bushman I had maintained the discreet relationship.

I turned to Kesi, my 'brother' Nxabase's wife, the only one of the three women with whom I could speak freely. 'What is wrong with her? Why does she say she will die?'

'Did you not see that she was sick? She has been for some time,' said Kesi.

'No, I did not know that, I did not go near her house and Namkwa did not tell me.'

'Have you no medicine?' asked Kesi.

'How can I give medicine when I don't know what is wrong with her?'

'It is the same sickness which took her voice, and which deformed Gruxa's nose,' said Kesi.

If that were correct it was tryponematosis, and she must have had it for a long time. I knew that Bechuanaland had been plagued by a non-venereal tryponematosis, an organism identical with that which causes syphilis, though it is not spread by sexual intercourse. A number of years ago, however, a World Health Organization team came to Bechuanaland. They inoculated thousands of people, and succeeded in bringing the disease under control. But obviously they hadn't got to Simmertchei, who had lived all this time with the disease, and now it was breaking out again. I thought, thank goodness, Namkwa and Nkasi had been spared. But Gruxa must still have it!

I decided to weigh Simmertchei. A significant loss of weight might confirm my suspicions. I unpacked my bathroom scale, and the weight that registered was alarming. She had lost about 18 pounds, and I thought, it must be.

'What has she been doing to treat her sickness?'

Kesi turned to the old woman and spoke with her before replying: 'Nxabase gave her something to drink, Tasa tattooed her with medicine, so also did Gruxa, and recently the old Nxabase spent time with her, but I don't know what he did. He is gone again so we cannot ask him.'

This was exactly what I might have expected. As far as I had seen, the XKos' medicinal knowledge was non-existent. Their remedies, to my scientific mind, were useless.

Despite their intimate knowledge of plant life they appeared to know very little about the therapeutic pharmaceutical properties of some plants, and have hardly come up with an effective herbal recipe (except one root recommended as a contraceptive) that could treat their many ailments and illnesses, whether TB, tryponematosis or boils.

When Nkasi fainted from what I diagnosed as heat stroke she was made to sit on the ground, practically on top of a fire. Blankets were placed in a canopy above her head, and women who had warmed their hands on the fire massaged her body. At the same time Gruxa sucked violently on her back to extract whatever it was that caused her discomfort. His effort at suction was so great that I feared he was also going to faint.

When I suffered from a bout of severe bacterial dysentery, Nxabase massaged my abdomen with such prolonged vigour that I'm sure I lost a pound or two of fat.

These particular remedies apart, most Bushmen sicknesses seem to be challenged by tattoo-type skin-deep inoculations of medicines endowed with special powers by the good god Guthe. To a plain medical doctor this would be absurd but to a social anthropologist it makes sense, for it is in the context of religion and the supernatural that the Bushmen, like many other peoples, try to understand and treat their sicknesses. It is their belief that enables them to tolerate the intolerable mysteries of their bodies, and stifles their medicinal initiative with a blanket of fatalism. After all, is not illness the manifestation of a conflict between Guthe and Thoa?

Although I've never tried to inflict upon them an attack on the veracity of their spirits, I have, over the years, persisted with more enlightened medical methods, and introduced them to the cures inside my box. Now my mother-in-law had come to me because of the failure of the customary job. She wanted me to help her, and hoped I had her cure in my box of medical tricks.

'Tell her that I do not have the right medicine with me. She should have spoken earlier,' I told Kesi. 'But I will give her something which will hold her until I come back in a few months.'

I gave Kesi some Cathomycin and explicit instructions on how it should be taken. I stressed that this medicine would not cure Simmertchei. That would come with injections when I got back. She must prepare herself, and be ready for a course of them.

In Johannesburg I acquainted myself with more details of the disease, before returning to Takatshwane equipped for two full courses of injections, for both Simmertchei and Gruxa. I tried not to think of the actual mechanics of delivery. I anticipated Gruxa might be difficult, but breaking through my mother-in-law taboo, no matter how willing she was, would be anything but easy.

I soon found that my mother-in-law's attitude towards me had changed. She greeted me and shook my hands with a 'morning!' She was all smiles and an expression that was pleased to see me, that said, 'Look, I'm still here, I'm alive.'

The Cathomycin had obviously done its stuff, and she had lost no more weight. The same couldn't be said for the rest of the village, or Namkwa. In the three months I'd been absent the drought had come with a vengeance, and everyone wore its hardship in their haggard eyes and protruding ribs. Namkwa was down to skin and bone, and I could hardly believe the change I felt when I held her.

Unbeknown to us then, the drought was settling in for several years. In the period that followed, conditions grew worse and worse. Not only did it not rain, but the land was barren. The great migrations of hartebeest and wildebeest that had recently come out of the central Kalahari had stripped the countryside of the foods Bushmen rely on. They passed this year, through the Takatshwane valley, decimating its tsama and gemsbok melons, its bush potatoes and bush turnips, and for a while the Bushmen had meat in great abundance. They passed on leaving almost nothing but a harvest full of famine.

What food remained was pillaged in the following year by an influx of starving Bushmen who came to Takatshwane because Takatshwane had been established as a distribution point for famine relief food. The area in the near vicinity of the borehole had been a main source of nutrition for my band, but it never really recuperated from the double rape.

On one occasion when I returned during the famine I failed to recognize Namkwa coming towards me. She dragged herself along, struggling on her digging stick. Her eyes were deep-hollowed, her cheeks drawn and her breasts hung empty. Her body looked fleshless, her abdomen wasted and her limbs all bone. I hadn't seen anything like it before. Moreover she was in agony because of a large suppurant ulceration just above the pubic area.

'Why didn't you come earlier?' Namkwa kept asking. And I wished I had. 'I've been crying three days because it was so painful.'

'But didn't anyone give you food?'

'We were all without food. Look at Nxabase's back, he's got the same sore. And look at the dog, Sibi, she has not eaten for days.'

It was shortly after this that the government introduced the famine relief which managed to tide the people through. In the meantime Dr Martini, who had arrived by plane, had gone through the band with multi-vitamin injections for avitaminosis, and we got Namkwa on her feet again. I was even able to find it amusing that a woman who could endure agonizing hardship became hysterical at the injection that would help make her whole again.

My injection problems with Namkwa's mother and father were of a different kind. And once Namkwa regained lost strength I was able to concentrate on handling them.

I let it be known that I had come prepared to treat them, and my mother-in-law seemed amenable, but Gruxa sulked and grumbled more than ever. I put his moroseness down to the hard times, and the diminishing supply of food. I didn't want to antagonize him any more than I had done already, lest I lose him altogether. So I played him carefully, trying to cultivate his confidence and listening intently when he talked.

When I thought the time ripe, I broached the painful question of the treatment again, telling them that they would each require an injection every second day. Under no circumstances would I only treat one of them. Both had to agree to the treatment, otherwise it would be useless, especially since they slept together and could make each other sick.

Gruxa refused point-blank. I tried every subtle ruse I could think of to change his mind. Not even Namkwa could influence him. Finally I decided to threaten him with the police.

'Look,' I said, 'you know that the police and some doctors were here several years ago to inject all the people. You were in the bushes while they passed through here, and you know you should have reported to the police afterwards. If you don't agree to have the same treatment as your wife I will go to the Ghanzi police tomorrow and then they must decide what to do with you.'

It was a hard threat to thrust at one's father-in-law, but I was getting desperate. He grumbled and said nothing. A short while later I asked Xamxua to talk to him. He came back after half an hour and said, 'He agrees.'

Then it was my turn to condition myself. I found I was back-pedalling, frightened again by the recollection of Namkwa that day, long ago, when I had tried to take a vaginal swab from her. I didn't want a repeat performance when I came to actually uncover my mother-in-law and face her naked buttocks. Besides, I had come to live by my taboo, and for a mother-in-law to expose her buttocks to her daughter's husband was, I think, unheard of.

Oddly (for Western minds) it is of no consequence for a Bushgirl to lift her front genital apron for a moment and expose herself. This she does when she is on completely informal, playful terms with a person, or when she wishes to show her disrespect, even disdain for him. But should a Bushgirl or woman expose her buttock for a moment by brushing aside her duiker skin she would be subjecting the object of her action to the gravest of insults, something worse than 'kiss my arse!'

On the day I had set aside to start the injections I sought more time. 'Build a full hut for your parents,' I told Namkwa and Nkasi. The privacy built, I had to go ahead. I lay Simmertchei stomach down in the hut, and knelt above her. I don't know who was the more afraid. Possibly I was. Quickly I plunged in the needle, rubbed around the spot with alcohol and dropped her duiker skin again. There! It was done.

Gruxa was no problem, and I handled him quickly and efficiently. When I had finished I threw the alcohol soaked cotton wool into the fire. Namkwa and Nkasi both flew forward and oblivious of burning their fingers flicked the flaming cotton wool aside to save the fire from contamination. I still made mistakes!

The dosages were increased every alternate day, and with them my qualms increased. Not so much with Gruxa, for he continued to be easy until the sixth injection, when his backside was so sore he refused to co-operate once more. I had to call in Xamxua again, rear divisions of police before his eyes, and mention Thoa. Only then could I go on.

My qualms with my mother-in-law rose as her buttocks also became painful, and I had to palpate her cheeks to find a suitable place for the needle. Somehow we survived even that, and to make up for our embarrassment I accorded her the keenest respect and deference outside. When I went hunting and came back with only two partridges, I gave both to her. Such consideration I'm sure she appreciated.

When it was over she said, 'It was very painful, but will I live now?'

'Only Guthe can answer that question,' I replied. 'I have done what I can, and I think you should get better now.'

It was now time to lay in food for my family, and the band, and I organized a four-day expedition to beyond Manyane Pan, where Bushmen had reported numerous stragglers from the migrating herds.

Although my petrol was dangerously low it was worth the risk, for we returned with my Nissan nolli loaded to capacity with four hartebeest and two wildebeest. Not a bit of meat was wasted, for the Bushmen eat anything that can be digested. They gathered up the blood and intestines, hooves and skin, to be cooked for every scrap of nourishment. Back at the village the meat was distributed sparingly, and a lot of it cut into strips and dried for the days ahead.

I now treated my parents-in-law as patients, and each day dished out to them their daily ration of venison. Gruxa remained incorrigible, but Simmertchei, in a radical change, abandoned our avoidance taboo. She would greet me openly, and often put her hand upon my shoulder. In the evening she no longer sat apart, but for the first time in the years I had been with her, she squatted down at our fire. For the first time she laughed and joked with me, and when the pipe was passed to her, she took two strong puffs and handed it on to me. After Namkwa had finished cooking, she took a hand in dishing out what was in the pots and pans, and she would rebuke her daughter for not giving me enough meat.

Her behaviour was not a fleeting whim. Her friendliness grew and at the same time we developed a new respect for each other. Her gratitude (for now she was getting better) was reflected in a number of different ways, and particularly in the presents that she gave me for my mother, and the way she interceded with Gruxa on my behalf. There was no doubt that I had gained a staunch friend.

'You have tamed your mother-in-law, for you have seen her bum,' the other Bushmen said. And that was true.

My changed relationship with Namkwa's mother paid further dividends in my life with Namkwa. She delighted in the relaxation of the rules, and acted as though a weight had been lifted from her mind. Though we continued to respect the norms of public behaviour, we became inclined to stretch them here and there, and show our affection openly. And whenever I came back, she would laugh her laugh, and let me know she had longed for my return.

Enthusiastically she would help unload my things and settle me down, practically herding me to my rest, for I was seldom other than weary when I arrived. Despite the comfort and reliability of my Nissan, and a slight improvement in the road, twenty hours on the go was still a gruelling ride, and Namkwa was aware of this. She would make up a bed for me under a large camelthorn tree and leave me to sleep.

While I slept she would go off and come back smelling fresh and soapy from her bucket bath, and the cream or powder that I had brought before. When I rolled and opened my eyes she was always there, only a few yards away. Often she would sit at my feet combing her hair, winding coloured beads around her waist and neck or lining her eyebrows with a charcoal crayon and rubbing oil on to her chin. When the sun shoved aside my shade, she would rise and weave more branches, grass and leaves into the camelthorn to mask the burning heat. With nothing else to do she would simply sit and wait for me to wake.

Hunger, usually, came with waking. Then we'd dig through my trunk for food to prepare. And the evening would come down to a fire of smells the Bushmen had missed for months. They'd come bubbling with hopeful good humour. They knew they'd have their fill.

The first evening was something of a ritual in our lives, invariably a ceremony of sweet pleasure, simple plenty and nonstop talk. At first it played around my arrival, shifting to the things that I had brought; perhaps the Puzemandle, or my new groundsheet, the blanket for Namkwa, and how much tobacco I carried. Ah; the tobacco! That came out and the pipes materialized, one a pipe of conical tin, another two metal cartridges stuck together, yet another a piece of half-inch water piping. They had probably been starved of tobacco for weeks if not months, so the pipes went round and round, puffed contentedly.

No one missed out on these occasions, certainly not the children who had, it would seem, been weaned on pipe tobacco. They too, like their elders, pulled hard through hollow cheeks, inhaling deeply and holding the smoke for maximum pleasure. The tobacco's bitter juice, however, was spat out on the ground, and quickly covered with a flick of sand.

Meanwhile the mielie meal would be stirred bit by bit into the boiling three-legged pot. Tchallo sprinkled it in and Thxale, the stirrer, would twist his four-pronged grewia stick between the palms of his hands. When it was ready to serve, the meal was dished out on an odd assortment of plates, a slab of bark, brown paper, a broken saucer and the lid. The children licked the stirring stick, and each person shared his portion with his neighbour, although I must say that the men would wait as long as possible before custom compelled their sharing with the women.

I, too, passed on my plate to one of the elders, Gruxa, Xamxua, Nxabase or even Midum if he was there. Namkwa would pass hers on to a woman. Each recipient would take a little and pass the plate on to others more junior, and the last one licked it clean. Finally the pot was scraped so clean it rarely required much washing.

Namkwa was in her element, the gay hostess. The gathering was told how tired I was, how she looked after me, how far it was to my place (though she had never been there), how we would now go hunting, and how there would be food for everyone. Yes, her husband would see to that.

She did not hold the floor all night. Xamxua for instance would seize his turn telling Nxabase the story of one of the hunting trips near Manyane. It was an old story that I had heard perhaps a dozen times and Nxabase many more times than that, but to show that he was really listening, Nxabase would repeat the last few words of Xamxua's every sentence.

The jokes that rose were crude, but not obscene. If someone let off they'd laugh and say, 'He's farting fat.' If I rose to get a cigarette and sat down again pushing my towel napkin tucked into my belt between my legs with the decorum of a woman, everyone screamed with laughter, Thxale and Gathua especially in near hysterics. Only here could I be so amusing.

The evening carried on and on until the jokes and laughs wore thinner, and tired yawns came thicker. 'Sit nicely,' some said as they got up. 'Go nicely and sleep,' we replied. Others simply left as they came, in silence. For a while we might have sat nicely in the silence, maybe have a last cup of tea and a swig of Marsala. Neither of us was in a hurry for bed, but Namkwa usually strained to keep her curiosity from my kit. She was impatient to inspect the tea, the coffee, sugar, powdered milk, potatoes, onions, jam, tomato purée, rice and shortbread that I usually brought. She came to expect these things, and the honey too. But there were surprises like the watermelon, which was a laughing, hand-clapping matter. For one thing it was red inside, unlike her

An old woman from Douté's band, aged about 60

Namkwa's sister Nkasi and her son Tonno

tsama, and to her amazement it was sweet. Oranges too were an unknown quantity deserving of some caution, but when she tasted them she smacked lips and tongue, and her face lit up. I could see she would want the oranges again.

Then she would scramble through my trunk, throwing out the toiletries obviously meant for her. After one such scramble there were two items that puzzled her. One was a tube of roll-on deodorant, which was easy to explain. The other parcel was a package of Tampax, which took more time and tact. I had been irritated by the taboo that required her to sleep apart from me while menstruating, so I was determined to introduce her to the discreet convenience of Tampax so that I could share her blanket.

After six years or so Namkwa had turned into a young woman approaching maturity. As I developed in my Bushman role she too kept pace with the changes and as my status evolved from ignoramus to a sort of honourable elder in the band, so she assumed some of the dignity and authority of an elder's wife. Yet she remained, in many respects, a rough-and-tumble tomboy, wrestling and running when she felt the urge, showing off her female strength and revealing flashes of her former naive and untutored youth.

I wouldn't have had it otherwise; and even when she had shed some of her child-smooth beauty she continued to surprise and captivate me with her many-sided personality.

In fact, each time I returned, I wondered what new face she would be wearing. There were many sides I knew. I had seen her extrovert and ecstatic, desperate and sad. I'd seen her starved and anguished, beautiful and brave. I'd seen her jealous, angry, sullen and sultry. But I'd also seen the humour in her eye and heard her laugh.

As a housewife she was efficient and conscientious without being absolutely devoted to her chores. She kept a clean place, swept daily, protected our dishes from flies and aired our blankets each day. She even took to mending my shirts, washing and ironing them (an art learnt from Solomon's wife). Her cooking, when she tried, was very good. But if she didn't feel like putting any effort into it, it was lousy. Her rice in particular always turned into one glutinous lump – until our meeting in Ghanzi with the Japanese anthropologist, Giro Thanaka.

'Mr Thanaka,' I said, 'would you do me a great favour? Would you teach Namkwa how to cook rice?'

I was I confess a little ashamed of Namkwa on that occasion. She paid Giro no attention whatsoever while he tried to demonstrate the vagaries of rice cooking in his minimal Nharo. As it turned out, Namkwa hadn't missed a thing, and her next batch of rice was as good as any you would get in an oriental restaurant.

With time and praise Namkwa developed greater pride in her cooking, and she picked up what tips she could from my visiting friends and scientists. I came back from Okwa once in full praise for a beefsteak that Ntumka's sister had barbecued for me. It was the most delectable steak I had tasted.

'Oh, she's a lot of rubbish,' said Namkwa.

'I'm not talking about her, though I think she is very pretty. I'm talking about the meat she roasted.'

'Huh!' said my wife. 'What does that rubbish know about cooking? She is just a wild thing from the bushes!'

Nevertheless the gauntlet was down, and Namkwa picked up her knife and carefully selected a springbok steak. She seasoned it and rubbed it with oil. She spread the meat on a grewia stick fork, and when she had judged her fire heat, lowered the angle of the grewia stick, which she had stuck into the ground. Close to the centre of the heat the meat sizzled and sealed its juices. Then she moved her coals around, and lifted the meat fork higher. From time to time she turned the stick, giving all her attention to the meat.

When she handed it to me, she said, 'This is no good. Give it to Sibi, the dog.'

It was, I'm bound to say, better than the steak Ntumka's sister cooked – it was exceptional. But Namkwa needed to be in the mood to cook like that.

The first portable radio I brought to the bush introduced Namkwa, first to another white man's marvel, then to the experience of Western music and the whole new world of classical music. Out of her dongo experience came an affinity with the music of the greats, and especially the piano concertos. Once, when I went down with acute dysentery, and grew delirious with fever, I recall music getting through to me. I seemed to be hearing Brahms's second symphony.

I asked Brian Maguire and Judi Roets, two friends who were with us, if they were responsible.

'No, that was Namkwa, we were out collecting plants,' said Brian.

She had no idea what made the music, but her ears pitched to an appreciation of its content, and she followed every variation with absorbed interest. This wasn't simply an impulsive interest in something new. In time her appreciation grew, and some years later when she actually attended a symphony concert she glowed with delight, and I with pride for her perception.

I guess pride would like me to say that Namkwa was intelligent, and quite the perfect little protegée that I'd pulled up from the sand. In some respects I was her Henry Higgins, and I couldn't help but teach her much, she knew so little, but I don't think her mind worked with any particular natural intelligence. Her qualities were something other, and what set her apart from all the Bushmen that I know was her initiative and ability to adapt. She was quick to grasp the significance of something new, and different, and adjust to the innovations that I brought. She was very much a girl of action, capable of leading and organizing others, and responding to the challenge of the moment. As she grew older her strength and initiative made her the most outstanding personality in her community, and ultimately the head of the band. That is another story, but in the early years, her self-willed independent spirit and the way she handled me gave hints of the woman she was to be. I, no less than Namkwa, had felt the changes ringing in me, and through her and her people I had got the taste of life that mattered.

It was not only sleeping on the earth and submerging oneself in the bush. I picked up lessons that I'd avoided all my years. I was introduced to fulfilment, and taught to recognize, if not to assume, humility. I think I saw a better person in me, if only because I could see my faults. I also felt I was a better person, who with some pride could say, 'Yesterday I was a stupid white man. Today I am a Bushman!'

Conceit (and convenience) enabled me to label myself a Bushman, but Namkwa never went that far. When she was particularly pleased with me, and wanted to praise me, she would exclaim, 'Now you are half-a-Bushman!'

If only she knew how right she was. Half a Bushman! I could never be anything more than that. For all my high-sounding chat about the real values of life, I couldn't submerge myself forever in the bush. I needed the lusher jungles of modern thought, the creature comforts, restaurant meals and intellectual drive, as much as I needed the Bushmen.

Namkwa would always sense it when I began to tire of the bush. When Gruxa's greed, Nxabase's continuous hunger for our mielie meal, the heat, the dust, the deprivations began to get me down, Namkwa would know. I was straining to get back, to leave her. 'I think now you will want to go,' she would say, and know that nothing could change that.

I often wondered if she realized the conflict that went on in me when the half-Bushman and the bespectacled academic came to grips. Could she understand that I was living two completely separate lives, and was selfish enough to want the best of each? That I, her jealous, demanding husband, was a loving, bleeding, rationalizing bigamist, married to his two cultures? And that out of her society she could never share the other with me, as other women might, as one day I hoped another woman would?

Would she forgive me though I knew exactly what I'd done?

There were, of course, sound practical reasons why Namkwa could never share my city life, even had I thought she might adapt and we could bridge the cultural chasm that separated the bush from Johannesburg. I speak of the laws of the Republic of South Africa, which laid down some strange taboos, such as the Prohibition of Mixed Marriages Act and the Immorality Act. These make it impossible to maintain any significant relationships across the colour line, and make a nightmare of any attempt to do so.

I could feel society breathing down my neck. I even felt friends eye me doubtfully, and I was sure as any paranoid is that my association with Namkwa was the core of the trouble with my academic adversaries. Many times I was tempted to bare myself and say, 'So what!' But I was never brave, or foolhardy, enough. I had too much to lose. My silence was tolerable while all went well, but it shamed me when my wife was raped.

On one of my trips back to the Kalahari, I remember wondering, as I always did when I neared Takatshwane, how Namkwa would present herself this time. What would I find? The primordial innocent nymph I'd married? The washed and perfumed glamour girl of the bush spun with beads and charcoal make-up? The laughing, tough tomboy? Would she be demure? Sulky? Healthy? Starved ... ?

She was none of these. Instead she was a broken Namkwa, overcome with crying and trembling, unkempt and dirty. Oblivious of the custom that required our greeting to be cool and not much more than a friendly handshake, she clung to me, mixing violent sobs with an inarticulate jumble of phrases.

I stood there hopelessly, trying to comfort her. Eventually, with her mother's help and Xamxua's calming tone, we pacified her enough for her story to make some sense. As we pieced it together, bit by bit, I wished I wasn't listening. It made ghastly sense.

Only a few days before I arrived, a farmer had come to Takatshwane. Apparently he had heard that a doctor from the Witwatersrand University was in love with a Bushgirl who was supposed to be exceptionally pretty, and kept by the doctor in nice dresses. He had been led to Takatshwane by one of his cattle drovers, and he hoped the XKo would now take him to her.

Xamxua (one of the XKo he had chanced upon) answered that he knew no such Bushgirl. Surely she must be at Lone Tree. The farmer was not put off, however, and that same night, when the Bushmen were asleep, he arrived at the village carrying his rifle. His arrival caused considerable commotion and consternation in the band, and before Namkwa could run off into the bush she had been identified by the cattle drovers and then apprehended by the white man.

When Gruxa protested and tried to intervene, the farmer, according to the Bushmen, threatened him with his rifle, and subdued any further protests.

Namkwa told me she was bound hand and foot and thrown into the back of the farmer's lorry like a mielie bag. She was then driven to his camp, where he sexually assaulted her. When it was over Namkwa asked him to let her get up to relieve herself. He released her, and she went off into the bush; when she thought he had grown drowsy, she fled.

She told me she ran as hard as she could, followed by her dog Sibi, who had either jumped on the truck or followed it to the camp. Near morning, she dropped exhausted under a tree, and despite the winter cold fell asleep. She was determined not to return to the village in case the man should find her there again, and possibly even beat her.

Meanwhile Gruxa and the others, wondering where he had taken her, and what had happened, set out to find her. When they learnt (I imagine from the drover) that Namkwa had fled, they searched for her spoor, and followed it until they found her. She was adamant. She would not go back to the village.

A few days later Ntumka went to her and offered to look after her at his family place. Still she was adamant, and only when Ntumka managed to convince her that the farmer and his cattle had moved on to Lone Tree did she agree to go with Ntumka. Ntumka told me that she was in a terrible state. They had hardly arrived at Takatshwane when they heard the familiar sound of my engine, and Namkwa, now beside herself, could only cry, 'My husband! My husband!' Then she ran out to meet me.

That in the main was the story. Namkwa didn't tell it like that, and if she had I wouldn't have recorded it so. All I was aware of, as her story grew more monstrous, was the gist of what had happened, and the tidal wave of rage rising in me. Had that farmer been there then, I don't know what I would have done. But he wasn't, and gradually I controlled my anger.

I couldn't do anything violent, I wouldn't do anything foolish. But I'd turn him in for his crime, I decided. Yes, not only for the rape he had inflicted on Namkwa, but also for the way he had defiled the village. That however would make it perfectly clear to the Court and to anyone else who was interested that this Bush-girl was my wife, and I her white lover. I tried hard to reassure myself and imagine a straightforward trial between the complainant and the accused. After all, it wasn't vital to the case that my name and my liaison should come up at all. But I wasn't reassured.

I would be bound to confess my true relationship with Namkwa, and thereby let loose the forces I suspected would destroy the very thing I was trying to preserve. I wanted retribution but I feared disclosure more. And the more I rationalized the consequences of any report or charge, the less I felt able to make one.

I took Namkwa to her hut, which had stood empty now for several days. I laid out the blankets and gave her a tranquillizer. Then I lay down with her, tucking my kaross around her and comforting her with my closeness. Soon she fell asleep, and I stroked her head for a long time before I too dropped off. I had made my decision.

The next day, after Namkwa had regained her composure and could talk about her experience more rationally, I explained why I didn't think it wise we should report the man. I reiterated the troubles we'd meet if we allowed our secret to be disclosed, and Namkwa understood all this. She too had come to obey the dictates of our secret, and she was as afraid of disclosure as I was.

There had been a number of times when strangers had come to the village, and Namkwa had always quickly picked up evidence of her things at our place and run off to hide our association. She was wary not to show me any intimacy in the company of outsiders, or say anything that could link us too closely.

I asked her about this farmer. She said she knew him. So did other Bushgirls over a wide area. He had slept with lots of them, she said, and several claimed his paternity. She then ran through a number of names of girls we both knew who had slept with him. None had the courage to oppose or expose him. In fact most Bushgirls consented more or less meekly according to the old custom that this was their lot.

With Namkwa however, the situation was different. She considered herself as my wife to be worth more than that. In fact she was indignant that he dared to look on her as a bedmate. She was not just an ordinary Bushgirl. She was the wife of a white man, and she would never have given herself to him without his coercion.

Besides, she was afraid of me, and she did not want a repetition of the trauma over Thxale or the Douté affair. That was why, she said, she was so anxious to tell me what had happened, lest I heard it from someone else and misunderstood.

'Were you not frightened to run through the night?' I asked.

'I was very much afraid later, when I thought over what I had done. But while I was running, I did not think of the lions which were about. We had heard them, because the cattle were afraid,' she said.

'And where you slept, all alone and without a fire, you never thought the lions would catch you there?'

'I was so tired. Too tired to care. But Sibi was always with me. She slept close by me to keep me warm, and I knew she would warn me. But I made a fire the next day.'

It must have been an intense shock to have forced Namkwa to a flight through the night bush, for in her opinion it was one of the most stupid, dangerous things one could do. How lasting and damaging the shock would be something that worried me for some time. I tried to analyse its effect on her, and measure her reaction against the sort of reaction one would expect from an assault victim in white society. There was no doubt it had been traumatic and might have been more serious had I not arrived when I did. At least I was there to reassure her and comfort her, and help her over the worst.

On the other hand, I believe that her deep involvement with me intensified her shock, and influenced her attitude to the whole experience. After all, she was no ordinary Bushgirl. Had she been like the others, a thing to be plucked at a white man's pleasure, she would probably have shrugged it off as the others evidently did. She certainly wouldn't have gone to Court, for neither she nor the others knew that they were protected against this sort of thing in a court of law.

As it was, Namkwa reacted in her own peculiar way. Her attitude was clearly influenced by her Bushman thinking and ignorance of the existence of the crime of rape. She saw it more as an act of adultery, an act in which she was forced to participate, and which in its consummation created a bond, ugly though it might be, between the raper and her.

According to her reasoning the man had taken, and she had given, something that was valuable to her and valuable to me. Reduced to its basic meaning this could only be made good with an adequate return payment. And as long as this was missing, the experience would endure.

I was told that on the following day the man gave Ntumka a rand to give to her. But this amount had no meaning for her, and she refused to accept it. When I spoke to her about this, she was scornful: 'He must pay,' she said. 'He must pay you. He knew you were my husband. He must pay you, but he can't just pay a rand.'

The aspect of payment goes as deep as the Bushman lore. A gift creates a bond between two people, and if the recipient is fond of the giver, he or she will wait sometimes years before making a return gift. So a special bond remains intact between the giver and receiver all that time. In this context it is a lovely piece of logic, but in this instance the logic worked miserably. Until the man made adequate payment, the abhorrent bond remained, and neither Namkwa nor I could ever forget it.

Consequently, Namkwa spoke frequently about the incident, and in later years when we travelled further afield and had occasion to pass the man's farm, she would grab my arm and say, 'You must stop! You must speak to him. He must pay you!'

But each time I would grit my teeth and accelerate past a confrontation. What good, I asked myself, would it do?

FIFTEEN

Flora and Fauna

There was one aspect of Namkwa's ordeal which pleased me, and that was the devotion displayed by her dog, Sibi. She was a mongrel, half bull-terrier, and had become an inseparable part of our home and hunting lives. She was undersized, smaller than a spaniel, but she had the courage of a honey badger and an air of friendliness about her that was irresistible. She was a city pup, but came out to the Kalahari after our experience with the jennets.

One day during a winter visit, Tasa of the Lone Tree people came to our camp with the skin of a jennet mother and four tiny jennet kittens. He asked me whether I wanted the skin, and whether he should kill the babies. I was aghast that he should have killed a mother with young, and told him so. Though it might have been more humane, I wouldn't think of killing the kittens, and to make his cruelty clear to him I said that I would look after them.

I took the kittens to our hut, and Namkwa was furious. She knew that 'looking after them' meant that *she* must do the looking after. She gave me and them a withering glance, and threw them into the corner. 'They aren't even weaned yet,' she said.

'That's all right – you will wean them, then,' I said, and stalked out.

About two hours later Namkwa came to me and said, 'You had better feed those things, they're hungry.'

She turned on her heels and left me with the problem. We had powdered Klim for our tea and coffee, and I decided to feed them with this. I took a chance on the composition, and mixed some milk that did not taste too rich. With one of my syringes I tried to squirt small amounts into their mouths. Since they were scuffling around in a cardboard box and protesting vehemently, it looked like an impossibility. But perseverance paid, and eventually I handed them back to an angry Namkwa.

She too, like the little spitting things, took to the process and from then on attended them with increasing devotion. It wasn't just duty. Every two hours she fed them, and worried about them. Out of their box they climbed all around our branch-roofed hut, and Namkwa was always afraid that they would get out and lose themselves. She seldom slept undisturbed, and wherever we went she took the jennets with us. Soon they were following her, four fluffy spotted bits of fur that scampered with life.

One evening Namkwa sat leaning against a tree with her babies curled up asleep on her lap.

'Why don't you give me a dog?' she said suddenly.

'What! Give you a dog? Look at the way you treat them. You don't feed them. You allow them to starve, and you're always beating them and chasing them. All I hear in a Bushman village where there are dogs is their howling and whimpering. No, I'll never give you a dog.'

'But why? I feed these little babies don't I? And you remember Nellie, Gruxa's dog, was she starved? Did we hit her?'

The argument went on and on, long after I knew I had surrendered.

In Johannesburg I hunted around for a suitable animal, short-haired with a reputation for courage and known hunting ability. I couldn't find a fox-terrier, which was my first choice, so settled for my second best – this bull-terrier mongrel pup. When the time came for me to return I gave her a tranquillizing shot to soothe her on the long ride, and delivered her to Namkwa.

At first Namkwa was more surprised that I had remembered than overjoyed by the gift. She called it Sibi, and carried it proudly all over the place. At night it slept in our bed, and more often than not on the pillow between us. There was nothing I could do about it.

Sibi's qualities weren't long in revealing themselves. She was likeable, for a start, which made her acceptable around the village. She was fast and courageous, which endeared her to the hunters.

She took an antelope, and though she was undersized and had a rather poor nose, she would herd a wounded buck from its fellows and go in for the kill, sometimes going in several times as springbok horns lunged at her. When Thxale took her hunting I feared for her life. With him she would go for gemsbok, with their long, deadly horns, which when harassed and cornered back up into a thorn bush and face the enemy.

Time and again Sibi stood before their horns. With the agility and timing of a mongoose, she would avoid the desperately flashing points, and at the right moment leap for the gemsbok's nose, grip it, and hang on like the bull-terrier she was. This gave Thxale his opportunity to come in for the *coup de grâce*.

Namkwa's pride in Sibi's prowess as a hunter was no less than her delight when I brought home the meat. She never failed to tell me how many antelope Sibi had brought down while I was away, and I dreaded one day coming back to hear that Sibi had missed the moment.

'One day, she will get just a bit older, and slower, and then those terrible horns will catch her,' I said.

Horns weren't the only killers Sibi had to beware. The kick of an ostrich is also deadly, and one time after I had slightly wounded one of these birds, I feared that the inexperienced Sibi would surely come off worst as she went in after it. But she leaped high and wide, latching on to the ostrich's breastbone.

The weight of the dog hanging from its breast must have been too much for the bird. Finally, its energy expended in its frantic kicking, the ostrich sat down. Only then did Sibi let go, lunge for its long neck. As the dog leapt and snapped, the neck broke.

Such fighting properties turned Sibi into the idol of the band. They had never seen such spunk. She was seemingly afraid of nothing, not even lion. When these beasts whoofed at night, Sibi would go outside the village and bark her challenge at them. Fortunately she never got close enough for her challenge to be taken up.

The attitude of the Bushmen to Sibi and the jennets was an eye-opener for me. I had almost come to believe the half-truth I had heard that no Bushman can keep and look after an animal without waiting for the moment when they can kill and eat it.

I had seen them seize young ostrich chicks waddling after their parent, and with utter nonchalance wring their little necks and throw them into the truck. Now ostrich chicks are the size of a duck or often a goose, and are a tasty and tender meal, so they must have been taken aback when, one day, I suggested that rather than kill them we should take the chicks back to the village and keep them.

We made a small enclosure of twigs and grass, and I fed them mielie meal moistened in water. Namkwa watched me for a couple of days, and then said, 'Why do you feed these things with mielie meal?'

'Because they eat it, and because I don't know what else they will eat.'

'Come with me, I'll show you,' said my wife.

She took a bag, and called Nkasi. The three of us set off towards the thicker bush, where we collected some plants she pointed out.

'This is what they eat,' she said. And to prove it, the chicks didn't stop until they had consumed what they had been given.

Her next question was: 'Why don't you give them some shade?'

'They don't need it. They're in the sun all day.'

This didn't satisfy Namkwa. She called a few girls, and in a few minutes had a little hut built for the chicks. Which, of course, they proceeded to make use of whenever the sun was at its strongest. We carried on collecting food for them, and after about two weeks, Namkwa showed me another bush with berries.

'They are old enough to eat these now.'

I took her word for it, and broke off some branches. Among that year's crop were almost as many of the previous year's berries. She sampled my harvest, and threw down the old berries.

'They don't eat those,' she said.

Curious, and not wanting to waste foodstuff unnecessarily, I picked up the old berry branches when she wasn't looking, and later gave them to the chicks. Not one of them deigned to give them a glance, let alone eat them. The newer berries, however, disappeared.

I could only shake my head, and wonder how Namkwa knew.

Then there was the case of the missing karakul, the African lynx. The year after the jennets, another Bushman brought me two young karakul. With their reddish fur, blue eyes and black tufts on their ears, they were as beautiful a pair of felines as I'd seen. Fully grown the karakul is not much bigger than an adult bull-terrier, but it is the fiercest cat you can find.

'Were this beast the size of the lion,' I joked, 'there would be no Bushmen left in the Kalahari.' The fierceness of the kittens intrigued me, and I wanted to see if they could be tamed. The Bushmen, however, just laughed at the mere suggestion, and to confirm their scepticism the little tigers spat, scratched and ripped at me whenever I went to feed them.

One evening, just before my departure, one escaped. This upset me, and angrily I chased all the youngsters to look for it. My anger amused Namkwa, and she sat down beside me.

'They won't find that kitten. They know it, but they just went because you sent them and were so angry.'

'Yes, but I wanted to take home the pair.'

'Call everybody back,' suggested Namkwa. 'Then let us sit quietly, and you'll hear where it is.'

I didn't think she knew what she was talking about, because I didn't understand her at all. But she insisted I listen to her, and when the boys had come back, and we sat 'quietly', we suddenly heard a distinct call that sounded like a lark or a similar bird.

'That's it!' said Namkwa, and at once the men got up, went straight to a thick bush where, with the aid of my flashlight, they found the kitten sitting. I was dumbfounded.

'That kitten won't go away without its brother,' explained Namkwa.

Then Nxabase elaborated: 'Those two are always talking to each other. When one is gone, the other will call it back. If we had not made so much noise, we could have heard them talking to each other long ago. But you were so cross you wouldn't listen to us.'

Once more I shook my head and marvelled at the extensive knowledge of wildlife these XKo possessed. It was almost as if they knew each instinct by heart. On the way back to Johannesburg it occurred to me that as far as I knew nobody had ever really tried to assess the depth of their insight into animal behaviour. So I decided it would be a worthwhile project to record and collate the biological repertoire of the Bushmen. From then on I devoted a lot of my time to doing this.

To help my research I gathered about me all the old men whose knowledge I respected, and got them talking about the creatures of the Kalahari, from the largest down to the tiniest insect.

For the zoologist in me these sessions were fascinating, but I noticed that children's ears – and the women's too – were also pitched to their elders' tales, and that they listened as avidly as I did. Here around a fire they, and I, were schooled in animal theory and I recorded masses of it.

Speaking about the spotted hyena, old Gocholu said quite casually, 'Oh, they are killers!'

This was a new one for me, and I protested my ignorance.

'They only eat dead things, what has been left behind by the lions,' I said. 'Surely?'

The Bushmen laughed at me for that: 'Look, the hyena hunts, and it can run. Why, it can even outrun a horse,' said one.

Speaking of the common brown hyena, old Duce told me, 'It sleeps during the day, but gets up in the afternoon to look for food. Just like its brother, the spotted hyena, and even the jackal, it watches the vultures. It goes straight to the place they are circling, for it knows there must be something to eat there.'

In her fascinating book *Innocent Killers* Jane van Lawick-Goodall writes: 'Indeed, it is by closely watching the movements of vultures in the sky that many earthbound predators are directed to new sources of food.' Jane van Lawick-Goodall had also published sensational pictures of hyenas pulling down a zebra. These followed an account by Kruuk on hunting hyenas in one of the 1968 *National Geographic* magazines.

My Bushmen provided me with this Bush intelligence long before any of these publications came out, but I was sceptical enough to disbelieve them. Even if they had seen hyena hunting, how could they possibly know these animals read the skies like mariners read the stars? Somehow they just knew.

'Hau! the jackal is a clever fellow,' said Xamxua one day. 'He always gets the hyena into trouble. When the lion is eating, the jackal annoys him so much that he leaves his food and chases the jackal. But what does this clever fellow do? He runs straight past the hyena, and in his anger the lion attacks the hyena and the jackal gets away. He's just the cleverest one, this chap.' And Xamxua chuckled.

Much of the information I gathered was from the Bushmen's eye-witness accounts, which taken out of context were scarcely credible. Dause, for instance, told me of the remarkable fear which leopards have of wild dogs.

'I came across one sitting in a tree, nearly starved to death, because a dead dog was staring at him,' he said.

It would seem that the dogs had chased the leopard into a tree. Jumping up at him, one dog had impaled itself just below the jaw on a sharp dead branch. Unable to free himself, he died with a terrible grimace, looking straight at the leopard which became so hypnotized he couldn't break its spell of fear and run off.

Gocholu verified this story by recounting a very similar one where the leopard had taken his duiker prey into the tree. Only Gocholu's arrival broke the spell, and enabled the leopard to escape. Both duiker and the dog had started to decompose by then.

I asked them about the solitary male, the rogue that wandered apart from the herd. One hears and reads often of the rogue elephant but other wild species also have their loners.

'Often we come across a wildebeest alone, is that like a rogue, one that has been thrown out of its herd?' I asked.

'No,' I was told, 'most of these have lost their herd. When someone wounds a wildebeest, his brothers will try to take it along. You have seen that. But sometimes the sore one can't keep up. Then it goes off into the bushes to lie down. Sometimes it recovers after a few days. Now it begins to search for its own herd. It has a special smell, and every other herd will kick it out. Finally it can only go alone. Though sometimes it meets another one just like it, and then the two go together because they need company.'

Once out hunting with Gruxa we came on a wildebeest, and I was about to shoot it when Gruxa warned me that the animal was sick and that we would not be able to eat it. Nevertheless, out of curiosity, I shot it. When we inspected it, we discovered a white fungus on it and, close up, it was patently diseased. Gruxa had diagnosed this from the way it behaved. I, of course, had seen nothing odd about it.

'The duiker (or any other buck) doesn't need the wind to smell you,' said Nxabase on another occasion. 'If you are creeping up on it, and a fly sits on your face, and then while you are resting or

Nervous at the prospect of going into the swamps, Namkwa plays her dongo to comfort herself

Namkwa boards the Jumbo for New York

Namkwa in New York

watching, the fly goes off and rests on the duiker's nose, it will run. Because the fly took your smell to him.'

Here out of the mouth of an illiterate Bushman came a sample of nuclear chemistry, and the simple acceptance of the fact that smell is transported in molecular form.

I soon found out that the Bushmen's anatomical knowledge was also impressive. Just as every animal had its name, so did every major muscle, organ or bone. These were people who, without the aid of microscopes, knew the function of the uterus, and the ovary, and the many machinations of the animal body.

Once, when we had opened a hartebeest, I asked why the intestinal contents were so liquid, but the droppings so hard. The explanation came with a sigh for the stupid white man.

'You have been with us so long, yet you ask this question. You know there is no water here. The animal must squeeze out the water' (and Nxabase imitated a peristaltic movement) 'and use it again.'

So much knowledge, and yet they thought with the heart and not with the brain. 'In my heart I knew it was not right, and I must not do it,' said Ntumka, after he was convicted of stock theft. It sounded the way we might say it, but it meant exactly what he said.

It was not only their comprehensive understanding of animal behaviour that was astounding. I never failed to be amazed at their detailed knowledge of plant life, and the way they used this knowledge. Here Namkwa (and other Bushwomen just as expert) proved to be an invaluable help and source of information.

When Brian Maguire, a skilled botanist, was with us, I asked Namkwa to accompany us on walks in the bush, and teach us something of her knowledge. She didn't let me down, and fed Brian's scientific enthusiasm with fascinating revelations of plant behaviour. Each day we could hardly wait to set out on the next excursion, and seldom did we get back before late afternoon.

Several times we had my mother-in-law along with us, and whenever Namkwa made a mistake, or hesitated, and that was only rarely, she invoked her life's experience as food collector and plant expert to correct her daughter.

By our count, Namkwa had a plant repertoire of over 300 plants, which she could recognize in almost any state of preservation. She didn't require anything as obvious as a flower to tell the difference between what seemed to us two identical species. Each plant had its own specific name, and never was there any confusion or synonymy. She could tell us where to find each plant, which were poisonous, and which were used by what animals as food.

Once she brought us plant leaves and gave Brian a name for the plant. He quickly leafed through his notes, and then, rather triumphantly said: 'Now I've caught you! Yesterday you gave me another name for this plant.'

Namkwa simply looked at him with that expression I had seen before: a sort of sigh-in-the-eye look. Then she turned and went off. A few minutes later she returned with two plants. She stood in a challenge in front of the botanist, holding up a plant in each hand. It was obvious to us that the leaves were identical, but the root systems were completely different.

I puffed a bit, and said, 'Well, she's got you beat, Brian.'

He could only agree: 'But how on earth does she know the difference without digging up the plant first?'

Whenever she separated similar-looking plants, Brian's incredulity grew.

'I know she is right. These are two different species,' he would say. 'But we botanists just don't know on what criteria we should distinguish them.'

Generally speaking modern botany separates species essentially on appearance, that is on morphological criteria. Namkwa, like any other Bushgirl, employed all her senses in order to assess the smell, feeling, texture, taste and appearance; which explains why she didn't need the flower to make a reliable identification.

If her knowledge of how a plant lives and eats and drinks – the physiology of plants – was impressive, it was no more than her taxonomic knowledge.

We've heard a great deal about environment in recent years, and how we should use it and nurture it to our best advantage. The Bushmen have never needed reminding, for they must use their knowledge wisely, husband their resources, or cease to survive. They must be able to read snake signs, avoid poisonous plants and recognize diseased wildebeest. They must know the instinctive habits of animals, otherwise how could they hunt successfully? They must know the living requirements of certain plants, otherwise how will they know how to find them? The Bushgirl knows that the food plant that she seeks grows in association with a number of other plants. When she sees such a community of plants, she knows that the particular plant she is after must be somewhere nearby.

Without this sort of lore, the Bushmen would lose his land-marks, and, I believe, some of his sense of direction in the vast uniformity of the Kalahari, especially if he should find himself in a wilderness beyond his own backyard.

The fact is that the Bushman does not get lost, and his sense of direction is unfailing. It is simply because he draws on all his experience and reads the signs around him, everything from the position of the sun to the subtlest breezes and the trails of creeper plants.

Once, on an extended tour over land completely new to Xamxua, my old teacher lost his knife somewhere. We returned six days later to the place where he suspected it might have dropped. He knew exactly where to stop, and within minutes he had found it.

It was easy the way Xamxua worked it. He had not relied on any one particular bush or tree (none of which look the same to a Bushman) but he had absorbed a picture of the entire plant community. This he sub-divided into its various plant suburbs, one of which he knew would be hiding his knife. So on the way back he merely looked for the specific plant community he remembered, and, having found that, his search was practically over, bar the shout of delight. He was a clever one, this Bushman.

With a similar application of her knowledge, Namkwa was also able to find without difficulty, and at night, a particular camp spot which she had only seen once the year before, also at night. This she did on a later expedition, 300 miles from her Takatshwane environment, and what made her feat the more remarkable was the fact that our approach on the second occasion was from a completely different direction. Such orientation defies my understanding.

Another time we arrived at a campsite near a Kgalagadi village, tired and hungry. I asked Namkwa, and Theugei who was with us, to prepare the meal, while I laid out our bedding. When

Namkwa came to inspect my effort she took one look, and was horrified: 'Can't you see that a donkey died there? Look! There are all its bones. He didn't die of a lion. He died of a sickness. The sickness is on the ground all around. We can't sleep there with that same sickness!'

With my fair knowledge of bacteriology what answer could I, a lecturer in a medical school, give to this Bushgirl? So I shifted our gear. The pattern of the bones was clear, and so was the correctness of her deduction. Only a highly civilized scientist would have failed to notice!

Bushmen, of course, learn these things from experience, and from years of listening to their elders. They have no such things as books, paid teachers, journals or organized classes. Bushmen learn as children, leaning up against the talk around the fire. A lot of it might sound the same old chat, but each tale retold is a piece of revision. Since the Bushmen go through life recounting old stories, repetition is a big factor in the learning process.

They also learn in practice from hunting trips, and food-collecting excursions with their parents, who take time out to tutor their children. Old Tasa, of Douté's band, for instance, always visited us with his little son. When I asked why his wife didn't come, he looked at his son: 'I want him to know the entire land between here and Okwa. I want to tell him about all the plants and animals, for one day I will die, and who can teach him then?'

In this basic way the experience of millennia has been handed down and along the route the Bushman has made of himself a scientist. He might not be able to analyse in highfalutin academic gobbledigook but his method is to all intents pure science: the acquisition of knowledge through the tested sequence of information obtained from minute observation and followed by correct deduction.

Their observations, even the most minute, are rarely incorrect; their mistakes where they occur lie on the plane of deduction. Which is hardly different from the experience of their Western counterparts who with all their erudition and the latest apparatus can still come up with wrong deductions, and who with all their information on life and history and people can still deduce that the Bushman is somewhat less than civilized.

This makes my hackles rise. We might have 'culture' in abundance, and all the paraphernalia of our super-society to go with it, but we probably do relatively less with our inheritance than the Bushman does with his. Our material and scientific progress, for all its moon walks, television sets, supermarkets and efficient abattoirs, is not necessarily an advance to something better, a straight line to good humanity. Would to God it were!

Nor do I offer this as some great original philosophical truth. All I know is that we have much to learn from the Bushmen, and though that sounds trite and clichéd, bear with it, for the Bushman has evolved a solution to life that, for all the indications to the contrary, isn't pure survival. For all his weaknesses, his jealousies and petty human traits, he does not live by meat or melon alone.

He has got nearer than we superior beings might ever do to the art of living in keeping with his environment. He has something of value – and we are threatening it – that he has nurtured down the centuries. In fact the forces now at work on the Bushmen are subverting the old sanctions that knitted the fragile fabric of their society. They are releasing the aggression which makes man anything but a noble savage, and it makes me sad to see it.

SIXTEEN

On the Hunt

It is clear to me that I am inclined to over-sentimentalize the Bushman's virtues, but my bias is understandable when I put it up against the racial prejudices that exist among my own kind. Then, indeed, they stand out as paragons, which of course they are not. Thank goodness, for my time among them would have been deadly dull if they were.

As it is I suffered from their quirks and was irritated and frustrated by their limitations, sometimes to the point of near-despair. But there is a resilience in their charm that overcomes and is all-redeeming. I don't have to romanticize my life with them to vindicate my time among them, or exaggerate its scientific side. I was not ruled by my research or any dedication to improving their lot. My motives were far more selfish.

I went to Namkwa and to Takatshwane because I was at home there, because I enjoyed their life, and found pleasure in sharing it with them, the hardship and the plenty. I liked the hours spent round the fire, watching and listening and sometimes contributing to their conversations in lively castanet, their concert of words. I liked to go hunting with the boys. I liked the feeling of achievement when I knew I had done it just right, because after all the years I was still eager to impress them that I was equal.

I enjoyed the hunt for its excitement and the stretching of the senses that it demanded. I liked the hunt because it proved my manhood, proved that I could provide for my mate. I enjoyed the aim, and the thud of a certain hit. Not because I enjoyed the killing, though I shot to kill. It's simply something that had to be done, and so much better if it were done well: the bigger the bag, of course, the better, because on the hunt you hunt for all.

I'm not a hunter by obsession, and I abhor those who kill for kicks. The horns I have in my lounge are not trophies displayed for their size and as a boast of marksmanship. Their length and size aren't worth a damn, but the stories and the bonds they recall stir my sentimental moods. I liked the hunt for the comradeship it provided, the understanding that was communicated when you were creeping side by side, barely breathing, on your bellies.

These are perhaps the most intimate moments of all, when you're dragging bellies and wriggling backsides together, talking only in silence with looks and gestures and knowing. In these moments you are earth brothers advancing hand in hand, and all your differences are lost and covered in the sand.

Most of my hunts have been with the men who came to take it for granted that I was one of them. Yet some of my most vivid memories include the times that Namkwa came along.

I cannot say that each time was all sweet harmony, although many trips were. No, some were soured by some of the more memorable quarrels that we had. Like the time she failed to pack the things I thought necessary for a hunting trip – the white man's luxuries (I called them emergency rations), such as sugar and rice, salt, pepper and pots and pans. It was her job to see that all these things were with us, including the snake-bite serum and the rope on which we used to hang the meat to dry, the proper bedding, karosses, springbok mats, groundsheet and pillow. Another necessity was a quantity of mielie meal to keep the men from hunger and thus save the venison earmarked for home.

As far as I was concerned this was important baggage, but Namkwa did not think so. Not on the first occasion, anyway. When we discovered a whole number of things missing we all heaped scorn on her, but her husband most of all. Then she was a 'bloody useless woman'.

Another time during a very hot summer we headed south to Manyane Pan. The rains hadn't broken, veldkos was scarce, and we were short of food. Early one morning, coming across signs of hartebeest, we stopped and told Ntonno and the two girls, Theugei and Namkwa, to make camp while we others went out to hunt. We came back not much later with two hartebeest, dumped their dismembered carcasses on some branches in the shade and asked the three to cut and strip the meat, and hang it up to dry. We hurried back to bag some more.

When we returned in the afternoon we found that the only thing Ntonno and the girls had done was to build a canopy of grass for themselves, under which they had fallen asleep. Our arrival did not even waken them. The meat we had left behind was lying in the scorching sun, and had already turned quite black.

We were incensed. With two extra hartebeest we'd already decided that four would last the village for a while, and when we had loaded the black meat we set off for home. As punishment (decided by our judiciary of hunters) the two girls and Ntonno were sentenced to the back of the nolli with no water or tobacco.

The afternoon became increasingly hot, so hot that the men took it in turns to sit up front with me. This did not bother Namkwa. What made her livid was the fact that we refused to give her a puff of the pipe, and I did not offer her a cigarette. I could see her grow more furious in the rear-view mirror.

About five miles from home we had a flat tyre. Quickly Namkwa jumped off and began to walk. I was too busy with the tyre to notice, but when we had finished I looked round.

'She's gone,' said Theugei.

A considerable distance further on we saw her walking in the bush parallel to the truck's spoor. I stopped and called to her, but she ignored me. I asked two of the men to jump off, and bring her back. It wasn't easy, for Namkwa was fast and strong, and when they did latch on to her she fought, biting and scratching and hitting as though her life was at stake.

Eventually they literally threw her into the back, and the others held her down. At the village I came to her with water, but she threw it in my face. She was unrecognizable, she was so angry. The look in her eyes was enough to put fear and trembling into anyone confronting her. She snarled at me with the viciousness of a karakul, and I carefully kept my distance.

It took hours before she calmed down and began to relax. I was relieved, for it was then, if ever, that I came to fear and respect her anger. This was real.

The anger that rose out of her jealousy was something else. I could handle it, provided I was quick enough to keep out of reach. When I teased her about other girls she entertained no humour whatsoever. She would suddenly lash out, hitting hard, without preference for any particular part of me. Sometimes when she was close enough and I was unprepared, she'd jab and dig her thumbs under my armpits, forcing genuine yells and excruciating pain.

To be fair, my jealousy was just as great, and my anger meaner. Though I tried to smother it, my jealousy was always there ready to rear when pricked. One evening in a village 15 miles from Takatshwane, Namkwa, Kathua (a girl from Midum's band) and I were sheltering in our hut from the rain. The two girls began to play the dongo and sing. As they harmonized they lulled me to sleep.

When I awoke with a start, the girls had gone. The rain had stopped and I could hear their voices behind our hut. There was a man's voice with them. Parting the grass and peering through, I saw the man was a young, flash fellow from Lone Tree. He was obviously doing a good job of entertaining both ladies. I felt the familiar lurch in the stomach, and the blood of jealousy rising. How could she go off without my knowing!

Soon Kathua ran in and asked for a cigarette for Namkwa. That really blew me.

'Tell Namkwa she'd better fetch it herself,' I said.

In a moment Namkwa was with me. I took her blanket and threw it outside. 'Sleep there,' I said.

And she did. She didn't go back to the fire, but rolled up in front of the entrance and pretended to sleep. In the morning I sulked about my work, sitting on my folding chair with my notes. Soon she came up and sat down beside me. Despite my sulk I put a hand on her head. Our eyes met, and we made up.

'But why were you so angry?'

'Because you went out without asking me.'

'But you were asleep, and I didn't want to wake you.'

'You should have woken me. Besides, how can you go off and sit with another man?'

'But he came and joined us when we were singing, and then he danced to our singing. I didn't go to him.'

What could I, this possessively immature husband, say in answer to his bush wife?

I have already described the things the hunt had done for me, but they are also an unavoidable factor in any analysis of the development of Namkwa herself. It was on our many trips, most of several days, that her talents for organization (the black meat day was an exception) and leadership began to emerge.

We usually took two or three girls along, as our domestics, and since we were usually away for days they had to work as hard as the hunters.

The men we took were selected for their hunting abilities. Usually we were about six. I had the rifle and the truck. Thxale had his eyes. Ntchumka and Txaunxua were expert after spoor; Nxabase lent his super insight into animal behaviour (he could take us on extensive short cuts, correctly anticipating the direction that animals would take). Xamxua came mostly for the adventure. Still, he made himself useful, cutting meat into strips for biltong, collecting firewood and digging holes for roasting heads.

In un-Bushman style we would move into game areas with the truck; the boys on the back scanning every sign. A bang on the cab-roof would indicate they had spotted something of interest, and from the stop on, all communication would be in sign language. Lifting the upper lip and tipping the nose meant 'straight ahead'. Each buck could be sketched with raised fingers; a flick of your hand as though you had burnt your finger would indicate that the prey was close.

On one such trip we stopped, and Ntchumka gestured me to follow. Creeping along the ground from bush to bush we followed the fresh spoor. Suddenly Ntchumka stopped, shook a burnt finger. A few more yards and he raised his head, a movement that told me where to look. I could not see anything. With a gentle hand he told me to stay behind him. We moved closer. Finally the wildebeest materialized ahead of me. I got in a shot, but the animal made off. We ran and followed. To Ntchumka it was obvious that the prey was limping, he could tell from the spoor, which at first was bloody. After some distance blood showed only occasionally on the sand, on a bit of grass, or a leaf. Ntchumka hardly hesitated. After about two miles we could see the wildebeest again. This time I dropped it. Within minutes the others, recognizing the sound of a hit, reached us, knives out. The first knife sliced the sternum to see if the animal had fat. Branches were laid out below the carcass to keep the meat off the sand. Then the skinning began.

The procedure is much the same with every kill. With dexterity and anatomical know-how, the body is dismembered, and each section placed on the bush. The blood is scooped into the rumen, and securely sealed with a sharp stick around which the end of the tissue is wrapped, over and over again. The bones adjacent to the hoofs are cut out, and thrown on the hot coals of the fire kindled nearby. The liver and kidneys are also thrown on the fire to roast. Then hands are washed by squeezing the fluid from the contents of the rumen, and Bushmen are ready for their hunters' meal.

The bones are removed from the coals, and cracked open lengthwise with a chopper to lay bare the hot roasted marrow. After the meal the hide is cut into strips and the hunters make parcels of meat, which are worn, much like rucksacks over their backs. Even distributed among four or five, the meat is a burden, and the several miles back to base can be heavy going.

In fact on the occasion I've described the trek back was an ordeal, but one quickly relieved by relaxing around the camp fire. Bushmen do not make fires that force you to flee from the heat, and rubbing shoulders close to the flames we reviewed the day, and joked at each other's ineptitude. I was often teased for being so clumsy at creeping, and this time for being so blind I couldn't see the buck when my nose was against it. I countered this by asking Xamxua why he couldn't look after his pipe and why he had to make us wait half an hour while he retraced his spoor to find it. We laughed too at Nxabase: 'What is wrong with your eyes, Nxabase, that you should almost step on a puffadder?'

Then Thxale turned on Theugei, and soon had us convulsed as he imitated her every idiosyncrasy. Finally we went to bed. I was weary and asleep almost before I touched the pillow, but I remember Namkwa pulling the kaross over us, cuddling into me and covering me with her arm.

In the days that followed this expedition Namkwa transformed our tiny settlement into a haven, kraaled by branches and leaves. The ground was swept clean, and kept spotless, the baggage piled tidy. The meat was stripped and hung from ropes tied between two trees, a hole dug for our rubbish. It was not all her own work. She had organized the others, the men included, into a co-operative unit. She did this with a minimum of fuss, and no one seemed to notice that slowly, but surely, her authority was increasing.

Even I was not fully aware of the subtle changes going on, except that I saw Namkwa grow more confident and decisive each time we were out. There was initiative in every move she made. What was happening was that Namkwa's personality was beginning to assert itself. When I looked at her in the firelight shadow she had none of the fawn-like innocence that I remembered when I first met her. The features were still the same, but the eyes had shed their timid look. Instead, there was a boldness in them, and a decisive grace about the way she moved. It was almost like a different person sitting there, another Namkwa waiting to come out.

SEVENTEEN

Going to Town

It was quite an outing, one way or another, whenever I took Namkwa up to Ghanzi. We did it a few times, and usually when the inside of the Nissan was like an oven. The petrol boiled in the fuel line, and I would sniff for the smell of rubber burning, half expecting the tyres to catch fire as we ploughed through blazing sand. The heat came up through the floor, and penetrated through the crêpe soles of my shoes. Perspiration ran in trickles down my neck, and the engine roared like a furnace in front of us.

The journeys through this inferno were only due to necessity when two weeks had passed since the orange squash ran out, when what beer I had was warm and undrinkable, when the drums of fresh Lone Tree water had been exhausted and when the salty Takatshwane brine was hardly palatable and gallons couldn't quench a thirst. So there we would be, Namkwa and I, and a few Bushmen in the back, on our way to Ghanzi for supplies; for fresh good water, and above all a cool beer, or even an iced vodka and bitter lemon. The thought would relieve some of the agony of the drive, which I could gladly have done without.

As ever, Namkwa and the men were unperturbed. Namkwa's feet, with their thick calloused soles, didn't even feel the heat. And she always chatted away as if the whole thing were a treat.

In fact that is exactly what it was. Namkwa, alive with anticipation, knew Ghanzi meant a few presents for her. And the boys licked their lips at the prospect of a can of beer or two, and quite possibly that luxury of luxuries, a white man's sandwich. They were on their way to town, and it was a big thing in their lives. There would be the store, the petrol pump, a peep at the butchery, the local police, buttons sparkling in the sun, and milling crowds of coloured faces; Nharo Bushmen, Kgalagadi maidens, dignified

Herero women, woolly-headed children of mixed races, tanned and sun-scored faces of white farmers, and their wives.

We would add a little colour of our own; my wild Bushmen in their skins and darting eyes, clutching their few cents to spend at the cash store on small presents for their wives and children.

We used to pull up at the store's petrol pump, and immediately be surrounded by a group of men and women, and snotty children sticking their inquisitive noses in the cab. Once a deranged old Bushwoman came begging and cajoling my chaps to sleep with her. They would jump off the truck, and stand around with sheepish delight on their faces, revelling in their arrival in this hive of peopledom.

Inside the store, a barn-like affair with long counters down each wall, the goods are stacked almost to the ceiling. To a Bushman it is a sort of Aladdin's cave, filled with an unimaginable wealth of surprises. Everything is sold here, from blankets to baby napkins, from dresses to shoes, canned goods and spice, saddles and brick presses, pots, pants, saws, sweets, door-frames, cold drinks, flower seeds, knives, belts and biscuits, sugar, mielie meal, and tobacco in little brown packets. Whatever cannot be fitted on a shelf is piled on the floor and dangled from the rafters.

While you watch, a little hand reaches up, puts its penny offering on the counter and runs out with a sweet. A farmer plants himself squarely at the counter and barks his order, each item a command. He buys enough to fill half his van, and has another cup of tea, before moving to other chores and some social chat. In pre-independence Botswana the social pecking-order was clearly visible. After the whites, the black government servants came in for preferential treatment, followed by the Hereros because they were usually rich enough to buy. Next were the Kgalagadis, then the farm Bushmen, and at the bottom of the rung, my veld Bushmen. They were made to feel so obviously inferior that it was painful to watch them dare the step up to the counter.

The store, located as it is at the main exit from Ghanzi, is both meeting place and departure point. Big transport lorries pull up outside it to take on piles of black and brown passengers, who perch up top with their bundles and bags and what-have-you. Then, like steamers, the lorries puff exhaust fumes and head off into the inhospitable Kalahari sea. Coming the other way are other desert steamers, loaded to the gunwales with post, newspapers, magazines, supplies and passengers. They arrive amid as much excitement as a liner arriving in port. And few seem to bother about the road sign: the only 'Stop' within hundreds of miles. There really isn't that much traffic.

From the store, I invariably moved on to the government offices to say hello to the Revenue man, and pay my respects to the District Commissioner. My visits were very polite and diplomatic. Then I would call on the local chief of police, which was also rather a decent thing to do. Then, at last, the official business done, I would pull up outside Ghanzi's only hotel, where I would leave my wife and Bushmen friends and become a thorough white man once again.

If I could manage it, I would time the visits to coincide with airmail day, when a little plane flew in with letters, the doctor and the bank clerk, and farmers' trucks lined up outside the hotel fence. The fence had a purpose, to protect the thick green grass and its enclosure of duiker and rabbits. It was also there to keep out dogs and Bushmen of all kinds. The owner, a cat lover, disapproved of dogs, it seemed, and convention wouldn't allow him to let the Bushmen in. That would be too much.

On the long cool verandah the wives and their white children drank and waited for their beery husbands. They would be in the bar, which had two doors; one leading from the verandah for whites and a side door for blacks.

The noise and laughter in the bar was enough to gladden any thirsty heart. Here the Kalahari-hardened characters in customary khaki gear and sweat stains under their arms soaked up beer and kept up rather raucous conversation. Outside their Bushmen servants sat docile in the sun, or crawled under the trucks for an extra foot of shade.

The hotel was a bastion of racial taboos, but I had my passport stamped on my skin and could enter at my pleasure. Not even my conscience stopped me, although I told myself that one day I would crash the 'hotel barrier', and I'd do it with Namkwa too. She, meanwhile, waited outside with the others for me to bring them cans of ice-cold beer and a tray of sandwiches.

I would make a few appropriate remarks but I didn't squat

down and break the bread with my wife and my Bushmen friends.
I went back inside for a fuller, better meal. The hotel food
satisfied my hunger, and a bottle of wine would give it the final
touch. But by the time I got up to leave I usually felt ashamed.

Not all my visits to the hotel gave me mental indigestion. For
other than some farmers who despised me for my relationship
with Namkwa I made happy contact with farmers whom I
respected.

I also recall one particularly rewarding meeting, although it
was some years later, with Botswana's Vice-President, Dr Quett
Masire. When I went up to him in the lounge and introduced
myself, he smiled back and said, 'I think we know each other.'

He wasn't guessing, and I couldn't place him or any occasion
that we might have met.

'Somehow I recall a red jeep stuck ... ' he said.

'Was that you?' I exclaimed. 'Were you the man who pulled
me out with a tractor and then refused to take my money?'

'Yes, that was me,' he said, obviously enjoying my surprise.

How he remembered staggered me, for he had only seen me in
the dark, and now I felt humiliated that I hadn't recognized him.

I've met Dr Masire many times since then, and on each meeting
he has impressed me with his charm, candidness and humility.
His record as Minister of Development speaks for itself, and there
is no reason to doubt that he should play a leading role in Botswana for many years ahead.

EIGHTEEN

Bushman Hospitality

A variety of character helps spice the bush life, and in a sparsely peopled land the web of visits that pattern it are very much part of the social order. The old Nxabases and the passing Somdakakazis are regrettably rather rare experiences, but even an ordinary new face about the place adds some excitement to the Kalahari round. In their isolation the Bushmen are a gregarious lot, and they enjoy the visits of other bands as much as they enjoy the adventure of going visiting themselves.

Most visits are bound by convention and the nature of the ties existing between the different bands. The visitors usually hover on the perimeter of the host's circle before joining the inner ring. So when a group of our Lone Tree friends came to trade tobacco, they seated themselves outside the circle we had formed around our fire, and even when they had begun to speak with our men, they did not put down their bags or their karosses. Nor did our men, though the talk was friendly and lively, deem it necessary to turn to face our new guests or make them comfortable.

Later on, however, the visitors rose and spread to various skerms and sleeping places where they chatted with particular friends. Only in the evening when our fire drew in the village did the Lone Tree visitors feel free to sit knee by knee and smoke among our people.

Bands from further away were received even more formally. Kathi's band from Hanahai, for instance, first gathered round Thakum's skerm. She was from Hanahai and one of Kathi's men was her younger brother. While they sat, Thakum rubbed eland fat under their noses and over their bellies. She then took out some powdered wood from her pouch of medicines which she gave the visitors to smell. She did all this because they came from a 'different air', and this treatment would ward off sickness and prevent them from falling ill at our village. This ritual would also protect us from contracting any sickness which they might have brought.

That night they all slept in the vicinity of Thakum's hut, and hardly mingled with our people. The next day the men were obviously more at ease and moved around the village. The women, however, took considerably longer before they mixed freely with our women. During the day they went out with the food-collecting parties – a privilege accorded to guests – and when they returned in the evening several came over to us with a gift of grewia berries and bush potatoes. Namkwa simply accepted these, offering no thanks.

The Kathi men had come with all sorts of things to barter for tobacco – bits of fencing wire, a penknife, arrows and bushels of ostrich feathers. The more valuable things – a python skin and a superb lynx skin – they sold to me for money.

In the evenings they brought out their supply of experiences and stories in exchange for ours, and they added laughter, dances and games to our village life. We were happy to have them, and as is usual when food is abundant, they stayed a long time. It is these lengthy stays when more than one band lives together that confuse strangers – as I was confused early on – over the size of Bushmen bands, their structure and territoriality.

Among the Kathi on this occasion was Nxabase the Elder. He was a remarkable man, with a reputation that ran wide across our part of the Kalahari, who the first time we met immediately impressed me, as a man full of strength and vitality.

My 'brother' Nxabase brought Nxabase the Elder to our fire, introduced me, and explained that because they bore the same name there was a special close relationship between them. He also pointed out that because of our own brotherly rapport, it followed that I should enjoy a friendly informal relationship with the old Nxabase. On this basis we took an instant liking to each other, and in the days that followed I spent many hours listening to his illuminating talk. His biological knowledge was vast, and as an ornithologist he had no equal in the bush. It was, however, as a powerful doctor that he had earned the abiding respect of the Bushmen. That is why we took Somdakakazi to him and why his namesake, the younger Nxabase, had (like others) gone to him that time when hunger had driven him to eat some honey badger, which was still taboo for him.

The doctor had the antidote for this sort of thing, which involved tattooing his patient to counter the ill-effects of a broken taboo – in Nxabase the younger's case the 'poison' he had absorbed from eating honey-badger.

A great dancer, he also had a hypnotic way with him that led Bushmen dances into the realms of trance and mouth-frothing conflict with Thoa's evil forces. I saw such an exhibition one evening during his visit.

Without any tangible explanation a 'mood' spread around the village at sundown. You could feel it creeping over the community and coming out in the hum of the people bent on their chores. It seemed to start with the men humming mournfully at first, then lifting their tunes into harmony. It was eerie and weirdly beautiful, and the whole mood increasingly irresistible. Soon the small children were gathered in a circle in the open centre of the village, the little girls, seated after the fashion of their mothers, clapping and ululating as their brothers stomped around them. Almost imperceptibly their movements gained in cohesion and the rhythm grew until the older girls and teenage boys were coaxed to join in and take up the lead. For a while the grown-ups remained apart, the men simply concentrating on their humming. But gradually each woman joined in, the young adults, including Namkwa, going first.

Soon old Theugei's voice had risen, resonating clear into the lead and I saw that all but the senior men were caught up. It wasn't until after midnight that they moved.

By then the dance, despite a series of breaks for an intermission of laughs and smoking, had developed its tempo and it was only a matter of time before the elders joined in: our Nxabase, Tasa, Kathi and Xauko. They rose from my fire circle crying, '*Ntchai! Ntchai!* Sing! Sing!'

Only the old Nxabase remained unmoved and seemingly unconcerned while the others went off to their huts for their dance rattles. They tied them to their legs, each length strung with hard moth cocoons filled with ostrich-eggshell chips to make rattles. At their own fires the men stamped the feel into

their bodies and then, again shouting '*Ntchai! Ntchai!*' they
closed in on the dancing circle. They came stomping and shuffling
their bodies bent forward, their arms raised and hands flapping
to the rattle of their feet and legs. Their entry encouraged the
others to step up their volume into a resounding harmony. The
younger men broke their circle and fell into line behind their
elders. Now all the men moved round the circle of singing women,
stomping and bending to touch lightly the head of each woman
in turn.

Old Nxabase next to me remained motionless, hunched in
himself. But I saw his eyes flitting to the dance, and I knew he
was listening intently, measuring the rhythm and biding the
moment when he too would get up. Suddenly he rose and wound
on his rattlers. Then like the others he stomped over to the dance
with outstretched arms and waving hands. At the same time he
let loose the song that must have been welling inside him.

His entry electrified the singing dancers. Their chorus, its
harmony already stretched to the utmost, rose higher in full cry
to meet him. Like a conductor with an ear for just the right
arrangement of sound, he took command. Shouting and scolding,
he moved one woman from her place to another, listened for the
effect, and proceeded to rearrange the group until he had guided
the harmony to an almost perfect pitch. Once satisfied, he began
his own stomp around the circle. In order of band seniority, the
men, none of whom would have dared to dance in front of him,
weaved in behind and abandoned themselves to the finale, dancing
until they were literally fit to drop.

What had started spontaneously on a 'mood' had grown into
an intense religious happening, and each stomp was a step in a
significant ritual. The XKo, like their neighbours the Gwi and
Nharo, believe that their women are exceedingly vulnerable to
the evil which Thoa, the opponent of the good god Guthe,
directs at them. Tensions and illnesses in a band are usually
caused by Thoa's evil influence, and women because of their
susceptibility are more prone to harbour this danger. By dancing
around the women and waving their hands, the dancers ward off
the evil. By touching their womenfolk they extract it and absorb
the evil into conflict in their own stronger bodies.

Not all men are equally powerful in combating the forces of

evil, and the younger men in particular must be shown how to master the devil. In such an exorcizing ceremony embracing the whole band, each has to give his everything and lose himself in the unity of the group. Otherwise the whole effect would be destroyed.

As the dance develops the evil accumulating in the dancer fills him with discomfort. It causes him to grunt and shout and rush into the bush, where he retches, spits or vomits it out. Slowly he collapses into a cataleptic trance.

While I watched the dancers started to falter. Their eyes glazed, and their stomps stuttered out of time. Tasa stepped into the circle and plunged ploughing, head first, into the glowing ashes of the fire. Young Nxabase kneeled before the pregnant Kobe wailing and chanting. Xauko collapsed completely and was rolled away to one side. I lifted his arm and let it drop again, lifeless as a rope.

Meanwhile, old Nxabase carried on in command. With his hands stretched out behind him, he led Thxale, holding on tight to his leader's hips, through the fire. Oblivious of its heat, the two men walked barefoot through the coals, kicking them aside. When Thxale let go of his teacher, his legs crumbled, and he would have fallen prostrate into the fire had not the women caught him and led him away to a spot where he lay rolling, moaning, sweating and groaning until his stupor calmed him.

Old Nxabase carried on, absorbing more and more evil into his body until it too could hold no more. Suddenly he bolted screeching and screaming into the dark bush. The dance didn't end with Nxabase's sudden departure; it went on, but it wasn't the same without him.

At the height of Nxabase's trauma, the clapping had accelerated wildly into an erratic unco-ordinated beat. The singing had pierced yet higher. Now the scene was littered with limp bodies and the heart of the dance pulsed sporadically. Some of the dancers still on their feet set about reviving the unconscious ones by massaging their chests. Moistening their hands with sweat from their armpits, and the oil on their heads, they rubbed the cure into the inert forms. Here the women turned to positive action, and some of the younger girls ran off to dig out pieces of the vile-smelling root of the camelthorn tree. I saw Nkasi chew a root, fill her mouth with water and swirl the bits into a mixture before showering out a fine spray of the smelly concoction over the face of an unconscious dancer.

She bathed several in this way until they were sufficiently revived to be picked up and returned to the ring. After a while old Nxabase returned. Had he not done so the Bushmen would have assumed he had turned into a lion, and as such he would not be harmed, which was all very well. But wives fear that they can lose husbands running off this way.

Nxabase's sprint through the bush had not run down his spirit, nor exhausted his power. He kneeled over the fire and allowed the flames to lick across his chest. Then he scooped up bare handfuls of glowing coals and threw them over his back, while the womenfolk rose to a new ecstasy.

It was 4 a.m. and the dance had passed to its climax. Gone was the emotional intensity, the violent physical side to the dance, and as the light grew the dancers stopped at last and moved off at peace with themselves. All but the very smallest children had been up through the night, and now it was time for rest.

Later in the day I made a point of studying carefully the participants in the dance, but detected no signs of hangover, burns or trauma. The village was back to normal, and the night might not have happened. Towards evening I went across to Thxale's hut when I saw old Nxabase there. The bush doctor made lateral incisions on Thxale's chest, shoulders and thighs, and into the cuts he rubbed carbon from medicines he had prepared, as well as the sweat of his armpits. My 'brother' Nxabase explained that the old man was satisfied with his pupil's performance of the night before, and was merely 'finishing him off'. From now on Thxale would be better equipped to grapple with the evils of Thoa. Old Nxabase had taught him.

Generally speaking the atmosphere is relaxed when Bushmen come together, and visitors do not abuse the hospitality of their hosts. The influx to Takatshwane during the great famine I have described was, however, exceptionally trying. Despite a common language the local Takatshwane distrusted and feared the many strange XKo who came to their valley for famine relief, and as it happened they had good reason. In normal circumstances the

Bushman makes an honest effort to husband his resources and harvest his veldcrop rationally, leaving seedcrop to provide food for the following year. But the foreigners had no ties with the land they had camped on, and, their occupation guaranteed by government decree, they not only lined up for the donated food-stuffs, but also ravaged the surrounding land of food and fire-wood. The locals were powerless to do anything to prevent this, and their morale deteriorated by the week.

When the rains finally broke and prospects for a veldcrop became better, the distribution of famine-relief food ceased, and most of the outsiders quickly returned to their lands, in some cases more than a hundred miles away. A few, however, remained behind, seemingly determined to stay.

With a solidarity uncommon among Bushmen, the Takat-shwane people, with their women, including Namkwa, in the front row, faced the foreigners and told them bluntly they had to go. Fortunately the foreign XKo, recognizing the strained tem-pers of their own kind, packed and left the same day.

Among other visitors the Tswanas, and especially the Kgala-gadis, are feared. When they are around the village becomes heavy with an air of submissiveness, and talks are spiked with a tense politeness. Government officials are treated with respect, but the arrival of whites is invariably a signal for the XKo to rush out like a bunch of beggars, hands out for tobacco.

Some of the visitors have no respect or regard for Bushman custom and their privacy. There have been whites who have come to our village, and without even introducing themselves have set about taking photographs. I've even been embarrassed by some scientists who have arrived too engrossed in their research to take any notice of etiquette. They barge into the Bushman's 'parlour', even his 'bedroom', clumsy with their curiosity. In pursuit of blood specimens, throat swabs, gypsum face-masks and dental casts, it doesn't occur to them that they are dealing with people who actually might not want all this attention. Again, a cigarette or a sprinkling of tobacco is too often thought to be sufficient compensation for the rudeness of their research. Besides, isn't it all for the Bushman's own good?

It isn't only this sort of thing that affronts the Bushman code. On one occasion we had a young white couple staying in the village who, in the bliss of their ignorance and love for each other, spent much of their time cuddling and fondling each other. They were oblivious of the taboo attached to this behaviour, but would have blushed had they known how critically the Bushmen watched them. Even the children took to crude repartee, throwing up their skin skirts and exposing their backsides or genitals. This they did from the safety of a distance, but Thxale and Txaunxua were more direct and far less discreet.

Once, after urinating, they turned round and in full view of the girl pointed their penises in her direction before tucking them away. I don't know what the girl thought, but I was taken by surprise. Then there was the evening the couple went to bed early, at about seven o'clock, when I was going to make a general announcement. From the fire, Nxabase, turned around and shouted, 'Stop fornicating now, the head man has something to say.'

In short, Bushman society is not 'permissive'. They adhere strictly to rules of conduct which they, in their naivety, think are common to all 'people'. For them, 'civilized' people don't behave like that.

Of course, not all our visitors have been discourteous, and many of my friends, such as the botanist Brian Maguire have been a joy to have around, and have earned the respect of 'my' Bushmen. Brian's success was built as much on his niceness as his remarkable knowledge of Bushman plant lore. But then he is nothing if not devoted, and in the field can lose himself from reality.

Once when we were limping home on a failing engine in the intense summer heat, the worst happened: our engine stopped altogether. Miles from anywhere the danger was vividly clear to me. But when Brian got out of the cab it was almost as though he did so to stretch his legs.

Outside, he looked around and his eyes widened in delight: 'Oh look!' he exclaimed. 'What a lovely Bauhinia macrantha!'

'Oh, for Christ's sake ... ' was all I could say as I tackled the engine.

Other scientists I've known have shown a greater capacity for anxiety. I think of the time I was taking a group of Americans from the Institute for the Achievement of Human Potential in

Philadelphia to Takatshwane. I was with Carl Delecato, and
following way behind in a slow Land-Rover was Glen Doman,
leader of the group, with the rest of the party. The night was one
of those ice-cold Kalahari freezers, but it did not bother me, lolling
in sleep against the window. Somewhere on the edge of Sukuma
Pan, Carl stopped and woke me.

'What has happened to them?' he asked.

I looked in the rear-view mirror and saw dim reflections in the
sky: 'They're coming,' I said. 'Can't you see their headlights in
the sky?'

Carl was not satisfied. He climbed out into the cold and got his
walkie-talkie going – 'Delecato calling Doman – Delecato calling
Doman – do you read me?' he called. Relieved by a reply he got
in again and set off. This performance went on for the rest of the
long journey.

At first I was somewhat amused by these Americans in the
bush, but I was soon impressed by their sincerity, dedication,
sense of purpose and their irrepressible humour. I was impressed
too by their attitude to Namkwa, whom they accepted as an
individual and woman of special quality. I didn't have an inkling
then that their visit would have far-reaching repercussions for
Namkwa and me.

Among the whites who passed through Takatshwane the
farmers were another breed. Men of the Kalahari, they brought
samples of their brand of culture to the Bushman. On the cattle
run they pick up XKo to work as drovers herding cattle to
Lobatse, where the Bushmen buy clothing and blankets for their
wives. The farmers also bring with them Nharo and other Bushmen drovers, some of whom are related to the locals and consequently welcome.

It is probably these visits as much as anything else that have
established and stretched kinship and other relationships way
beyond Takatshwane as far as Ghanzi. I was bewildered on
occasions in that metropolis when Namkwa casually introduced
me to some woman or other saying, 'This is your auntie.' (Or
whatever she was to me.)

Not only the Tswanas are feared; among the Bushmen who
pass through XKo land there is one group that causes trembles.
These are Kaukau, the southern group of the XKung. The Nharo

might be admired because they are 'tamed', and 'have much more sense', but the Kaukau are genuinely feared. Even the taming of the Kaukau on Ghanzi farms and their intermarriage with the Nharo will not dispel the fear.

'No, these are the strongest of all Bushmen,' Xamxua told me. 'These people produce the greatest, most powerful doctors. When their men change into lion, they never return, and no lion is safe from them. They go off killing and eating antelopes much better than any lion can. They have medicines which can kill you without even touching you. But their men are strong; they are the best fighters; they can easily overpower you without even resorting to their medicines.

'Their women are tall and beautiful. Yet what man can marry such a woman? She will kill you before the year is out. And their dances! They are not like ours. We tire by morning. They continue for three days, and then go off to hunt. Besides, who can understand their language?'

Xamxua had a strange story to tell which backed his belief, and he told me it one day when I was recording the genealogies of the various bands in and around Takatshwane.

By his first wife, Domku (Gruxa's younger sister, who was named after Musomo's wife), Xamxua had one child: Ntonno. His present wife, Betchei, bore him three children.

'The eldest of these, Nkisa, is dead. But you knew her,' he said.

I couldn't remember.

'Yes you did,' insisted my old friend. 'When you were here the first time and stayed with Douté's people in the Okwa. You saw Nkisa. She was there for she told me about you.'

'But how? What did she tell you?' I asked.

'She said you made her and two other girls walk towards you while you looked at them through your little black box.'

'You mean I took a picture of her! The pretty one? Was she Nkisa, your daughter?'

Xamxua sighed. 'Yes, my only girl child.'

'But why ... how did she die?'

'It was a Kaukau,' said Xamxua, and there was sadness in his eyes. 'Some time before you were here, a Kaukau came to our land. He saw Nkisa and fell in love with her. He returned on the next cattle trek and saw her again. No one could understand his language, but he also spoke Nharo, and he spoke to Nxabase who knows this language well, just as your father-in-law does. So Nxabase told Nkisa that the Kaukau man wanted to marry her.

'Nkisa came to me and asked how could she marry a man whose language she did not understand. How could she go off into his land without understanding what her mother-in-law was saying?

'When next he returned, Nkisa refused him. But this man was persistent, and now told Gruxa that he would return. And he did return, but Nkisa and I were away. He asked Nxabase what her answer had been, but no one could tell him. Neither Nxabase nor anyone else knew that Nkisa was weakening. She told me that perhaps she should go off with him and marry him. She said, he keeps coming back, so perhaps he will be a good husband to her.

'Nxabase didn't know this, and could give the Kaukau no hope. So he got angry, as all those Kaukau easily get angry. He said, "Tell Nkisa, one day she will go out into the veld and find a dead jackal or a dead bird. She will feel hungry and bring home that thing to cook and she will eat it. Yes, she will eat it. But that thing is me. And it is then that I will kill her."

'Nobody took him seriously. They didn't believe him. Months passed, and one day Nkisa did come back from collecting with a jackal that had just died. My wife prepared it, and we all ate it, but next day Nkisa was sick and on that night she died. There was nothing we could do to save her.'

'But when did this happen?'

'Just a short time after you left on that trip to the Okwa.'

I could say nothing. There could be a dozen medical explanations for Nkisa's death. But I didn't bother to think them up. I just sat back and remembered Nkisa – her striking features, the beauty and harmony of her body, and especially the strength of character in her face. That was the time Douté tried to get his sister-in-law Nkobe, into my bed. Had it been Nkisa instead, his idea might have succeeded, but he wouldn't have dared go that far, for Nkisa was his uncle's daughter.

Suddenly it struck me: I had obviously taken a picture of Nkisa, so I must have a print in Johannesburg. I would give it to Xamxua.

'You were very fond of your daughter?' I asked.

'I loved her very much,' said Xamxua. 'She was the only girl among three boys, and she was always by my side. The finest things she brought home from the veld she would give me, and when I was sick she looked after me better than my wife. My Nkisa! My only girl ... I cried for days and I was not ashamed.'

The next time I returned to Takatshwane I took with me Nkisa's photograph. When I gave it to Xamxua I bit my lip to hold back the tears that rose as I watched him.

Unbelieving he stared, and whimpered to himself as his tears ran: 'My Nkisa ... my child ... my little girl.'

From that moment Xamxua carried, well protected, that little photo in his shoulder-bag. At times he would take it out and look at it and shake his head again, before wrapping it up again with his memory.

NINETEEN

Parents and Children

'Do you want our baby?' I said one day.

'Will it be pretty?' asked Namkwa, without looking up or showing any sign of surprise at my question.

'Well, look at Freddie Morris's children,' I answered. 'Aren't they pretty? What about Lissy? Do you think she is pretty?'

'Oh, she is pretty.'

'Well, my darling, you are pretty, your sister is pretty and so was your mother. Why should our child not be pretty?'

Yes, why not. It should be pretty enough. But this was not the question that bothered us down the years. Our problem when we first spoke this way a number of years ago was whether we should have a child at all.

'I would love to have a baby with you,' said Namkwa as she cuddled Nkasi's little Ntonno. But she was afraid, as was I. A child born of Namkwa with as much white as I could give him would be just the sort of evidence that my enemies would latch on to to prove that I had unscientific and ulterior motives in the Kalahari. Our child in all its innocence would be the weapon they would need to separate its parents.

I could see that Namkwa needed a child, for she showed her motherly drive in so many ways. But far more compelling was the fear of what might happen to us if we were found out. One could only sigh and shut the thought up.

Times have changed since then. By the grace of Guthe we have our baby, and in the climate of Botswana today it could hardly be used in evidence against us. It was born in December 1972 ... but that is, as they say, another story.

Long before she became a mother Namkwa knew as much as

any Bushwoman was expected to know about children, their development and their behaviour. Here again she was a valuable informant for the scientist who was concerned with the behaviour patterns of the Bushchild and the conditioning it underwent to conform in its grown-up social role.

In this sphere I was fortunate to learn from Professor Eibl-Eibesfeldt, of the Max Planck Institute in Munich, who with one of his students, Heidi Sbrezny, spent long periods in our village observing Bushmen children. Watching him at work, and listening to him, stimulated my interest in them. If anything it was the German scientist who really opened my eyes to children's playgroups, and the forces at work in the child community. Without the Professor's influence, his observations and deductions, this particular chapter might not have been written. Certainly things I'd taken for granted assumed a fresh importance for me, and casual comments became significant statements of anthropological value.

So when Namkwa nursed Ntonno and quite casually remarked that for a baby that wasn't even a child he had a stubborn head, I sat up, ears open.

'What do you mean?' I asked.

Namkwa put on her patient look, and explained: 'It takes about six years before a baby becomes a human being. Only then is it old enough to recognize a snake; that is when it has reached its first sense.' Looking down at Ntonno, whom she was keeping at bay with pieces of shortbread, she added, 'And this one is going to give its parents two very big fights.'

'Why two fights?'

'Oh, don't you know how babies fight when you stop giving them the breast?'

'Yes, I know about that but what about the other fight?'

'Well, that happens when his uncle stops carrying him – and that should have been you!'

I understood this one. Bushmen in their roaming life must carry their small children, and this responsibility normally falls on the mother's older brother's shoulders. Since Ntonno didn't have such an uncle, the duty (which Namkwa seemed to assume would not be carried out) fell on me, the mother's elder sister's husband. In the circumstances of my absence the parents would probably have to do the carrying, and when the time came that the child was considered old enough to walk alone, they would refuse to carry it. This would lead the youngster into a severe crisis, and his objections to what he might see as a form of rejection would explain the 'fight'.

Namkwa continued to play with Ntonno, and gave him several pieces of our shortbread. I pulled out my favourite – a gingernut – which Ntonno grabbed and hung on to. He protested when Namkwa forced it away from him.

'Oh, let him have it,' I said. But Namkwa thought the biscuit was too hard for him. She bit off a piece, chewed it, and pacified the protestor by feeding him the biscuit from her mouth to his mouth. This form of feeding is common among the Bushmen, and it is interesting to note that Eibl-Eibesfeldt says that this is where the kissing began; that kissing is nothing more than ritualized mouth-to-mouth feeding.

Namkwa then tried soothing him by offering her breast, and when he had quietened she bent down and went through the motions of delousing him. Then she blew a Bushman kiss over his face and lifted the wide-eyed Ntonno, laughing and smacking kisses on his cheeks, his belly and right on his penis.

'If children get their first sense when they recognize a snake, when are they grown up?' I asked.

'Oh, not until the girls bleed and the old men think a boy can support a wife and send him to the bushes with the men. Then the children are at the end of their second sense. But they are still not grown up. At this time brothers and sisters must sit apart, and the brother must never enter the hut of his sister. Both know they will be sent to the seclusion hut, you remember Tkose's hut, to learn to be a grown person.'

While she played with Ntonno, Namkwa spoke on. Little girls, she said, learnt to cover themselves in front at a very early stage when just over a year old. Boys took a little longer, and when a girl reached her first sense she was told to cover her buttocks as well.

Suddenly Namkwa got up, saying, 'I think Nkasi is back from the borehole. I'll take him back now.'

In pursuit of the next instalment in my new interest, I went with Namkwa to Thxale's hut, where we found Nkasi and several other couples sitting around. Soon they were joined by my in-laws who brought with them Nkasi's 3½-year-old first-born, Tchallothoa, my particular favourite.

Taking a back seat, I watched as tiny Ntonno crawled or walked from hand to hand, from person to person. Hardly a moment passed without his being cuddled or comforted. This is par for the Bushman's daily round, for according to Heidi Sbrezny the Bushbabies spend 72 per cent of their 8-hour waking day either in the hands of their mother (48 per cent) or with others (24 per cent). The remainder of the time they spend sleeping or occupying themselves. Compared with European babies the Bushchild gets far more adult attention during this most plastic era of his life.

One can only be impressed by the love the XKo exhibit for their own and others' children. An adult will seldom pass a child without kissing it or hugging it and these feelings are reciprocated by the children who have no qualms in cuddling up to one or another 'auntie' or 'uncle'. This behaviour is an expression of the ties that bind a Bushman band, and that have their roots in the early life of the children. The band of my experience is an extremely cohesive group, and to deny its integrity or even existence as anthropologist Richard Lee, working among the XKung, has done, simply means rejecting or failing to observe and recognize the binding power of these ties of adult–child life.

When Tchallothoa became obstreperous, Nkasi picked her up and soothed her by offering her a breast to suck. Immediately Ntonno, without any sign of hostility, I should add, went over to his mother, pulled out her second breast and also began to suck. If nothing else, this was an indication of how Bush children are taught to share from the very beginning of their lives.

This need to share is crucial to the Bushman's way of life. It has nothing to do with altruism and children themselves soon become guardians of the norm. For example, on one occasion when some sweets were handed to the older children, young Gathua, the orphan, took it on himself to teach Tchallothoa, three years his junior, that she had to share hers with her baby brother. Something like a sweet ought to be shared from mouth to mouth if necessary.

After a while the group at Nkasi's got up and drifted over to Kesi's place where Nxabase was working on a bark quiver that was giving him some bother. While Nxabase worked, several children were playing around Kesi as she bent over her three-legged pot. She took out a piece of meat and gave it to Guanaci's 2-year-old daughter, who had shyly sat down beside her, carefully pushing her little front apron between her legs. None of the other children, including Kesi's own, objected to the preferential treat handed out, and they ran off to join a game.

An older group of children, about eight or them, boys and girls, were playing boisterously nearby. Nxabase's 12-year-old daughter Tchetchei seemed to be the leader, asserting herself and sorting out arguments between the others. There was good cause for her intervention, for among the laughs there was a lot of hair-pulling, sand-throwing, teasing and sticking out of tongues. The little boys were quite aggressive, hitting back at each other and even confronting each other with grewia sticks. Two especially were angry with each other. They glared, heads lowered at each other for probably two minutes before each slowly turned away and withdrew.

The rough stuff, the bumping, tripping, cuffing and kicking, was not confined to the boys. The girls, too were party to the horseplay which also saw the children form sides against each other. Although there was plenty of pretence, there was no real violence, for Bush children know that they must control their anger. They learn this within the context of their play-groups which are an important factor in the moulding of children in their social behaviour.

As Eibl-Eibesfeldt, writing on the XKo, says, 'XKo children are extremely socialized within their play-groups. It is here that the child learns to harness its aggressive impulses. Older children aid each other in their upbringing by interfering with punishment. Social inclinations of children are encouraged. They share and receive, comfort their companion and aid him, and also resolve arguments. While playing they learn to co-operate and become acquainted with the rites which serve to create ties. Of particular importance is the play dance of the children, one of their favourite games.'

Tasa soon arrived on the scene, curious to see how Nxabase had fared with his quiver. He came home carrying his little grandson with the child's mother following. Tasa was not a grandfather in the European sense. He was actually the father's oldest brother, but 'grandfather' nevertheless because of his age. His relationship with the child was also that of a grandparent who by custom is very close to the grandchildren. Not only are they joking partners, but the relationship allows the children to run frequently to their grandparents when hungry or in need of comfort.

As an illuminating example of the relationship between 'grandfather' and 'grandchild', Eibl-Eibesfeldt cites the occasion when the little grandson sat between Tasa's legs, crawled over and around him and on a baby's whim defecated next to him. Quickly the mother cleaned its behind with grass and then carefully scooped up the soiled sand and carried it away to a bush. (Mothers, muttering disapproval, will also clean up like this when a baby urinates. From this the baby learns it is not the done thing to do it like that, and by the time it is a year and a half old it is usually thoroughly house-trained.)

Its lavatorial exertion obviously did not relieve the child altogether, for it was soon crying. The old Tasa tried to comfort and distract him from his woes by lightly pulling his penis. He did this several times, but when the child turned his attention from crying to trying to touch his penis, himself, Tasa carefully removed the little hand. Tasa nevertheless continued casually playing with the child's penis but when the child tried again to pull at it himself, the old man once more removed the hand and proceeded to distract the child with a plaything of pumpkin rind.

On another occasion several girls were sitting around, one of them eating a melon which she had found. The others waited for their turn at the fruit, but one, impatient, snatched the melon and immediately got a slap for her greed – a punishment which the rest thought quite legitimate. Just as a hunter has first choice in the antelope he has killed, so did the little girl lay claim to her ownership before sharing the melon with her companions.

Slapping is an accepted form of chastisement among the Bushmen, but they will strike a child only as a last resort, and then only in the form of a slight slap. In most cases the parents try to distract a child, and by so doing lead it to other less harmful or annoying activities. The children themselves are not as placid in return.

Once, when Txaunxua hid an object from a baby, thinking it would be a dangerous toy, the baby and a 6-year-old girl tried to find it by searching and feeling his whole body. At first he was good natured and tolerant of the search though he and the girl did exchange slight slaps. One of his slaps turned out to be too hard, and the girl got furious. She ran off, and returned with a barrage of bones and melon rinds. That went on until her father soothed her and stopped the bombardment.

Another time Nxabase had to discipline one of his daughters for snatching a piece of meat from a smaller boy. She was so angry with her father that she threw sand at him, and a clout from him only served to increase the vigour of her assault.

When I asked Xamxua why I never saw the boys practising with bow and arrows, he laughed and said, 'We know our children. Are they not our flesh and blood? We have terrible tempers, and our children are no better. They might easily in their anger take a poisoned arrow and shoot us. No, they must be in their second sense before we can allow them to go with poisoned arrows.'

Bushmen are not averse to rearing up bogeymen to bring their children into line. When Tchallothoa wanted to go off with Nxabase's children one evening, Thxale soon had her scurrying to cuddle between his knees. He took a digging-stick and a dish to act as a resonator, and by rubbing the stick placed over the dish, produced an odd and eerie sound. Then he called to Tchallothoa saying that an evil spirit in the bush would rush out and catch her. The effect was immediate. She ran back and didn't move or at least wasn't moved until she grew sleepy and sleepier and Nkasi placed her in the skerm on their hartebeest kaross.

Generally, the children will sit around the fire with their parents at night. Seen and cuddled but not heard, they listen attentively to all the talk, and no subject of conversation is hidden from them. The older children might stay awake for hours, but the small ones, like babies anywhere, are soon asleep. In this manner they bridge the dangers of what we call the 'generation gap'.

Another feature of the Bush-children's life is the way they look after their younger brothers and sisters. The XKo teach their children very early their responsibilities towards the young ones, and even $3\frac{1}{2}$-years-old Tchallothoa was expected to keep a mother-ly eye on Ntonno. Once she went off with him to defecate and neglected to watch him properly. The baby began to put the faeces in his mouth, and was only stopped by my mother-in-law who rushed up to clean Ntonno's mouth. Meanwhile she berated Tchallothoa and gave her several hard smacks. For good measure Nkasi added a few more.

As they grow older the relationship between brothers and sisters changes. The responsibilities remain, but the relationship is formalized. Little boys and girls play and fight, tease and hit each other, but not so older brothers and sisters. At the age of about ten a brother and sister are expected to sit apart and girls, when a little older, are expected to leave their parents' house for a hut of their own.

On the same night of the day Nxabase made his quiver, I took my observations to bed with me and plied Namkwa with questions. Talking about the relationship between brother and sister she said brothers had to look after their sisters very strictly.

'If I had a brother, you could not have married me without asking him,' she said.

Then she asked, 'Do you remember the fight last year about Ntumka and his sister Gakoma?'

'Yes,' I said, 'but I never understood what that was all about.'

'Gakoma and Xamxua's son, Tanate, were always together. Some people said that they might marry. But Ntumka objected. He wanted Xamxua to speak to him first and get his permission. He didn't like his sister to be with Tanate like that. Then he found that Tanate had again slept with Gakoma and he became angry.'

'Yes, I remember he shouted at her, but why did the entire village suddenly get involved?'

'Because in his anger he was rough with Gakoma, and when he pulled her, he caused her apron to be pushed aside so that he and all the others could see her organ.'

'But what did that have to do with the others?'

'Well, they said if a brother can treat his sister in such a way that he sees her bare, then he can also sleep with her. It's the same. They scolded Ntumka, saying he must never get that close to his sister. He must keep his distance.'

'And what about the time Ntumka spilled the petrol in his

eyes? Gakoma was all over him then, screaming and crying. She didn't keep her distance.'

'That was different. Her brother was in pain, in danger, and then as his sister she was the one who had to help him.'

'Does he love her?' I asked. 'Does she love him when he can hit her and be so rough with her?'

'Oh, he loves her very much. They are very close, those two. Much more than Nkasi and I, because since Nkasi got married we often fight.'

The relationship between children and their parents also intrigued me. Namkwa couldn't tell me why she always referred to her father as 'Gruxa', and never called him 'father'.

Nor could she suggest why she sometimes referred to her mother as 'mother' and other times called her Simmertchei. But she explained that the close relationship between parents, especially the mother, and small children gave way to a more distant relationship based on respect when they grew older. 'Otherwise the parents could not bring up their children properly.'

'Children listen to their mother and father much more than to their grandparents because they can joke with their granny,' she said.

We had got back again to joking partners, and the joking relationships which have a socializing influence on a child. The greatest influence comes from the joking relationship between peers because these partners can tell another what he is doing wrong and can ridicule him into step. Grandparents however, are inclined to be too soft, they spoil a child, and are not sufficiently critical. They will even take a child's side against the parents.

By the time the child is thirteen, it knows all its joking partners, and those towards whom it must behave with the greatest respect. In this knowledge it is equipped to conform to the behavioural patterns that bind his society and keep the structure viable. We who exist in more 'civilized' climes could do well to consider the ways of the Bushman. Here we find a tightly knit society with no generation gap to mend; old and young, men and women, boys and girls, are thoroughly integrated.

Compare it with our society so far removed from the values of the Kalahari hunters and food-gatherers. We are practically light-years away, living as we do in our high-density urbanized wastelands. We like to think ourselves advanced, but we fail where society starts, in our homes, to provide sufficiently the basic needs for our children.

Among the Bushmen, children are socialized by each other and by the rest of society at such an early age that their entry into the adult world does not bring with it trauma when they are forced to face their responsibilities. There is no room for loneliness because children grow up with a feeling of being wanted by all members of their society. Even marital discord is buffered by the love a child receives from the rest of society. There are no 'step-children' in a polygamous or a widower marriage, for wives speak only of 'my' or 'our' children, and would not think of them in any other terms. Here are sound bases for emotional security.

Man, though a social creature, is highly aggressive, as Dart and many others who have studied both history and prehistory have emphasized. A hundred thousand years from Boskopman, his offshoots, Mongoloid, Negroid and (especially) Caucasoid live on the threshold of self-destruction. Much more can and doubtless will be said about man's inhumanity to man. But for all his faults there is next to nothing of this inhumanity among Boskop's direct progeny. Like all men, the Bushman is aggressive, yet he has retained a multitude of means to bridle his impulse for aggression, not least of which is his ability to ritualize impulses.

The Bushman's 'freedom' is nothing like the anarchical licence that some imagine freedom to be – it is the tolerance which he shows towards his fellow-man, and his subscribing only to the most necessary norms of behaviour.

He does not encumber his life with stifling religious dogmas, or marital codes which prohibit polygyny or polyandry. He lives a socialized role by allowing each of his fellow-men the opportunity to live his life as long as he does not interfere with the peace and tranquillity of the society to which he belongs.

This, I think, with all its limits, is true freedom.

But the Kalahari was never Utopia, and never will be. Everywhere man is in chains, the Bushman too. The Bushman is a slave to his environment, and cannot lay claim to freedom from want, freedom from disease and freedom from fear. Nor has he escaped entirely the anti-social streak in man that after so many years of survival still threatens his vulnerable society.

TWENTY

Another Trial of Strength

The year after my discussions with Namkwa about having a child, I returned to Takatshwane and noticed a radical change in her appearance. It was almost as though nature had caught up with her too soon. She looked older, and her skin had lost its shine. I had seen her haggard from starvation, but this was different, for she was obviously in good health. I was struck particularly by the condition of her breasts. They hung; their firmness was gone, and her swollen areolae had flattened completely.

'What has happened to you, Namkwa?' I asked. But she wouldn't reply, and there was something in her attitude that was perplexing.

The next day I spoke to Nxabase, but he too was evasive. 'I don't know. She is your wife. You had better ask her, she must know.'

I felt that he did know but wasn't telling, and my curiosity was unsatisfied. When Xamxua joined us I said something had happened to Namkwa while I was away. What?

'Oh, she was sick, and the old women had to treat her,' was all he would say.

Gradually the truth dawned. Namkwa had been pregnant; this could be the only explanation for her change. I guessed she must have had a miscarriage or that the old women had aborted her. I put this to Namkwa, but again she would tell me nothing. However, she was clearly disturbed and I interpreted this as an admission of a guilty conscience.

Next day I spoke again to Xamxua and told him outright what I thought. He then admitted, and so did Nxabase, that Namkwa had been aborted. They couldn't tell me what had taken place and I did not find out – it was a 'woman's matter'. But I was told that Kesi and my mother-in-law had performed the abortion.

Apparently the entire band had been shaken at the sight of Namkwa's pregnancy, for fear of exposure had come to permeate the whole village. Rather than have the baby betray my true relationship with Namkwa and endanger the group, they decided to take the extreme measure.

I was moved by the loyalty of the band. But the motive behind the abortion did not lessen the shock I felt. I could see and feel Namkwa's deep hurt, and I blamed myself. My fears and warnings had come home to roost in a dreadful manner, and the abortion sat heavily on my conscience for a long time. It contributed to a state of depression aggravated by my financial difficulties and an awareness of my own failings.

After seven years in and out of the bush, I was finding it increasingly difficult to finance my trips. Costs had risen but likely sponsors had gone to ground, and my University salary was hard put to cope.

Even the source of my 'petrol money' had dried up. For some time I'd obtained quantities of lion fat at Muramush Pan on the Lobatse Road for sale to inyangas and herbalists in Johannesburg, but now supplies were practically nil. In addition my father-in-law, Gruxa, still expected me to come to Takatshwane loaded down with the horn of plenty. At the village he looked to me as the provider of all his material wants, and, after years of looking kindly on his idiosyncrasies, I rebelled.

It was not only his greed that got me down; it was also his hold over Namkwa. I knew that he sometimes irritated Namkwa, but she was always too much the daughter to object greatly to the pressures he exerted on her. He insisted on her loyalty as a priority, even when I was around, but by then I knew enough about Bushmen lore to see he was too demanding of her.

My father-in-law and I were heading for an inevitable show-down. I did not rush too boldly to this confrontation. For one thing I remembered too vividly the hold Ntchumka had over his daughter Shucre. When Shucre's husband Ntonno contracted glandular tuberculosis, Ntchumka forced a divorce because he claimed Ntonno couldn't support her. Though Ntonno went to hospital and returned healed, Shucre remained with her father and did not re-marry. I feared that Gruxa might exert the same influence over Namkwa and I would lose her.

Nor was I reassured by Xamxua, who said that fathers were frequently reluctant to let their daughters go after a son-in-law had worked off his three years' 'bride service' and wanted, as is the custom, to take his wife to his own band. Such a strongly possessive father would rather insist on a divorce.

Gruxa knew I was in no position to take Namkwa away from her people, but he was determined to prevent her from slipping out from under the wing of his authority.

Matters came to a head after a series of incidents, and when I had had enough of Gruxa's grumbling about me.

There was the time we came back from a hunt with nine guinea-fowl and Gruxa complained bitterly about receiving only one of them. A few days later several of us ran down a wounded wildebeest that I had shot. Sitting round eating the kidneys and liver Ntumka said, 'Well, we won't see much of this meat', and told me that my father-in-law would object: 'He says that you are his son-in-law and you must feed him. But you're away so much you can't feed him throughout the year, and that is why the meat we shoot must go to him.'

'But surely you don't give it to him?'

'Yes, we do, so that we can keep the peace. Otherwise he fights with us all the time. He does this when you are not looking. He is not like other fathers-in-law.'

Shortly after this Namkwa asked me if she could go to Lone Tree to trade some of her father's skins for tobacco.

'But why?' I asked. 'Surely he still has some of the last lot?'

'Yes, he has, but he says you will be going soon, and then he'll be without tobacco. He wants me to go now.'

'But you can wait until I've left and then you can go.'

'No, he says he then wants me to go back to the place near Barachu where you found us that time.'

I remembered 'that time'; it had taken me days to find Gruxa, who had kept Namkwa away from Takatshwane hoping that I wouldn't find her. Now, to say the least, Gruxa's plans did not coincide with mine. I was planning a trip to Noyane with Namkwa, as well as some others, before returning to Johannesburg, but Gruxa threw down the gauntlet and said Namkwa could not go with me unless I left behind enough food to keep him while we were away.

In anger I called the Bushmen together. My differences with Gruxa had to be thrashed out in front of the village elders. It was the only way. Otherwise I would carry on simmering with discontent and this would do no one any good.

Looking at Gruxa, and then at the others, I said, 'See here, I'm sick and tired of fighting my father-in-law all the time.'

Then I turned to Gruxa and, talking straight at him, went on: 'Your daughter has been married to me for eight years. I can't see what right you still have over her.'

Facing the others again, I said, 'Namkwa is supposed to be my wife, yet Gruxa tells her what he likes. He takes what he likes; he makes her give him what he wants and he continually insists that I feed him. What kind of a man is this that can do these things after he gave his daughter in marriage eight years ago?'

I could feel the meeting tensing under my outbreak of disrespect. I didn't know whose side the Bushmen would be on, but I was past diplomacy or tactful advocacy.

'If you want her under your authority,' I said to Gruxa, 'there she is sitting over there; tell her so. Take her home! Tell her she must go to your place. I will not stand in her way, and I will not stop her.'

At this, shock and excitement clicked on tongues around the circle. The Bushmen shook their heads and seemed to exclaim in unison. Suddenly old Tasa raised his voice: 'When you gave Namkwa to this man, you never asked me, her uncle. You should have asked me and received my permission. Now we have trouble and fight. I am hungry and he gives me no food. Perhaps you should take your child back.'

This incensed Xamxua: 'What are you saying? You, Tasa! How much meat have you stuffed into that stomach of yours which he has given all of us? Have you not drunk his beer and eaten his mielie meal?

'Gruxa can still hunt, why must he sit back and wait to be fed? We all agreed to give him this daughter of Gruxa. You were not there, it is true. You were away hunting. But when you came back you had no objections. You were happy to get your meat and tobacco. Why do you only speak now after all these years? When he was at the *tshomma*, why did you not object, why did you tattoo him? Huh, your mind is getting old and very foolish. You don't sit quietly like other old men. You sit, but you talk shit!'

The Bushmen had quietened to listen to Xamxua's prolonged attack, and when he had finished they broke out again into an excited babble. Namkwa alone sat staring unemotionally at the fire. I turned to her.

'Namkwa, you have heard what I said, you heard what your uncle Tasa said, and also what Xamxua had to say. Now I'm speaking to you. You must make up your mind to whom you are married: to me or to your father. If you feel that I am your husband, then you cannot listen all the time to your father. But if you decide for your father, then you must go home to him today. You can go, I will not stop you. But one thing you must also remember; if you do that then you will stay with him. You cannot decide otherwise tomorrow. Think hard about this.'

Namkwa in reply said nothing. She acted as though she hadn't been listening. Casually she reached forward, teased a piece of glowing coal from the fire, stuffed it into her pipe and blew smoke around her head.

Once again I faced Gruxa: 'There is your daughter, tell her to go to your place.'

Gruxa said a few words to her but in the noise and excitement I couldn't catch what they were. Whatever they were, they didn't stir Namkwa from her impassive attitude.

To the assembly and to Gruxa I said, 'I want all of you to go away and think about what is best. Whether you want to support Gruxa or me. I'm also speaking to you, Namkwa, and I want you to think hard. If you come to my bed then I'll know you have chosen me, and that all the nonsense with Gruxa must stop.'

At this I got up and wandered off to our hearth-fire. I threw off my sandals, pants and shirt and slipped under the kaross.

One by one the village dispersed, leaving Namkwa, as emotionless as before, and Gruxa sitting opposite her. I couldn't hear what he was saying but after a while he too got up, and returned to my mother-in-law, who had remained conspicuously apart from the fray.

I watched Namkwa sitting there, and was dozing off when

Gruxa suddenly appeared. He squatted down next to me, without saying a word. Finally, after an agonizing silence, he spoke.

'I see that you have been married to my daughter for a long time now, and she is used to you. I must consider that because she no longer listens to me.'

Not knowing what to say, I said nothing. After some minutes, Gruxa got up again and as unceremoniously as he'd arrived, went back to his fire.

Namkwa gave no indication of having seen Gruxa come and go. She continued to stare at the fire, and blow smoke around her head. Gruxa's words I interpreted as a surrender, but I feared Namkwa's next move.

What if she decided her loyalty was to her father, as Shucre had done? Could I accept that with the simple magnanimity that Gruxa had just displayed, when I knew, despite my bravado in front of the others, that I did not want to lose her? Was it too late to forget my pride, go to her and plead?

I was just about to get up when Namkwa moved. My anxiety lurched and I lay rigid as she rose. I watched her select two large logs from the pile of firewood and place them on the fire as we always did before turning in for the night. Then she ambled towards our bed, stood above me for a moment and suddenly gave me a violent kick: 'Move over,' she said.

I lifted the side of the kaross and she slipped under it. As I hoped she would, she nestled spoon-like against my back and put her arm over me. That was all. Neither of us said a word before we fell asleep.

TWENTY-ONE

Namkwa
the Businesswoman

In retrospect, Namkwa's decision that night became the cornerstone of her subsequent development. When she kicked me and
said, 'Move over,' she kicked over the traces binding her to her
father and the tightly knit Bushman life. She became free to do
with me what she wished.

Soon afterwards we celebrated our independence by going on a
trip with Glen Doman and Carl Delacato up to Maun and the
Okavango. It was the first of a series outside the XKo backyard
which culminated in one to the United States; a history-making
trip, for Namkwa was the first Bushwoman ever to visit America.

The trip to Maun started rather traumatically, with Namkwa's
first dress. While we stocked up in Ghanzi, Carl took Namkwa
into the shop. When we met outside again he was in a state of
considerable excitement.

'Heinzie!' he said, 'I could have gotten killed in there. We
went into the left side of the store where they sell dresses. There
was a young Tswana serving us. I told him that I wanted a small
dress for the lady. He handed me a tiny baby's dress. I handed it
back to him and pointed to some that were hanging over the
counter. At this moment I suddenly noticed that Namkwa and I
were surrounded by Africans. At first I thought they were only
curious, but then they started to shout at us and to spit on us. I
drew Namkwa close to me and leaned over the counter, out of
sheer fright, I might add. I took out my knife and brandished it a
bit and they backed off, but every time I turned my back they

came closer and spat on Namkwa and me, shouting all the time. I had no idea what they were shouting but it was obvious that they wholly disapproved of Namkwa and me being together.

'I reached up and pulled a dress down that was hanging above the counter and put it on Namkwa. In the midst of all the shouting at us and the hostility, Namkwa loved the dress. I threw a few rand down on the counter and started to leave. Again the shouting built up but, as I left, I put my arm around Namkwa and shouted, "Get the hell out of my way!" and they backed away. I must say I was frightened.'

Namkwa seemed altogether unperturbed. She loved the dress and climbed on to our truck preening herself like a fashion model.

'But Carl promised me a jersey too,' she said, ready to go back. Carl however, grunted that he'd go back alone, thank you.

Later he was still disturbed by the incident and shook his head over the cruelty he saw in the experience. But he admired Namkwa's calm and said, 'Perhaps the Bushmen have more to teach us so-called civilized people than we have ever dreamed.'

I, of course, knew that already, but Namkwa never failed to impress me with the equanimity she showed in the face of insults and in other frightening situations. For her this trip was potentially full of them. There was so much that was new. But she absorbed it all with delight, unlike poor Ntumka, whom we took along and who suffered acutely from fear and homesickness.

He was not afraid, however, of travelling at speed, and both he and Namkwa revelled in zooming along at 70 m.p.h. This was on the Maun–Francistown road, hard and fast, which we travelled part-way before saying goodbye to the Americans.

On the way back to Maun I decided to turn off the road for a three-day visit to the Moremi Game Reserve; a wild area and to all intents void of the amenities and restrictions that cosset visitors in more 'civilized' parks.

Long before we reached the south gate of the Reserve we ran into a pitch-black night and the remainder of the drive was an eerie experience. Trees shrouded in creepers filled the imagination with weird and shadowy fears.

Nor did the strange road help. Sudden steep humps sent our headlights skywards, clutching frantically for something to hang on to, before coming back to the spoor with a jolt. On one occasion as we bumped and our fears leapt into the unknown, Namkwa screamed and flung her arms around my neck.

She was still afraid when we reached the camp and even the rangers' warm welcome was not enough to remove her from the cab's cocoon. 'You make the fire and the bed and then I'll come,' she said.

I tried some gentle persuasion and suggested that it was her job to help. Reluctantly she made a move but as she stepped out a lion's 'mmmmmmuph, mmmmmuph, mmuph ... mmuph' sent her leaping back into the front seat.

Notice, the ranger, laughed: 'Tell the woman she musn't fear the lion. He only makes a noise, but he does not come into camp.'

Since the lion was only about five yards away, his assurance wasn't much comfort and Namkwa only stepped down when its whoofing had retreated into the bush.

Around our fire I spoke to the ranger's young assistant who on arrival I thought was a young boy. He turned out to be a Bushman, one of the River bushmen or Bugakwe. He told me about his people who lived north of the swamps and warmed my interest in his remote breed.

The following days bounded with all manner of wild things, Namkwa shed her fears and took to spotting game with obvious delight. She had never seen elephant before and was duly astonished by their strange appearance. She would have been even more impressed had she appreciated how big the lumbering giants were, but in the foreign environment and from a distance neither she nor Ntumka could properly assess their size.

They were quick to identify and name other animals however. Impalas were recognized as the springbok's 'brother', the zebra galloping beside the vehicle were 'horses' and the tsessebe was clearly a close relative of the hartebeest.

At night – one of them spent at a spot aptly known as 'Lion's-roar' – we camped carefully between the protective cover of the Nissan and the camp-fire and though we began our sleep some feet apart, morning found us wrapped up against one another, Ntumka, Namkwa, me and my Mauser rifle.

It was all too much for Ntumka. Thoroughly demoralized, he refused to eat and insisted on going home. Namkwa and I wanted to stay on, but to do so might have broken our Bushman colleague. He only began to revive when we reached Maun. Beyond Maun, on the haul to Ghanzi, he had recovered and the three of us jabbered incessantly about the excitement we discovered in Moremi. How mountainous the elephant droppings, how long the leguan lizards, how plentiful the geese and ducks, how abundant the antelope, and how close the lions!

Turning off into our Takatshwane valley, Namkwa sighed, 'How green and wet everything was there! Everywhere you looked there was so much water and look how dry it is here.'

Some time after our trip, a young doctor at the Witwatersrand Medical School, Dick van Hoogstraten, led a mixed team into the Okavango swamps. His was an expedition to discover a legendary lost tribe of river Bushmen.

He came back with a fascinating account of his team's adventures and the people they found in the swamps – in particular the survivors of the Tannekwe people. This was more than just confirmation of what the Bugakwe in Moremi had hinted at. This intrigued me and the more I thought about the mysteries of the swamp people the more determined I became to explore for myself.

Several months later, having secured the backing of the Wenner Gren Foundation, I assembled my team. An unusual team, it consisted of myself and Namkwa, Nkasi and Thxale, and Bolo Bolo, a Lone Tree Bushman with an ebullient personality. These were all Namkwa's recommendations and we were agreed that Ntumka should stay at home this time.

Gruxa fortunately made no effort to interfere in our plans or prevent his daughters from leaving, and general enthusiasm acompanied our preparations. Namkwa, in particular, ran around with excitement, telling the team what to expect and organizing our departure. She told Thxale what he should take and what he should leave behind. She pulled me over to old Tasa, handed him her bundle of medicinal roots and sticks and told him to 'teach my husband how to use these medicines so that we can eat the meat of the animals where we are going.'

It had not occurred to me that we would be taking our taboos with us and I asked Namkwa why then had she and Ntumka eaten tsessebe meat in Moremi. Her reply made sense. They had discussed it and decided that since the tsessebe was the harte-beest's brother it was all right.

Tasa then showed me which roots I should carry and how I had to roast the first piece of meat cut from a carcass, and sprinkle it with shavings from the roots before feeding each of the Bush-men separately. This done I had to rub my armpit sweat on to their bellies and their heads.

Fortified with this security and loaded with the paraphernalia of a safari, tents, mosquito nets, axes, shovels, planks for muddy places and provisions, we set off for more than a moon away from Takatshwane.

Our first camp, about 70 miles north of Ghanzi, found Namkwa strangely quiet and pensive. She took out her dongo and played it with her eyes closed, drawing comfort from its melodies. What-ever doubts and fears she might have had – and she must have had many – seemed to come under the control of her concentra-tion and relax with the gentle swaying of her body.

Into Ngamiland, the minds of my Bushman companions ran with rivers and water which they'd never imagined existed. Typically they chatted away, alive to the whole adventure ahead of them, and the green stretching for miles around them.

In Maun we took on an interpreter who usually accompanied teams of crocodile hunters to the Okavango swamps and set off for the western perimeter of the marshes.

Here I would start my study of the people living within, and around, the great Okavango Delta – a remarkable phenomenon of nature. Unlike practically every other river in the world, the Okavango, rising in Central Angola, never reaches the sea. Its waters are lost in the 16,800 square kilometres of swampland in the Okavango Basin which stretches towards Lake Ngami.

The Delta is a labyrinth of main- and side-streams. There are innumerable islands of all sizes, right down to tiny ones which cling to the base of fig and other swamp trees. The main-streams meander through patches of reed, which in the upper reaches of the swamp rivers largely consist of papyrus. Hippos are a con-stant threat to the safety of a boat, and tsetse flies – the carriers of sleeping sickness – are another hazardous nuisance, coming at you as they do like mosquitoes.

The people are a mixture: hybrid Bushmen, and Bantu. None

of our journeys discovered the mysterious, unknown tribe of the legends, a fact however which hardly detracted from the fascination in the customs and people we did meet.

My companions on this first expedition were equally fascinating. To all intents a family unit, we got along with a stumble here and there, and each one of us added some individual talent to the total contribution.

Yet again I was amazed by the Bushmen's acute powers of observation and their lively curiosity convinced me the whole exercise was worth while. I believed they could only benefit, as I knew I would, from expanding their experience of other people.

The Bushmen of the River Tannekwe, we discovered, maintain cattle as their chief source of wealth, though they also indulge in primitive agriculture.

The Thandakwe on the other hand subsist mainly by agriculture and hunting and also keep goats. These and others are, when compared with the XKo, generally affluent and their progress impressed my companions. They saw how differently their cousins lived. After all they ate the meat of goats and herd cows, they poured hot milk over the cooked millet which they had grown themselves. They did not walk distances, but rode on horseback and made donkeys carry their belongings.

After this exploratory trip I made several expeditions to Ngamiland accompanied by Namkwa. Her confidence grew with a sense of adventure and she adapted readily to changing circumstances. I was, I think, happily aware of this but I hardly expected she was brave enough to fly. Let alone insist!

At the end of one of our trips at Maun we were watching mine-labour officials loading their immigrant cargo on to a plane bound for South African mines when Namkwa stated quite simply that she would like to go up in one of the 'fly machines'.

Decorum demanded that Namkwa dressed for the occasion. We stripped her of her beaded genital apron and covered her in a blue polka-dot dress. Whether this reinforced her dare I am not sure, but she strode boldly to the aircraft, and three hours and 500 miles later she stepped down as lightly as she went up. Her reaction seemed as fussless as that of a seasoned traveller, but a week or so later as we bumped along the Botswana earth, she turned to me and said, 'You know this car of yours is awful. It shakes and knocks us about and my head gets sore, but up there it's smooth. Now we must drive and drive and still sleep along the road. Up there we arrive long before the sun is high.'

All these experiences and especially her observation of affluent domestic lives led Namkwa to arrive at a single question.

The answer to Namkwa's question was to radicalize the Takatshwane way of life, change her and her people.

'Why can't we have goats?' she said.

I offered to buy a goat when we returned; it was to be a token payment for the help my Bushman friends had provided on our expedition. Namkwa however took the initiative from my hands. As it happened I did not get the goat, for at the end of the first adventure I had to hurry my return to Johannesburg. The next time I went back to Takatshwane, there was the goat. Namkwa had traded a sweater given to her for a pregnant nanny goat and all that remained for me to do was to suggest that a nanny was not enough. We bought a mate and a goat herd was started.

At the same time the interaction of several factors bore down on the XKo and encouraged me to guide the Bushmen into a settlement scheme and a more advanced economy. I believe I was careful not to push them too fast, or force new ideas on them, hoping that the initiative would come from them. But I was quick to build on any signs of progress, the mate for Namkwa's goat being an example.

The role Namkwa played during this time, from late 1969 to October 1971, was crucial to the entire future course of events. The Okavango experience had encouraged her to try growing maize, but the drought thwarted her. Then she revealed herself as an entrepreneur of sorts when she sold some fortified maize I had left for her. With the five rand she collected she found herself with a new commodity to play with – money. It was a concept that the Bushmen had no name for in their wild days, but Namkwa at least was to learn something of its value.

She showed me the money, and rather shyly said she might have got more but she did not know how much the maize was worth. It was then that I decided to put her into business. Her people had developed a taste for tobacco, sugar, maize meal, tea and coffee. They had come to find useful cups, basins, files and other utensils, which were really only available in Ghanzi. So Namkwa's little Bushman shop was started with fifteen to twenty basic items. She could not, nor could the others, read or write. Their language did not even provide for numbers above three. But prices gained a meaning, and Namkwa kept them in her head. As her savings grew, her thoughts turned to investment.

'How much money does it take to get a cow?' she asked. It cost sixteen rand. So Namkwa owned the band's first cow.

Prior to this significant deal other Bushmen, encouraged by the presence of Namkwa's goat, had also earned themselves some goats. Two nannies were killed by a lion and the people decided to build a kraal. This was to me a symbolic act, for with it they surrendered their mobility.

I must say at this stage that a brake had already been placed on the band's mobility. The drought and the famine relief I have written about drew Bushmen to the Takatshwane water pump, and though most of the foreign bands returned to their own backyards, Midum's band, Douté's Okwa people and the Gruxa–Ntchumka group maintained their links and were later to be drawn into the same settlement.

After Namkwa bought her cow Thxale and Nxabase followed suit, although Nxabase did need plenty of coaxing to do so. At about this time I discussed the possibility of a development plan for the Takatshwane area with the District Commissioner of Ghanzi.

I saw that extensive ranching development was envisaged, and with it a displacement of all the Takatshwane nexus to foreign land east of the main road. It was then that I made a more concerted effort to encourage development at Takatshwane, including particularly the acquisition of cattle and the planting of crops. My thinking was clear: if ranches were going to be proclaimed and developed in this area, the Bushmen of Takatshwane were to have the first ranch. Not only would this enhance their social status in the larger, cattle-conscious community; it would stabilize them economically and protect them from outside exploitation. It would also make them less reliant on hunting ever-diminishing herds.

When the veterinary officer, growing provocative, wanted to confiscate the livestock – mostly that of the Okwa band – for watering at government expense, and for feeding on grass on the Ghanzi–Lobatse trek route, it became necessary to drill a borehole outside this route.

From this the present Bere (pronounced bearer) settlement was born, for it was decided to drill alongside the pan there. Here too, in order to appease the Ghanzi District Council afraid of Bushmen squatting on farms planned along the road, it was decided to amalgamate the Okwa with the Takatshwane Bushmen. It would also forestall a confrontation with the veterinary officer, and increase the personnel available for the anticipated ranch.

The role that Namkwa played during this time was of prime importance. Apart from her acquisition of livestock she built the first Tswana-type hut (later a guest-house); she learned thatching; she cultivated land and encouraged others to do so; she had the men fence in the living area against goats; at Bere she organized the men to clear an airstrip; she assumed simple first-aid duties; she insisted that a school be built for Bere; she began her shop and often gave out mielie meal for communal work; and was invited to visit the Institute for the Achievement of Human Potential in Philadelphia.

Meanwhile money was being raised in the U.S.A. and South Africa to cover the drilling expenses. It was partly to stimulate these monies that Namkwa went to the States.

TWENTY-TWO

The Land of Plenty

There was another motive; Carl Delacato and Glen Doman had been very impressed with Namkwa, and were struck with the thought that she would be an ideal choice to demonstrate to Americans the intellectual capacity of the Kalahari Bushmen.

The first Namkwa knew about our going to America was when a friend of mine, and a complete stranger to her, plucked her from Takatshwane and took her to Gaberone, Botswana's capital, to wait my arrival. She had no idea what to expect. America was simply a place name where Carl and Glen lived, but because they were good and happy people she was sure their land would be good and happy too. She had nothing to fear.

Six days after my friend left her at a mission school in Gaber-ones, I arrived to pick her up. I found she had brought with her all those worldly goods which she considered valuable and impor-tant. She had her little moneybox, but she also had an awl and sinew to string up the beads which she had brought in abundance. She also had a beautifully beaded handbag gift for a girlfriend whom she hoped to see and a few unfinished leather skirts. Other-wise she had packed the two dresses with which she had visited Gaberone the year before, several tasselled skin skirts decorated with beads and some ordinary bush wear. She had also brought her dongo.

To avoid the possibility of any suspicion of our relationship arising, we travelled to Johannesburg chaperoned by two other young women friends who took it on themselves to equip Nam-kwa properly for her journey. Namkwa was rather puzzled and perturbed by the impersonal attitude I adopted towards her, and couldn't understand why she was made to sit in the back of my car. Or, later, why I didn't stop and walk with her, why I ignored her in the Jan Smuts Airport lounge when we came to leave for New York.

The answer was that I was afraid. I was simply paying obeisance to South African taboos.

The only positive attention I paid her in Johannesburg was at a special dinner with a close friend. This meal, complete with waiter, was her first and only lesson in Western table manners. We gave her some idea of the procedure but once again simply by observing our behaviour she quickly learned.

On the aircraft she showed no undue concern and coped confidently with the usual packaged tray meals.

In America too she was to take in her stride the strange and extravagant dishes that we met at the numerous dinners to which we were invited. No Bushman could have ever imagined such plenty. Namkwa certainly hadn't, and America was therefore a colossal happening. It was not only the foods she ate; she had never anticipated so many people, especially so many fat people, so many buildings, so much water, so much greenery, so many different dogs, motorcars, and roads. Nor so much attention.

When she got back to Takatshwane she tried describing all that plentitude and the mass of idiosyncrasies she had observed. Her Bushmen listened wide-eyed. But she turned to me and sighed, 'These Bushmen just don't believe what I tell them.'

Perhaps what impressed Namkwa most was the beauty of the countryside, the lush lawns, the fruits and flowers. Aeroplanes, television, elevators and machines were remarkable enough but too removed from her experience to boggle over. She accepted them for what they were. But nature was her background and she could compare how poor her dry Takatshwane was.

Bushmen look on plant life with a strictly practical eye, and the Kalahari flowers which explode into ephemeral colour after the rains have no aesthetic value for them. But Namkwa was fascinated by all the decorative arrangements that she saw.

On one occasion she drew me to the window of a florist's shop and asked whether these plants were sold because they contained medicine. My explanation that they were simply decorative brought her to a new awareness and when, one day, Raymond Dart picked a rose for her in the Institute's grounds, she smiled her delight. Later she added it to the four flowers she had already collected, and had arranged in a milk-bottle in her room.

Namkwa also came quickly to terms with dress styles, and she gained in poise and self-confidence, knowing that her clothes conformed to the fashion around her. Only when she was cold did she abandon fashion for anything that would keep her warm.

For the Institute's banquets an appropriate dress had to be bought. Her choice fell between three sky-blue mini-dresses, to which I added another, thinking it was very becoming with its plunging neckline. She tried it on but rejected it immediately, saying that it would expose her too much.

'But, Namkwa, at home you often wear nothing on top!'

'That is at home!' she retorted, settling for one of her preferences.

Our pride was her African jackal cape, which she had worn with a leather skirt and a matching jersey when we left Johannesburg. Wearing it on the street one day she was suddenly stopped by two young Americans: 'Excuse me,' said one, 'what lovely fur is that you're wearing?'

Namkwa was taken aback, but I replied, 'The lady does not speak English, but this cape is made of ordinary African jackal.'

The girl smiled. 'There's nothing ordinary about that fur,' she said, as we walked on. She might have been even more impressed if she had known that Namkwa herself was more than an ordinary personage, as one man we met had wondered.

'Is this charming young lady an African dignitary?' he asked when his curiosity got the better of him. In her way she certainly was.

At the Institute itself, Namkwa was a great success. She responded to stimuli, and in only four short lessons she learned to read almost two dozen words, began to write her name, learned to count, recognize numbers up to 100 and master simple additions.

When it was suggested that she was of exceptional intelligence, I said, no, she was average among Bushmen. But where she outshone the others was in her adaptability and initiative. It was this that made her a leader among her people.

At the beginning of our three-week stay in America Namkwa was self-conscious and shy in the presence of others. But as she adapted she dropped her inhibitions. When we visited a dance-hall she succumbed to the beat of the music and leaped up to dance alone on the floor. I followed her out of propriety more than inclination, and as she fell in step with the white man's conventional way of dancing her enjoyment was spontaneous and obvious.

There were many other things that took her fancy; from window-shopping to riding escalators, from television to a beer in a tavern. And when she saw the ocean liner *QE2*, she threw her hand to her open mouth in astonishment.

In the mansion of our host Institute, a piano attracted her attention, and, oblivious to the goings-on around her, she would sit down to experiment with its sounds. In a small tavern she took a place as near to the piano player as she could get, and sat with eyes glued and ears tuned to the keyboard. It was, however, a symphony concert that held her truly spellbound. As she watched and listened – the first of her people to attend such a concert – she kept whispering in her words how beautiful it was.

A second concert in New York provided another unforgettable experience, but her appreciation was just as great for the performance of two Greenwich Village folk-singers we heard. I had few doubts that she would enjoy her introduction to such live music. Even in the bush she had shown her liking for the radio and notably its classical music programmes.

Despite the non-stop excitement, Namkwa still found time for moments of homesickness, then she would turn to the security she held in her dongo. It was her playing it one evening in a hotel room that provided for me one of the most poignant moments of the trip. She sat on the floor with closed eyes rhythmically nodding her head to the flow of melodies that came with her improvisation. For a long time she played her tiny hand-piano, picking sad and wistful sounds from it. Then she raised her eyes and asked, 'Where is the road to Ghanzi?'

Moved, I pointed and said, 'It's in that direction, but it's far and were you to walk it you would soon have wet feet.'

And so we flew back to Africa.

TWENTY-THREE

Yesterday I Was a Bushman

Time since then has increased the traffic on the Ghanzi road, but it remains a rough road in a hard uncompromising country. Progress has introduced new values, new fears, new conflicts, and set in motion a breakdown of the sanctions that have maintained the Bushmen personality all these years.

For me it has brought disillusion and long periods of bitter soul-searching and self-recrimination. Nor has Namkwa escaped the changes that have exploited the vulnerability of her people. So many unforeseen things have happened, so many hopes and ideas have withered in the bush since I set out with Namkwa to show her life beyond the Bushman's ken.

Above all the social integrity of the Kalahari Bushman, which had survived for centuries, has become a thing of the past. Their hunter-gatherer culture has been bludgeoned by the invasion of other forces, and at a rate I, one of the agents for change, certainly hadn't anticipated.

With the opening up of western Botswana, especially in the few years since independence, Bushmen have been drawn increasingly into the growing cattle economy. More and more are employed on the farms odd-jobbing and fencing, or tracking cattle to Lobatse.

Road development and maintenance has attracted Bushmen to road camps for temporary employment and food rations. Money has become a factor in their lives. The trappings of Western materialism clutch at them, and as the traffic increases and communications are improved, Bushmen find it more profitable to stay where the opportunities are for their ha'porth of tobacco, for gifts, for famine relief.

Even the Bushmen of the Central Kalahari Reserve, said by some to be the most 'untainted', make more periodic trips to growing towns such as D'Kau, Rakops, Tsetseng and Kang for supplies or to squat when their water dries up. Bushmen also congregate at other water places, at the new boreholes that have been drilled in the desert. The effect has been to blunt a band's old habits and obliterate customary boundaries.

The pressure of cattle farming has increasingly affected the game distribution. More than 30,000 head of cattle are pushing in all directions from Kang into Bushmen land and forcing game removals from traditional areas. The Bushmen now employ new hunting methods too; they buy horses to run down their prey, and use spears and dogs. Even the XKung in the north of the Reserve have surrendered their hunting tradition.

At the same time new and stricter game laws, often misunderstood, have made Bushmen prey to the law-enforcing bodies, even turned numbers of them into fugitives.

Streams of scientists into Bushmen areas have also accelerated the rate of change, inevitably bringing new ideas and money into communities. I was one of this group, with Tony Traill and others in the south, the Japanese Thanaka in the Central Kalahari Reserve, and the Harvard group with Wiessner and Wilmson in the north.

Along with scientists there has been an increase in the visits of journalists and television film-units, with misguided rates of remuneration for the Bushmen co-operation they seek. As a result many Bushmen have had a distorted introduction to the money culture. The increase of missionary activity has also led to a distortion of old values. At Lone Tree, for instance, I have discovered boys refusing to be initiated because it is now suddenly wrong.

On the other hand medical attention is more readily available and the Flying Doctor service has filled an urgent need.

Tourism, too, is taking its toll of custom. The lone traveller has been followed by organized groups who with their cameras and their insensitivity and their demand for artefacts have exploited the Bushman's good nature and ignorance. I am particularly incensed by the shameful exploitation of their work. Some tourists think a cigarette or two is enough for an artefact many hours in the making. At least in Bere the locals gained a better idea of the value of their articles, which they sold through Namkwa's shop.

Namkwa herself I see as a symbol of a changing culture and her future is tied to the success or otherwise of the Bere settlement. In its early days a meeting of the bands expressed their wish that I be confirmed 'headman' of the group, and I pledged myself to do all I could for the advancement of their settlement.

It struck me as vital to get government permission for the development and in 1972 Bere became a scientific project of anthropology, a pilot scheme for further reference, supported partly by the Max Planck Institute in Munich, partly by money and material I had been able to raise in South Africa. Additional grants were also obtained and student and other volunteers came to the Kalahari to help in the settlement construction. The result was an ablution block, a teacher's house, a partly built school, Namkwa's shop and a house for her. Later two guest-houses, a tannery, a dispensary and a workshop were added.

When the school was built Bere obtained the services of a teacher who in eighteen months produced a sizeable crop of youngsters able to speak, read and write English, and do elementary arithmetic. In 1974 a replacement teacher arrived to continue the development of a curriculum especially adapted to the evolving community.

Outside the classroom the range of livestock had grown to include goats, horses, donkeys, cattle, chickens and dogs. Namkwa, thanks to a disproportionate run of female calves, established herself as the largest cattle-owner in the Bere herd, which grew to more than 100 beasts.

Initially the progress was dramatic. But gradually the hope inherent in the scheme ran into traumas. Bere had grown too fast.

In my ignorance of basic economics and the facts of Bushmen private ownership, I had envisaged Bere as a co-operative. But these were concepts the Bushmen were not ready to grasp, and unhappily it became apparent that the adults had little or no sense of responsibility in matters affecting the community as a whole. Community service was foreign to them.

Nor did the amalgamated bands come together with any degree of beneficial social adhesion. The bands to all intents maintained their distance, physically and psychologically. The incidence of violence increased and band members could no longer disappear as they used to when conflicts threatened. Their children were at school, their livestock was kraaled, and the shop provided a better type of food than that found in the veld.

Another hampering feature was the reluctance of the Bushmen to think of their future. The adults showed no propensity whatsoever for applying their minds to even the simplest potential of the ranch.

While I was inclined to despair at so much complacency, Namkwa kept my hopes alive. She alone of all her people could see her cattle as an insurance and investment for the future.

In a pilot scheme of this nature and amid the pressures of intruding interests, it was inevitable that I would be criticized and blamed for its failings. My administration was criticized as bourgeois and paternalistic. It was said that my headmanship prevented the Bushmen from identifying with the land and that they considered it to be my land, my ranch.

Some would say my methods were crude, my ideas fanciful and my Namkwa just a plaything whom I tried to mould into a petty capitalist. The criticisms have hurt.

It has also been argued that I was an outsider and my headmanship did not encourage self-government through responsible people in the Kgotla, a sort of representative local authority and an innovation borrowed from the Tswana. Nor did my long absences from Bere help the situation. My authority was steadily eroded, I was unpopular in influential quarters, and in a heap of problems, bitter and disillusioned, I resigned my headmanship in 1974.

Despite requests by some members of government to retain my official lead, I felt I could not carry on in the prevailing atmosphere.

During a Kgotla meeting in May the community was requested to elect my successor. The immediate responses were significant. At first the people said there was no one there who could be a headman. The government should send someone, and if they could not then a Bushman from Ghanzi should be appointed. And then if that were not possible there was only one person who could fill the post and that was Namkwa.

Although the community with a little coaxing put up another

two candidates, Namkwa was a clear winner. She got 28 votes and the other two only 4 between them.

In some respects this achievement might be seen as the culmination of Namkwa's experience. Certainly she had matured to the point where she was an obvious choice to be a leader among men. Beyond that she symbolized the hope for a new era of progress and an adaptation to new ways.

Unfortunately the forces at work undermined the hopes. My old friends who taught me to be a Bushman failed to rise to new responsibilities. I even think they feel deeply unhappy and frustrated by demands they would rather have ignored. Nor has Namkwa been able to stir them into assuming a community pride. They have, to all intents and purposes, made a mockery of Namkwa's leadership. Her authority has also been eroded and few have shown an inclination to follow her example. When I bring myself to think about it, I see her as a symbol too of the Bushman tragedy, and it saddens me. After all, I have played a role.

Hope for the future of course lies with the generation presently at school. For with guidance and understanding they can adapt to the demands they face.

As for me, I have lost much of my fight, the old drive has diminished. I too have been on the receiving end of the critical forces that have infiltrated the old ways, and have restricted my movement among Bushmen. Time and nature are also making uncompromising demands on me. Even when the spirit wills, the sheer physical strain of trekking to Bere daunts me. It is not merely the long, hot haul; it is the attendant discomforts that offer themselves as aches to a tired body – the makeshift repair jobs, the sleeping out, the search for firewood ...

I have discovered the limits within me. I have felt too my inner communion with my old friends fading. Yesterday I was a Bushman, but today I am something else. And though I am bound to Africa I seek my security in a style of life from which I could never entirely break away.

My ties with Namkwa, however, do remain. She has my child, for one thing, but I am too selfish, too old and too much a prisoner of my background and the hardships of my present circumstances to fancy myself forever as her Prince Charming. I even allow myself to think, since it is inclined to assuage the guilt that sometimes visits me, that we were never properly married anyway. Didn't Namkwa herself say that?

A greater consolation is that Namkwa understands. Or so I believe. I am not crucial to her wellbeing. I might have been, perhaps, but she too has slipped beyond our mutual dependence, aware that she must not rely on me.

I cannot conjure up happiness for her, nor for her people who changed my life, though Heaven knows I wish I could. All I can hope is that my role has been for the best. That it is just the nostalgic romantic in me that mourns the gone 'wild' days, and my shy thirstland maiden who, somewhere along the way, was left behind.

Afterword

by MARSHALL LEE

It was inevitable that the South African press would catch up with Dr Heinz's controversial attachment to Namkwa. The remarkable thing is that it took so long.

The headline in the Johannesburg *Sunday Times* (of September 21st, 1975) blazed across ten columns. It said: 'WHITE BUSHMAN KING EXILED'.

Underneath this, the report said that Dr H. J. Heinz, a professor who gave up his university post in South Africa to marry a Bushman woman and become the headman of a Bushman tribe in Botswana, had been forced by the Botswana Government to leave Bere, the settlement he created.

Even allowing for journalistic licence, this introduction was not accurate. Dr Heinz was not a professor. He did not leave his university post to marry Namkwa, and let us say that circumstances drove him to leave Bere.

The remainder of the long report did not redeem the start. As an exposure of a controversy it had a certain validity in newspaper terms, but despite the attempt at balance written into it, my opinion is that it erred in favour of superficial sensation and was defamatory.

It quoted Miss Liz Wily, Bushman Development Officer for the Botswana Government, as saying she had been forced to recommend that Dr Heinz be kept away from the Bere settlement because he set himself up as a virtual god.

She was further reported as saying, 'Dr Heinz has decided that the young son he had by his wife Namkwa will eventually become king of the Bushmen. It's a terrible thing to say about a living legend – which is what Dr Heinz has become – but his actions have become erratic.'

As background the report then said that when Dr Heinz developed the Bere scheme in the late 'sixties it received international acclaim as being the first settlement to provide the Bushman with means of changing his traditional way of life from hunter to pastoralist; that he had helped the Bere Bushmen to buy their own cattle – an important symbol of wealth in Botswana – and to establish their own store, a village community and even a school. The job of teacher at the school Dr Heinz gave to Miss Wily, a New Zealander travelling through Africa.

At first (according to the article) she 'idolized the "Doc" ', but she 'began to think his approach to the settlement was a bit off-beam. I found that he would not allow anyone to disagree with him or argue with him. He was the headman and his wife was the biggest cattleowner and ran the store.'

At the request of the Botswana Government, she wrote a report on Bere 'as objectively and as truthfully as I could'. It was very critical of Dr Heinz. Soon afterwards, and despite her relative inexperience, she was appointed Bushman Development Officer, a post that gave her virtual control of all Bushman affairs, and enabled her to recommend who could have access to their areas and who could conduct research among them. She was even able to vet research proposals of reputable scientists.

'I cannot allow Dr Heinz to do any further work with the Bushmen. His ideas are all wrong,' the newspaper article quoted her as saying, and went on: 'She said she believed that Dr Heinz tried to create an aura around himself. He has created an enormous myth. He revels in his belief that he has become a legend in his own lifetime.'

After his interview with Miss Wily in Gaberone, the reporter found Dr Heinz recuperating from a major abdominal operation performed at a mission hospital in a small village, Malelolope.

He described Dr Heinz as angry and distraught, and in carrying his denial that he 'set himself up as a virtual god', quoted him as saying he had been victimized, along with the retort: 'So Miss Wily thinks I'm a lunatic, does she? All I want is to be left alone to live my life and do my work.'

He said the Bere settlement was 'falling apart since he had left', that Miss Wily had got him to resign as headman and tried to push the most respected person there, Namkwa, out of the picture.

'I went, but my wife stayed on. Namkwa is a remarkable woman.'

The report described how Dr Heinz spoke of his work, the unique material he had gathered and his knowledge of the Bushmen, and it ended with an extract from an editorial in the *South African Journal of Science*. This was mildly critical of Liz Wily's appointment as Bushman Development Officer:

> By sad irony, the person appointed to the job has relatively little sympathy for one of the first independent settlement schemes established several years ago with the purpose of teaching the Bushmen the fundamentals of stock farming within a free enterprise economy, and also providing basic education for the children.
>
> Partly for this reason, Dr Heinz resigned from the supervision of Bere last year. Although views vary on what, if anything, should be done to 'advance' the social development of relatively primitive people this turn of events is to be regretted.
>
> Botswana is quite big enough to accommodate the conflicting attitudes of Dr Heinz, the Bushmen Development Officer and those few other people concerned about the welfare of the Bushmen.

This sound reasoning was not enough to defuse the anger and shock that followed the newspaper report.

Dr Heinz struggled to Johannesburg a few days after his talk with the reporter, arriving just after the report was published. If he was distraught when interviewed he was even more so when he called me.

Already hammered by surgery and a long period of depression, the report practically devastated him.

He said he had spoken to the reporter, who had spurred him with Liz Wily's allegations, only after repeated assurances that nothing he said would be published. The last thing he wanted was to be drawn into a public conflict that would harm his standing with the Botswana Government and threaten his continued residence in the country.

He had left South Africa to devote himself to Botswana, his anthropological research and his domestic life which, for most of his adult life, I believe one could only fairly describe as unconventional.

What the report did not mention was that Dr Heinz had settled in Maun, alongside the Okavango swamps, with his third and latest civil-law wife. Here, away from South Africa and the pressures of a metropolitan existence, he had set his sights on a peaceful and productive old age.

He was only too aware that his body was losing much of its stamina for the bush life. He was growing to fear the rigours he once welcomed and it was only realistic that he should decide to make a new domestic bed and lie, so to speak, on his 'Western' side.

God, health, and domestic harmony willing however, he also hoped to preserve the Bushman links that bind this story, in particular his relationship with Namkwa and their Gustel.

Unfortunately things seldom turn out as planned in such a varied life as Dr Heinz's. In the years I have known him, to say nothing of the earlier years I have come to know intimately, he has been well and truly married to extraordinary and sometimes traumatic problems. Mixed with his ambitions they have stimulated considerable energy, much soul-tearing and above all a remarkable contribution to our ethnological record.

The Johannesburg *Sunday Times* report presented another crisis; one from which he says he has not recovered. I saw it as damaging his reputation, for not only did it suggest he was a crank but the suggestion that he wanted to set up his son as 'king' of the Bushmen was defamatory of a scientist whose research had been internationally acclaimed.

Whatever his ambitions for Gustel, this idea was utterly ridiculous, for the Bushmen have no concept of kingship, even between quote-marks. The reporter probably went too far.

Dr Heinz, however, resolved not to take the report to court. Even assuming he were successful, he felt he could not handle the publicity that would surely accompany a case. Nor did he want to risk embarrassing the Botswana Government, thus jeopardizing his life in Botswana. Time and dialogue, he prayed, would restore all.

Long before the newspaper report, Dr Heinz's fears made him determined to protect Gustel as much as possible from outside publicity that would render him an oddity to be stared at and photographed by tourists. He resented the undignified nature of the exposé.

At the same time he was acutely distressed by the effect the story might have on his latest wife and their domestic security. Quite reasonably, I believe, she was not fully reconciled to the Namkwa relationship, and this publicity could only humiliate her. As it was, it upset her.

It also upset Liz Wily who, according to another reporter in an unpublished message, was 'hopping mad – mad enough to wish a plague on the houses of all journalists, and particularly a Johannesburg Sunday newspaper.' She hotly denied Dr Heinz had been ousted from Bere at her instigation. She said it was nonsense and that Dr Heinz had himself decided to discontinue his interest in the Bere scheme.

She said she had only agreed (reluctantly) to an interview because she understood the article was to be about Bushman Development and not about any personalities.

She described the report as 'totally manufactured and grossly inaccurate'. She denied Dr Heinz had been prevented from visiting Bere or that she had ever recommended his restriction because he had 'set himself up as a virtual god'.

'It is hard work getting to see Miss Wily now,' was the reporter's comment. 'In fact she is out of town to journalists. Only Bushmen need apply for an appointment. Of the two Miss Wily has a distinct preference.'

The Johannesburg *Sunday Times*, as it happened, was prepared to 'stand by the story in all its details'. But the newspaper was not called on to defend it publicly.

Whatever departmental ructions in Gaberone might have followed the report, they did not appear to change Liz Wily's attitude to Dr Heinz. If anything, their differences and Miss Wily's opposition were probably more entrenched.

Other men might have forced the issue, but Dr Heinz preferred not to. After all he was in an extraordinary and vulnerable position and, subject to extraordinary fears and pressures, he chose a more passive and placatory stance. Up to now this has not solved his problems, personal or official. What is more, and contrary to one view that he has enriched himself at the expense of the Bushmen, financial worries have added to the problems.

He has been forced to change his lifestyle completely and pick up a new career, trucking cattle along Botswana's diabolical roads.

'I tell you, Marshall, I've never worked so hard,' he said on one of his rare trips to Johannesburg. On that occasion he was considerably healthier. At least he was a year away from the depths to which he had plummeted at the time of his operation and the Johannesburg *Sunday Times* report. He had also regained his interest in this book. But he had not been to Namkwa and Gustel for many months.

I have no doubt that, when in a less vulnerable position, he will return – irregularly – to Bere. But, of course, trite though it sounds, it will never be the same; nothing like those days, for instance, when I first went out there and enthusiasm was working wonders.

Then his Bushmen gathered round him and he was obviously at home. We had actually flown in, landing on a rough strip cleared by the Bushmen under Namkwa's direction. It was four miles to the settlement and long before we reached it the soft insides of my walking shoes had turned to granulated leather.

I was so blistered I could hardly appreciate the laughs and greetings as little Bushmen ran to join us. One of them was Namkwa, who stopped a short way ahead of us. She stood waiting, with a coy expression and little gestures of self-conscious casualness, until we reached her, and she fell into quick step with her Caucasoid lover's long strides.

Up until this trip I had spent a lot of time doubting, as others had and probably will, the sincerity behind this odd, even incongruous, relationship. But when the early sun woke me the following morning I eavesdropped quite innocently on their intimacy as they lay together. I could hear the affectionate tone in his teasing and Namkwa giggling as any woman might with a lover just returned.

If this convinced me that I was involved in something genuine, it did not overwhelm my cynicism altogether. Despite my friendship with 'Doc', or 'Heinie' as other friends call him, I have, I hope, been sufficiently detached to recognize the flaws in the man brought on by the attacks of ego or the emotional outbursts that are inclined to overtake the rational scientist.

There have also been a number of occasions when people might say he rationalized himself into errors of judgment. Others might believe they would have acted differently.

Dr Heinz has had to spend a lot of his thinking time vindicating his actions and behaviour, but he is only too aware he is not a paragon of scientific virtue and that his emotional traits sometimes shoved the objective scientist aside. But this is what makes the man and his Bushman life a remarkable study.

His eccentricity took him into a unique situation, his strength made it productive, his ego and vulnerability added drama, and the sum total of circumstances took it close to tragedy.

The following years might repair the situation, but meanwhile this book is a record of a man's infatuation with a Kalahari way of life, his growing attachment to a pre-literate, Stone Age people and particularly his love for a Bushwoman.

As a work of fiction it could be regarded as imaginative, but the story is not mere romance. Its value is just as much scientific, for there is probably no other account of Bushman life to match it.

Whatever social anthropologists might say of his methods and his subjective submersion in his work, Dr Heinz has emerged from years of conscientious observation with priceless material. As an authority on a fading culture he has been rewarded by academic recognition and a certain fame. But the gains have been more than balanced by sacrifice, the fulfilment reduced by the doubts and antagonistic forces that beset him.

This book details some of the forces that worked against him and which for years he weathered or evaded by hiding the truth of his Bush life. Although some of his colleagues, both critical and encouraging, knew of his relationship with Namkwa, he dreaded the possibility of an exposé that would kill it. Consequently he kept superficial diaries and scattered more personal notes among his research papers, lest they fell into the wrong hands.

When he came to write this book he found years of incidents had wandered out of chronological order. But not seriously. In parts of the book we have also used some licence to lodge scientific descriptions more neatly into the story. Certain liberties have also been taken with conversations, but only to make them flow coherently. Many of these Dr Heinz recorded on tape, so the gist is always accurate, and before he learnt Namkwa's language he made careful use of his interpreter.

The learning covered a painstaking period during which Dr Heinz overcame the intricacies of the Bushman tongue, and particularly the complete arrangement of clicks that characterize it. In scientific papers these are written into words with exclamation marks, single strokes and double strokes; but to ask a lay reader to cope with names that look something like /a!um would be asking too much. Instead of !Ko and N//amkwa we have resorted to 'XKo' and 'Namkwa', a pretty enough name even without the click. In other words and names we have used 'X' or 'ch' and 'th' where the different clicks should be. The pity of it is that the reader cannot hear the sounds that make the Bushman tongue the fascinating instrument it is.

Not all the information is based on Dr Heinz's research. The history of Ghanzi was taken from a paper written by Dr John Clement, who kindly made this material available. Furthermore the chapter on child behaviour is a synthesis of Dr Heinz's own research and the invaluable work of Professor Eibl-Eibesfeldt and his assistant, Heidi Sbrezny. Dr Heinz owes thanks and much of his inspiration to the Professor. With the permission of Dr Clement and the Professor we have personalized the relevant chapters to maintain the autobiographical flow and to avoid the jargon and esoteric depth of more academic accounts.

Otherwise it remains for me to acknowledge and thank my wife, Kate, not only for typing the manuscript but also for her advice and the objective eye she kept on my involvement. She, for one, was quick to see when Dr Heinz's male chauvinistic streak was showing, as it does along with his many other traits, the weaknesses and the strengths which are bared for assessment.

The major portion of the book deals with the old way of Bush life before the Bere settlement experiment, and the events leading to its rise and decline are treated relatively briefly to provide some sort of end.

The story, of course, has not ended. Miss Wily's resignation from her government post raises new possibilities. Dr Heinz's role among the Bushmen has not been fully analysed and there is much more that this book could not hold, or that could be told in newspaper reports. It could not be otherwise with such a controversial man who, yesterday, was a Bushman.

Index

WITHDRAWN
No longer the property of the
Boston Public Library.
Sale of this material benefits the Library

BOSTON PUBLIC LIBRARY

3 9999 00063 569 6

namkwalifeamongb00hein

namkwalifeamongb00hein

namkwalifeamongb00hein

Sale of this material...

Boston Public Library

DT797
.H44
1979

87801339-01

The Date Due Card in the pocket indicates the date on or before which this
book should be returned to the Library.

Please do not remove cards from this
pocket.